Springtime of the Liturgy

CLASSICS IN LITURGY

Springtime of the Liturgy

LITURGICAL TEXTS OF THE FIRST FOUR CENTURIES

by

LUCIEN DEISS, C.S.SP.

translated by

MATTHEW J. O'CONNELL

THE LITURGICAL PRESS

Collegeville   Minnesota

Library of Congress Cataloging in Publication Data
Main entry under title:

Springtime of the liturgy.

   Edition for 1967 published under title: Early
sources of the liturgy.
   Includes bibliographical references and index.
   1. Liturgies, Early Christian. I. Deiss, Lucien.
II. Deiss, Lucien. Aux sources de la liturgie.
English.
BV185.D413   1979   264'.01'1   79-15603
ISBN 0-8146-1023-4

Contents

Abbreviations

CCL	*Corpus Christianorum, Series Latina*. Turnhout, 1953–
PG	*Patrologia Graeca*, ed. J. P. Migne. Paris, 1857–66.
PL	*Patrologia Latina*, ed. J. P. Migne. Paris, 1844–64.
SC	*Sources Chrétiennes*. Paris, 1942.
TDNT	*Theological Dictionary of the New Testament*. Grand Rapids, Mich., 1964–74.

Introduction

Springtime of the Liturgy presents the principal texts relating to the Christian liturgy from its beginnings to the fourth-fifth century. The following are the main sources which we now have at our disposal for knowledge of this early liturgy:

— The *liturgical texts of the Jewish tradition*. These texts are precious to us Christians, for just as Christ Jesus "fulfills" the Scriptures (Mt. 5:17), so the prayer of the Church, heir to Christ, "fulfills" the prayer of the synagogue. To be acquainted with Jewish prayer is to have a better understanding of Christian prayer.

— The account of the *institution of the Lord's Supper* according to the synoptic tradition and the First Letter to the Corinthians. This account, as everyone knows, is at the heart of every Eucharistic celebration.

— The *doxologies, blessings, and hymns of the New Testament*. The "letter" of these texts is frequently inspired by the Old Testament. Their "spirit" shows us how the first generation of Christians was able to see the face of Christ "in the law of Moses and the prophets and the psalms" (Lk. 24:44). They thus attest to the permanent relevance of the Old Testament in the Christian effort to understand and celebrate the Lord who is at the heart of both Testaments. As Irenaeus of Lyons put it, "The writings of Moses are the words of Christ."[1]

— The *Didache*, and especially the "eucharistic" prayer that it contains. This prayer of thanksgiving may have served as framework for a Christian meal that included, in all probability, the celebration of the Eucharist.

— The *Letter to the Corinthians* of Clement of Rome, which gives us the earliest witness we have to the liturgical prayer of the Church of Rome. It dates from 95–98 A.D.

— The witness of St. Justin, who in his *First Apology* describes the rites of baptism and the Eucharist as well as the celebration of the Lord's day. This document goes back to the middle of the second century, about 150.

— The *Homily on the Pasch* of Melito of Sardis, in the second half of the second century. This masterpiece of rhythmic prose shows us what fruit paschal joy can yield when combined with a splendid literary form.

— The *Apostolic Tradition* of Hippolytus of Rome. This extraordinarily important document attests to the state of the liturgy and Christian practice in the Church of Rome at the beginning of the third century.

---

1. *Adversus Haereses* IV, 2, 3. See also A. Rousseau *et al.*, *Irénée de Lyon: Contre les hérésies, Livre IV* (SC 100; Paris, 1965), p. 400.

— The *Anaphora of Addai and Mari*. In all probability, this anaphora is contemporary with the one in the *Apostolic Tradition*.

— The *Didascalia of the Apostles*, which likewise dates from the beginning of the third century.

— The *Euchology of Serapion*, bishop of Thmuis in Egypt, written about 350.

Beginning in the fourth century, the witnesses become more abundant but are of unequal value. We may divide them into two groups.

The first group consists of liturgical texts and collections. They are anonymous compositions, for the most part, and for this reason it is not easy to date them. The exegete also finds in them many a snare and surprise, for the manuscript tradition by which they have come down to us has sometimes added more recent elements, to the point that critical scholarship has difficulty in restoring the original movement of the text. Frequently, therefore, we find ourselves unwillingly drawn onto the treacherous ground of risky hypotheses. And yet, despite this danger, we can find in these texts, buried there under the layers of dust laid down by time, the gold of the ancient formulas. In this first group we may locate the following texts:

— The *Strasbourg Papyrus*, which probably goes back to the fourth century and contains the so-called Liturgy of St. Mark.

— The *Apostolic Constitutions*, which draw upon the *Didascalia of the Apostles* (in Books 1–6), the *Didache* (in Book 7), and the *Apostolic Tradition* (in Book 8). This is the most extensive of the liturgical books; it was compiled toward the end of the fourth century.

— The *Euchology of Der Balyzeh*, which was rescued from the sands of Egypt. Although it was edited at a relatively late date (fifth-sixth century), the prayers it contains may in all likelihood claim to be much older.

— In a section entitled *Klasmata* (Greek: fragments, crumbs), we have gathered fragments from various periods that could not be classified under any other heading but are nonetheless worth our attention.

The second group comprises writings that are based on the liturgical rites and texts, and endeavor to explain them or to derive exhortations from them. As the reader may guess, these explanations are of the greatest interest for our own understanding of the early liturgy. We may mention here:

— The *Catecheses* of Cyril of Jerusalem, which were preached about 347. To these are usually added the *Mystagogical Catecheses*, although their authenticity is suspect; they could date from around 400.

— The *Baptismal Catecheses* of John Chrysostom (discovered October 4, 1955, by A. Wenger), which were preached between 386 and 398.[2]

— The treatises *On the Sacraments* and *On the Mysteries* of Ambrose of Milan.[3]

---

2. A. Wenger, *Jean Chrysostome: Huit catéchèses baptismales* (SC 50; Paris, 1957).

3. *De sacramentis: PL* 16:417–62; *De mysteriis: PL* 16:389–410. See also B. Botte, *Ambroise de Milan, Des sacrements, Des mystères* (SC 25bis; Paris, 1961).

These are a series of catechetical instructions for the use of neophytes. They were preached about 390 and copied by one of the hearers.

— The *Pilgrimage of Etheria*, which describes the liturgy at Jerusalem as Etheria saw it during her pilgrimage to the holy places about 400.[4]

— The *Catecheses* of Theodore of Mopsuestia in Cilicia (†428).[5]

In order not to make the present book too long, we shall present only the *Catecheses* of Cyril of Jerusalem. These are undoubtedly the most important of the group, and we believe them to be also among the most beautiful.

As in the past, we have avoided taking sides in the controversies to which the texts must inevitably give rise. These discussions are often interesting and at times absolutely necessary. They are the means by which we obtain light; they help us to achieve a better understanding of the sources. Here, however, we prefer to leave the questions open whenever possible and let the reader retain the happy responsibility of making up his own mind (even if he can sometimes see where our own preference lies). Our purpose is simply to bring together the data supplied by the tradition — data sometimes scattered through many books not readily available — and to present them to the reader.

Many of the texts gathered here appeared in my book *Aux sources de la liturgie* (Paris, 1963). When the time came for a fourth edition of the English translation, *Early Sources of the Liturgy*, I was asked to revise my work. I have profited by this opportunity to go back over all the texts, to introduce, where pertinent, the results of more recent research, and, above all, to turn the original work into a more complete collection. To the edition of 1963 I have added the sections on the Jewish liturgy and the texts of the New Testament, the *Letter to the Corinthians* of Clement of Rome, the *Homily on the Pasch* of Melito of Sardis, and the *Catecheses* of Cyril of Jerusalem.

It is my hope that this revised edition will continue to be of service to all those who are tired of drinking their water from the pitcher of routine and prefer to drink it from the fountain of tradition. It is from this fountain that it flows, like spring water, in its original freshness. The journey back to the sources is a marvelous one, for knowledge of the past brings the promise of youth and newness for the future. Under the action of the Spirit, says Irenaeus of Lyons, "the faith we have received from the Church, like a priceless perfume that has been kept in a superb vessel, constantly rejuvenates, and communicates its own youthfulness to, the vessel that contains it."[6]

---

4. *CCL*, Excerptum 175 (Steenbrugge, 1958). See also H. Petre, *Ethérie: Journal de voyage* (*SC* 21; Paris, 1948).

5. R. Tonneau and R. Devreesse, *Les homélies catéchétiques de Théodore de Mopsueste* (Studi e testi 145; Vatican City, 1949). See also A. Hänggi and I. Pahl (eds.), *Prex Eucharistica: Textus e variis liturgiis antiquioribus selecti* (Spicilegium Friburgense 12; Fribourg, 1968), pp. 214–18.

6. *Adversus Haereses* III, 21, 1. See also A. Rousseau and L. Doutreleau, *Irénée de Lyon: Contre les hérésies, Livre III* (*SC* 211; Paris, 1974), p. 472.

1

The Sources of Jewish Prayer

THE SOURCES OF JEWISH PRAYER

At the source of the Christian liturgy lies the Jewish liturgy. Just as Jesus, according to the forthright statement in Scripture, was born "of the seed of David according to the flesh" (Rom. 1:3; cf. 2 Tim. 2:8), so too the liturgy that celebrates the Messiah, the Son of David, borrowed its prayers from the people of Abraham and David. It was in the school of the synagogue that the Church learned how to read the word of God, compose its Gospel, and discover the words for its own prayer.[1]

The Jewish liturgy is to the Christian liturgy what the flower is to the fruit, the promise to the fulfillment. Just as the ancient Scriptures were, as it were, "pregnant" with Christ — that is, carried the Messiah in their womb — so also the Jewish liturgy was the womb from which the Christian liturgy was born. In fact, the very richness of the New Testament prayers bears witness to how rich the Jewish soil was in which the infant Christian liturgy sank its roots.

In making our modern pilgrimage back to the sources of Jewish prayer and liturgy, with the purpose of gaining a better knowledge of the origins of Christian prayer and liturgy, we have had to hold ourselves in check while choosing texts. Moreover, we have had to provide a framework for the testimonies, so that the latter might fit properly into our book with its limited scope. Therefore we have proceeded as follows:

We have decided not to cite biblical texts from the Old Testament, although these are, as everyone knows, at the heart of both the Jewish tradition and the Christian liturgy. For example, by way of shedding light on the account of the institution of the Lord's Supper, we could, with good reason, have cited the account of the covenant-making on Sinai as given in Ex. 24:1-11 (since Jesus' words, "This is the blood of the covenant" repeat the words Moses used), the text on the new covenant in Jer. 31:31-34 (since the covenant celebrated in the Eucharist is called "new" in Lk. 22:20 and 1 Cor. 11:25), the fourth Servant Song

---

1. On the relationship between the two Testaments, see H. de Lubac, *Exégèse médiévale*, Part I (Théologie 41; Paris, 1959), pp. 318–55. When we speak here of Jewish liturgy and Jewish prayer, we are thinking of these in their entire range, both private and public, and making no distinction between these two sectors; the distinction is not required for our purposes.

3

in Is. 53 (which makes its presence felt throughout the account of institution[2]), and finally the psalms of the Hallel (Pss. 113–118), which Christ sang with the Twelve at the Supper (see Matthew 26:30). We believed, however, that these references were readily available and the texts accessible to everyone. We have therefore limited ourselves deliberately to the Jewish tradition that is not contained in the Bible.

On the other hand, while the entire Jewish tradition deserves esteem and respect from a Christian, it does not follow that all its texts shed the same light when it comes to understanding the Christian texts. It seemed reasonable, therefore, to limit ourselves to the Jewish prayers that directly influenced the Christian liturgies.

Within this frame of reference, we have chosen the following:

The *Kiddush* for the Sabbath and feast days, which has provided the Roman Missal with its prayers for the presentation of the bread and wine;

The *Birkat ha-mazon*, a blessing recited after meals;

The *Shemone Esre*, or "Eighteen Blessings," in the Palestinian and Babylonian recensions;

The *Birkat Yotser* of the prayer *Shema Israel*;

The *Kaddish*, which underlies the Christian Our Father.

These last three texts provided models for the elaboration of the first Christian anaphoras.[3] They show that the isolation of the words of institution is only apparent, for it is a solitude that is in fact filled with the presence of Jewish prayer.

An unbridled apologetic approach to these marvelous texts could well reduce them to a state of enslavement. Such an approach might assert, on the one hand, that "there is nothing new, since the Christian liturgy was born of the Jewish liturgy." On the other hand, it might claim that "everything is new, since the Christian liturgy broke away from the Jewish liturgy."

In fact, the texts should not be appropriated in either way. The most authentic respect we can give them consists in respecting fully the letter of them. For this Jewish letter is of royal dignity, inasmuch as it reflects the prayer of the people whom God loved more than any other in the world, the people of whom the Lord said: "You shall be my own possession among all peoples" (Ex. 19:5). Such prayer has no need of pseudo-honors. It possesses its value in itself, just as do "the sonship, the glory, the covenants, the giving of the law, the worship, and the promises; to them belong the patriarchs, and of their race, according to the flesh, is the Christ" (Rom. 9:4-5).

It is true, nonetheless, that when the Christian liturgy read these texts, it filled them with newness. But the newness is to be found not in the letter but in the realities to which it now refers: the coming of Christ Jesus among men and his

---

2. On this point, see L. Deiss, *It's the Lord's Supper: The Eucharist of Christians*, tr. E. Bonin (New York, 1975), pp. 18–19, 42–43.

3. On the ritual of the Jewish Passover and the hymn of the Four Nights, see Deiss, pp. 33–39, 51–67.

presence at the heart of his liturgical prayer. Irenaeus of Lyons writes: "What did Christ bring when he came? Know that he brought complete newness, because he brought himself."[4] Thus, when the liturgy prays the Our Father, it makes its own the formulas created by the Jewish *Kaddish*, but it gives them the depth of meaning that only the Son, "full of grace and truth," could give to the invocation "Father." Similarly, when the liturgy recites the words of the *Shema Israel*, it repeats the ancient words of Deuteronomy: "You shall love the Lord your God with all your heart," but it endeavors to love God as no one had previously been able to do, that is, to love him with the very heart of Jesus himself. And when it recites the Eighteen Blessings, it continues to ask for the coming of tender love and mercy upon the world, but it also knows that the Father's tender love has acquired a human face in Jesus Christ.

It is not enough to say that we must approach these texts with sympathy. Rather, we must, as far as is possible, read them with the eyes of Christ Jesus; when he was still a little child, he learned them from Joseph and Mary. And it was he who, as his soul awakened to adoring love of the Father, gave these texts the fullness of meaning that the Christian liturgy today sees in them. Across the gulf of the centuries, we continue the reading of them that was begun by Jesus, for, as Paul said, "we have the mind of Christ" (1 Cor. 2:16).

The Kiddush *for the Sabbath and Feast Days*

The word *kiddush* means "sanctification"[5] and is the name of the blessing pronounced at the beginning of each Sabbath and feast day, at the moment when the first stars appear and the Sabbath lamp has been lit. It separates profane time from time more specially consecrated to God.

The prayer comprises a blessing over the wine, a blessing of the day, and a blessing over the bread. These blessings are said at table by the father of the family, with his family and guests around him.

As we know, the blessings over the bread and wine have been taken over in the ritual of the Roman Mass for the presentation of the offerings.

BLESSING OF THE WINE

The master of the house stands, holds the cup of wine in his right hand, and, with eyes raised to the lamp, recites the text of Gen. 1:31b–2:1-3, which tells of the institution of the Sabbath. He then directs his gaze to the cup and says:

---

4. *Adversus Haereses* IV, 34, 1 (*SC* 100:846).

5. On the *Kiddush*, see Hänggi-Pahl, pp. 5–7; I. Ellbogen, *Der jüdische Gottesdienst in seiner geschichtlichen Entwicklung* (4th ed. Hildesheim, 1962), pp. 107–12; G. F. Moore, *Judaism in the First Centuries of the Christian Era* 2 (Cambridge, Mass., 1927), p. 36; J. Jeremias, *The Eucharistic Words of Jesus*, tr. N. Perrin (London, 1966), pp. 26–29.

You are blessed, Lord our God,
King of the universe,
you who created the fruit of the vine.

He then adds this blessing in order to sanctify the day of the Sabbath or the feast.

You are blessed, Lord our God,
King of the universe.
You have sanctified us by your commandments,
you have given us as an inheritance the Sabbath of your holiness,
out of love and good will,
as a memorial of the works of your creation (Lev. 23:3).
This day is the first of your holy convocations.
It is the memorial of the exodus from Egypt.
You have chosen us among all peoples,
you have sanctified us,
you have given us as an inheritance the Sabbath of your holiness,
out of love and good will.
You are blessed, O Lord, who sanctify the Sabbath!

All those present then receive a bit of the wine from the cup into their own glasses, and drink it after the father of the family has drunk.[6]

BLESSING OF THE BREAD

The father of the family lays his hands on the bread, then raises it while saying:

You are blessed, Lord our God,
King of the universe,
you who have brought bread forth from the earth.

He then breaks the bread and distributes it to the guests.

Birkat ha-mazon

BLESSING AFTER MEALS

The *Birkat ha-mazon* is the blessing recited after meals.[7] It contains four parts: the *Birkat ha-zan*, which blesses the Creator; the *Birkat ha-aretz*, which gives thanks for the land, the covenant, and the law, and is thus a memorial of the history of salvation; the *Birkat-Ierusalayim*, which is a prayer of intercession for

6. According to the school of Hillel, the blessing of the wine precedes the blessing of the day; according to the school of Shammai, it follows it. See Tractate *Berakoth*, in H. Danby, *The Mishnah* (Oxford, 1933), p. 8.
7. See Hänggi-Pahl, pp. 8–12, for a Latin translation and some bibliographical references.

Jerusalem and the house of David; and the *Birkat ha-tob we-ha-metib*, which is a general blessing at closing.

We should note that to the second and third blessings embolisms[8] could be added that would develop the reasons for praise and the intentions being prayed for, especially on the feasts of Purim and Hanukkah.[9]

While the *Birkat ha-tob* may date from the time of the rebellion of Bar-Kochba († *ca.* 135), the first three blessings seem to be very old. It is thought that the third goes back to the second century B.C., while the first two seem older still. Jesus himself, therefore, recited them.

The whole of the *Birkat ha-mazon*, with the elements that structure it — thanksgiving for creation and for the history of salvation; memorial; intercessory prayer — seems to have been the basis on which the Christian anaphoras were developed.[10] This is especially the case for the earliest anaphoras, such as the anaphora of Addai and Mari and the Egyptian anaphora of St. Mark, as preserved for us in the Strassburg Papyrus.

We give here two versions of the *Birkat ha-mazon*. The first represents L. Finkelstein's attempt to reconstruct the primitive text.[11] The second is the liturgical version as given in the *Siddur Rav Saadja* (tenth century).[12]

Birkat ha-mazon

(Primitive Text as Reconstructed by L. Finkelstein)

You are blessed, Lord our God,
    King of the universe,
you who nourish the entire world
with goodness, tender love, and mercy.
    You are blessed, O Lord,
you who nourish the universe.

We will give you thanks, Lord our God,

---

8. An "embolism" (Greek: *embolismos*, "something inserted") is a prayer that has been inserted within the original text.

9. The feast of Purim, or Lots, celebrated the story of Esther (Est. 9:26-32). The feast of Hanukkah, or Dedication, commemorated the dedication of the Temple under Judas Maccabeus in 164. On these feasts, see R. Martin-Achard, *Essai biblique sur les fêtes d'Israël* (Geneva, 1974), pp. 133–51.

10. See L. Ligier, "De la Cène de Jésus à l'anaphore de l'Eglise," *Maison-Dieu*, no. 87 (1966), pp. 32–36; L. Bouyer, *Eucharist: Theology and Spirituality of the Eucharistic Prayer*, tr. C. U. Quinn (Notre Dame, 1968), pp. 78–88, 97–103.

11. L. Finkelstein, "The birkat ha-mazon," *Jewish Quarterly Review* 19 (1929), pp. 243–59.

12. In I. Davidson, S. Assaf, and B. I. Joel, *Siddur R. Saadja Gaon* (Jerusalem, 1941), pp. 102–3.

for you have given us a desirable land for our inheritance,
[that we may eat of its fruits
and be filled with its goodness].
You are blessed, Lord our God,
for the land and the food.

Lord our God, take pity
on Israel your people and Jerusalem your city,
on Zion, the place where your glory dwells,
on your altar and your sanctuary.
You are blessed, O Lord, who build Jerusalem.
You are blessed, Lord our God,
    King of the universe,
(you who are) good and filled with kindness!

You are blessed, Lord our God,
    King of the universe,
(you who are) good and filled with kindness!

Birkat ha-mazon

(Liturgical Text According to the *Siddur Rav Saadja*)

You are blessed, Lord our God,
    King of the universe,
you who nourish us and (nourish) the entire world
with goodness, grace, tender love, and mercy.
    You are blessed, O Lord,
you who nourish the universe.

We will give you thanks, Lord our God,
for you have given us for our inheritance
a desirable land, good and widespread,
the covenant and the law, life and food.
For all these (blessings) we give you thanks
and we bless your name eternally and for ever.
    You are blessed, O Lord,
for the land and the food!

Lord our God, take pity
on Israel your people, on Jerusalem your city,
on your sanctuary, on your house,
on Zion, the place where your glory dwells,
on the great and holy dwelling.

In our day restore to its place
the reign of the house of David,
and build Jerusalem soon.
    You are blessed, O Lord,
who build Jerusalem! Amen.

You are blessed, Lord our God,
    King of the universe,
God our Father, our King, our Creator,
our Redeemer, good and beneficent King.
Day after day you are solicitous
to do good to us in many ways.
It is you who give us increase for ever
through grace, tender love, spirit, mercy, and every good.

Shemone Esre
(Eighteen Blessings)

The *Shemone Esre Berakot*, or "Eighteen Blessings," are "the most official and most representative prayer of Judaism."[13] They are also called the *Amidah*, from the verb *amad*, "be standing," because they are recited while standing, or even more simply the *Tephillah*, or "Prayer," because they were regarded as being the prayer par excellence. They comprise three introductory blessings, which are followed by twelve prayers of petition (these also end with blessings), and three final blessings.[14] The text could be expanded by means of embolisms; the most important of these is the *Kedushah* containing the *Sanctus*, which is inserted before the third blessing. On the Sabbath and feast days, the twelve prayers of petition were not said.

The influence of tradition and the changes wrought by piety have combined in a single prayer formulas that evidently date from different periods. It is thought that the *Shemone Esre* existed as a unity in the first century.[15] The first three and last three blessings go back to the pre-Christian period; the twelfth and fourteenth blessings are later than the destruction of the Temple in the year 70 A.D. (the twelfth blessing mentions the "heretics" (*ha-minim*), a reference to Jews who have gone over to the Christian "sect"). The prayer in its entirety must have acquired its

---

13. J. Bonsirven, *Textes rabbiniques des deux premiers siècles chrétiens* (Rome, 1955), p. 2.

14. The text of the prayer has deep roots in the biblical tradition. The reader will find in A. Z. Idelsohn, *Jewish Liturgy and Its Development* (New York, 1967), pp. 92–110, all the scriptural references for each blessing. For a short bibliography on the *Shemone Esre*, see Hänggi-Pahl, p. 41.

15. See Idelsohn, pp. 109–10; H. Strack and P. Billerbeck, *Kommentar zum Neuen Testament aus Talmud und Midrasch* 1 (Munich, 1922), p. 407.

definitive structure in the time of Gamaliel II (about 90 A.D.). This does not mean that the text of all the formulas was fixed, but only that the order of the eighteen blessings was established.[16]

Jesus knew the *Shemone Esre* and alludes to it in the Gospels. In fact, the beginning of the "Hymn of Jubilation" (Mt. 11:25-27; Lk. 10:21-22) and the title "God of Abraham, Isaac, and Jacob" (Mt. 22:32; Mk. 12:26; Lk. 20:37) are borrowed from the first blessing.[17]

What influence did the *Shemone Esre* have on the Christian liturgy? At the level of generalities, we may note that the twelve blessings in the middle, which are in fact petitions, are situated between praise and thanksgiving.[18] From this the Christian liturgy learned never to separate petition from praise. We see this union in the anaphoras when the liturgy integrates prayers of petition into these. These prayers of petition can, then, claim great antiquity, while at the same time they find their power magnified, as it were, by the context of praise. As for the more specific influence of the *Shemone Esre*, we may observe that the first three blessings, together with the *Sanctus*, recall the opening of the Eucharistic Prayer, while the blessings *Abhodah* and *Hoda'ah* recall respectively the epiclesis and the doxology.[19]

The *Shemone Esre* have come down to us in two main recensions: the Palestinian, which S. Schechter discovered in 1898 in the Cairo Geniza, and the Babylonian, which, while also originating, it seems, in Palestine, later on acquired a certain literary independence. The differences that have been observed between the recensions show that the great synagogal traditions retained a certain flexibility, the flexibility proper to living prayer. These differences do not alter the general movement of the prayer.

A. Palestinian Recension[20]

Lord, open my lips,
and my mouth will declare your praise! (Ps. 51:15)
1. *Abhoth*. You are blessed, Lord our God *and God of our fathers, God of*

---

16. See Moore, 1:292. Note that the name *Shemone Esre* was used even when the number of blessings exceeded eighteen.

17. See J. Jeremias, "La prière quotidienne dans la vie du Seigneur et dans l'Eglise primitive," *La prière des Heures* (Lex orandi 35; Paris, 1963), pp. 50–51.

18. Ellbogen observes: "The petitions were to be preceded by a section devoted to praise, and followed by a thanksgiving" (p. 31).

19. For more details, see Bouyer, pp. 70–78, 121–35, 197–200, 233–37.

20. Our translation follows the text as given in D. W. Staerk, *Altjüdische liturgische Gebete* (Bonn, 1910), pp. 11–14. There is a Latin translation in Hänggi-Pahl, pp. 41–43. The Hebrew words at the beginning of the paragraphs are the names given to these blessings in the Mishnah. The italicized words are considered to be additions to the primitive texts.

Abraham, *God of Isaac, and God of Jacob*, God great, powerful, and to be feared, God Most High, Lord of heaven and earth, our shield and the shield of our fathers, who make our trust increase *from generation to generation*. Blessed be you, Lord, shield of Abraham!

2. *Ghebhuroth*. You are powerful, *you humble the proud*; you are strong, *you judge the tyrants*; you live eternally, you give life to the dead; you bring back the wind, you pour down the dew; you feed the living, you give life to the dead; *in the twinkling of an eye you make salvation send forth its shoots*. Blessed be you, Lord, who give life to the dead!

3. *Qedushah*. You are holy, your name strikes fear; apart from you there is no other god. Blessed be you, Lord, holy God!

4. *Binah*. Grant us, our Father, the grace of the knowledge *that comes* from you, as well as the understanding and the discernment (that come) from your law. Blessed be you, Lord, who grant us the grace of knowledge!

5. *Teshubhah*. "Make us return to you, Lord, and we will return. Renew our days as of old" (Lam. 5:21). Blessed be you, Lord, who take delight in conversion!

6. *Selihah*. Forgive us, O our Father, for we have sinned against you. Wipe away *and remove* our sins from before your eyes, *for your mercies are many*. Blessed be you, Lord, who hasten to multiply forgiveness!

7. *Ghe'ullah*. Look upon our affliction, take our cause in hand, redeem us for your name's sake. Blessed be you, Lord, Redeemer of Israel!

8. *Rephu'ah*. Heal us, Lord our God, of all the anxieties of our hearts, *keep sadness and groaning from us*, place a medicament on our wounds. Blessed be you, Lord, who heal the sick among your people Israel!

9. *Birkat ha-shanim*. Bless this year for us, Lord our God, *let it abound in every kind of fruit. And make the year of our redemption come soon*. Let the dew and rain fall on the surface of the earth. Give the world its fill of the treasures of your goodness. *Bless the work of our hands*. Blessed be you, Lord, who bless the years!

10. *Qibbuts galuyoth*. Make the great trumpet sound for our deliverance, raise the standard for the gathering of our captives. Blessed be you, Lord, who gather the exiles of *your people* Israel!

11. *Mishpat*. "Make our judges what they were in other years, our counselors what they were of old" (Is. 1:26). Reign over us, you alone. Blessed be you, Lord, who love justice!

12. *La-meshumadim*. For the apostates let there be no hope. Root out quickly the rule of pride. Blessed be you, Lord, who humble the proud!

13. *La-tsadiqim*. For the proselytes (who seek) justice, let your mercies be stirred. Grant us the *good* reward with those who do your will. Blessed be you, Lord, who increase the confidence of the upright!

14. *Ierushalayim. In the multitude of your mercies*, Lord our God, take pity *on your people Israel*, on Jerusalem *and Zion, dwelling place of your glory, on your sanctuary, on your house* and the reign of David, the One Anointed with your justice. Blessed be you, Lord, God of David, *who build Jerusalem*!

15. *Tephillah*. Hear the voice of our prayer, Lord our God, *and take pity on us*, for you are a benevolent and merciful God! Blessed be you, Lord, who hear prayers!

16. *Abhodah*. Make it your delight, Lord our God, to dwell on Zion. May your servants serve you at Jerusalem. Blessed be you, O Lord, whom we wish to serve with reverence!

17. *Hoda'ah*. We thank you, Lord, *for you are the Lord* our God *and God of our fathers*, for all the benefits, *for your kindness, your mercies by which you have made us grow*, which you have lavishly bestowed on us and on our fathers before us. *When we said, "Our feet stumble, then your love, O Lord, is our support"* (cf. Ps. 94:18). Blessed be you, Lord; it is good to give thanks to you.

18. *Shalom*. Give peace to Israel your people, *to your city, to your inheritance*. Then together we shall praise you: Blessed be you, Lord, who give peace!

B. Babylonian Recension[21]

Lord, open my lips,
and my mouth shall declare your praise! (Ps. 51:15)

1. *Abhoth*. You are blessed, Lord our God and God of our fathers, God of Abraham, God of Isaac, and God of Jacob, God great, powerful, and to be feared, God Most High, who fill us with your blessings, sovereign of the universe, who are mindful of the fidelity of our fathers, who send a redeemer to the children of their children out of love for your name, O king, helper, savior, and shield. Blessed be you, Lord, shield of Abraham!

2. *Ghebhuroth*. You are powerful for ever, Lord, you give life to the dead, you feed the living out of kindness, you give life to the dead by your countless mercies, "you raise up the fallen" (Ps. 145:14), you are faithful to those who sleep in the dust. Who is like you, Lord, (who do) marvelous things? Who is like you "who give life and death" (1 Sam. 2:6)? You make salvation send forth its shoots quickly; you are faithful, who give life to the dead. Blessed be you, Lord, who give life to the dead!

3. *Qedushah*.[22] The multitudes of heaven crown you, together with the congregations here below. Together they will thrice proclaim your holiness, as the prophet says: "They were crying one to another and singing:

Holy, holy, holy, the Lord Sabaoth.
The earth is full of his glory!" (Is. 6:3).

---

21. Text according to the *Seder Rav Amran*; Latin translation in Hänggi-Pahl, pp. 44–54.

22. In this third blessing, the text down to and including the citation from Ps. 146:10 is an embolism that was inserted into the prayer when it was recited by the celebrant in the presence of a congregation; in some traditions, the congregation responded with the three quotations from Scripture.

Then, with the crash of resounding thunder, marvelous and mighty, they will make their voices heard and, rising toward you, they will say:

"Blessed be the glory of the Lord
in your dwelling place!" (Ezek. 3:12).

Shine forth from your place, O our King, reign over us, for we await you. When will you reign? Reign in Zion soon, in our days. In our lifetime establish your dwelling. Be glorified and sanctified in the midst of Jerusalem, your city, from generation to generation and for ever and ever. May our eyes see your reign, according to the word that was said in the songs of your power through the mouth of David, the One Anointed with your justice:

"The Lord will reign for ever,
your God, O Zion, from age to age!
Alleluia!" (Ps. 146:10)

From [23] generation to generation we proclaim the kingship of God, for he alone is the Most High, the Holy One. May the proclamation of your glory, O our God, never leave our lips, for you are the great King, you are the Holy One. Blessed be you, Lord, holy God!

4. *Binah.* You grant man the grace of knowledge, to mortal man you teach understanding. Grant us the grace of the knowledge that comes from you, as well as understanding and discernment. Blessed be you, Lord, who grant us the grace of knowledge!

5. *Teshubhah.* Make us return, O our Father, to your law; grant that we may serve you, O our King. Bring us back into your presence through a complete conversion. Blessed be you, Lord, who take delight in conversion!

6. *Selihah.* Forgive us, O our Father, for we have sinned. Pardon us, for we have committed violations. Blessed be you, Lord, who pardon and multiply forgiveness!

7. *Ghe'ullah.* Look upon our affliction, take our cause in hand, hasten to redeem us soon for your name's sake, for you are a mighty Redeemer. Blessed be you, Lord, Redeemer of Israel!

8. *Rephu'ah.* Heal us, Lord our God, and we will be healed of all our infirmities. For you are a God who heals, you are merciful. Blessed be you, Lord, who heal the sick among your people Israel!

9. *Birkat ha-shanim.* Bless this year for us, Lord our God: let it abound in every kind of fruit. Blessed be you, Lord, who bless the years!

10. *Qibbuts galuyoth.* Make the great trumpet sound for our deliverance, raise the standard for the gathering of our captives, proclaim our liberation, bring us together from the four corners of the earth. Blessed be you, Lord, who gather the exiles of your people Israel!

---

23. When the embolism was not said, this third blessing consisted of only this final paragraph.

11. *Mishpat.* "Make our judges what they were in other years, our counselors what they were of old" (Is. 1:26). Reign over us with justice and judgment. Blessed be you, Lord, "who love justice and judgment" (Ps. 33:5)!

12. *La-meshumadim.* For the apostates let there be no hope. May the heretics perish in an instant, may all the enemies of your people be quickly annihilated. Root out quickly the rule of pride, break it and bring it low in our days. Blessed be you, Lord, who break the wicked and humble the proud!

13. *La-tsadiqim.* For the just, the devout, the proselytes (who seek) justice, let your mercies be stirred, Lord our God. Grant a good reward to those who trust faithfully in your name. Grant us a share in their (happiness), may we never have to blush with shame. Blessed be you, Lord, protector and hope of the just!

14. *Ierushalayim.* Because of your mercy, return to Jerusalem, your city. In our days build your everlasting dwelling in her. Blessed be you, Lord, who build Jerusalem!

15. *David.* Make the shoot of David soon blossom anew, exalt its power [lit.: its horn] through your salvation. Blessed be you, Lord, who make the power [horn] of salvation blossom anew!

16. *Tephillah.* Hear our voice, Lord our God; in your mercy and good will accept our prayer. For from eternity you are a God who hears our prayer and our petition.

17. *Abhodah.* Find your delight, Lord our God, in your people Israel, have regard for its prayer. Restore the (liturgical) service to the sanctuary of your dwelling. In (your) love, accept soon the sacrifices and prayers of Israel with good will. Let the service of your people Israel be always pleasing to you, and may our eyes see your return to Zion. Yes, let our eyes see your merciful return to Zion. Blessed be you, Lord, who come again to dwell on Zion!

18. *Hoda'ah.* We thank you because you are the Lord our God, the rock of our life, the shield of our salvation, from generation to generation. We will thank you, we will tell your praise because of our lives which we have placed in your hands, because of our souls which you preserve. You are good, for your mercies do not fade. You take pity on us, for your kindnesses do not cease. For ages we have put our trust in you. You have not sent shame upon us, Lord our God, you have not abandoned us, you have not hidden your face from us.

For all these benefits, may your name be blessed and exalted without end, O our King, through eternity and beyond! May all living creatures thank you for ever, may they praise your name in truth. Blessed be you, Lord; your name is good, and it is right to give you thanks.

19. *Shalom.* Give peace, happiness, blessing, compassion, mercy to us and to your people. Bless us all, our Father, with the light of your face. For it is by the light of your face that you have given us, Lord our God, the law of life, love, compassion, justice, mercy, and peace. May it seem good in your eyes to bless your people Israel at every time. Blessed be you, Lord, who bless your people in peace!

Shema Israel

BIRKAT YOTSER

The *Shema Israel* is Judaism's profession of faith. At the same time, it is the basic assertion of the Jewish law that is also the law of Christianity: "You shall love the Lord your God with all your heart, with all your soul, with all your strength." It includes Dt. 6:4-9, which begins with *Shema, Israel*, "Hear, O Israel," and thus gives the entire prayer its name. To this passage have been added Dt. 11:13-21 and Num. 15:37-41, which recalls the rescue from Egypt.

Jewish tradition likes to think of the practice of reciting the *Shema* as going back to the patriarch Jacob or to Moses.[24] This shows that Jews have regarded the practice as very ancient; certainly it goes back to the pre-Christian period. When a scribe asks about the first and greatest commandment, Jesus immediately recites the beginning of the *Shema Israel* (Mk. 12:29).

The *Shema* was originally not a prayer but a profession of faith. Nonetheless, it later became, according to D. W. Staerk, "the principal prayer of Judaism."[25] And in fact the tradition has chosen to place the profession of faith in a context of praise and blessings. Thus the two blessings *Birkat Yotser* and *Birkat Ahabah Rabbah* form a kind of doorway of praise that leads the Jewish soul to its profession of faith, while a third blessing, the *Birkat Emet-we-yatsib*, concludes the profession.

We give here the *Birkat Yotser*.[26] It begins with praise of the Creator of light and darkness: each new dawn that he causes to break over the world is like a new creation. This blessing was especially suitable when the *Shema* was used as a morning prayer. The praise then continues with a blessing of God who creates the world of the angels, and with the *Sanctus*, the acclamation of the seraphim in the Book of Isaiah.

The *Birkat Yotser* may have served as a model for the Christian anaphoras, which begin with a blessing of God the Creator and lead to the singing of the *Sanctus* acclamation.[27]

You are blessed, Lord our God, King of the universe, "you who form the light and create the darkness" (Is. 45:7); who shed the light of your mercy upon the earth and those who dwell on it; who, out of goodness, constantly renew every day the works of your creation.

"How splendid are your works, Lord! You have done them all with wisdom; the earth is full of your riches" (Ps. 104:24). Sublime king, the one and only from before time, glorious, magnificent, exalted since the days of eternity!

---

24. See Strack-Billerbeck, 4/1 (Munich, 1928), p. 191. On the *Shema*, see the bibliography in Hänggi-Pahl, pp. 35–36; Latin translation, pp. 36–37.
25. Staerk, p. 3.
26. Hebrew text in Staerk, pp. 4–6.
27. See Bouyer, pp. 62–70.

God of the universe, in accordance with your many mercies, take pity on us, sovereign Lord of our strength, rock of our refuge, shield of our salvation, our refuge!

The blessed God in his great wisdom prepared and formed the rays of the sun. He created this good thing for the glory of his name. He set the stars in place in accordance with his power. The leaders of his armies are his holy (angels). Ceaselessly they extol God, they proclaim the glory of the Almighty and his holiness. Be blessed, Lord our God, for the splendid work of your hands and for the lamps that you have created. May they glorify you!

Be blessed, our rock, our king, our redeemer, who create the holy (angels). May your name be glorified for eternity, our king, who create the angels! Your angels stand in the heights of heaven; together, in a loud voice, they proclaim with reverence the works of the living God and king of the universe. All of them [the angels] are holy, all chosen, all powerful; with respect and reverence all do the will of their Creator; all open their mouths in holiness and purity, they sing melodiously, they bless, they glorify, they magnify, they adore, they proclaim the holy king and the name of God. . . . They say with reverence:

> "Holy, holy, holy is the Lord Sabaoth!
> The earth is full of his glory" (Is. 6:3).

And the *Ophanim* [28] and the holy Living Creatures (*Hayyot*), with a thunderous noise, rise up to face one another; they give glory and say:

> "Blessed be the glory of the Lord
> in the place where he dwells!" (Ezek. 3:12)

To the blessed God they offer their songs; to the God who is king, living and eternal, they sing hymns and proclaim his praises. For he alone does wonders; he accomplishes new things, this master of battles. He sows justice, makes salvation bear fruit, creates healings. He is revered that he may be praised, the Lord of wonders.

Out of goodness he ceaselessly renews, every day, the works of his creation, as it is said: "He creates the great lamps, for his love is everlasting!" (Ps. 136:7).

Illumine Zion with a new light! Let us soon be made worthy of your light!

Blessed be you, Lord, who create the stars!

---

28. The *Yotser* here alludes to the inaugural vision of Ezekiel (ch. 1). In the Jewish tradition, the angels surround and support the divine throne on which the glory of Yahweh rests. These angels are the seraphim of Is. 6:2, the cherubim of Ezek. 10:3, the *Hayyot* or four Living Creatures of Ezek. 1, and the *Ophanim* or four Wheels in which the Living Creatures dwell (Ezek. 1:20). (At Babylon, the wheel, an ideogram for the sun, was a symbol of the divinity.) The praise offered by the angels is normally linked to the creation of the stars, for the angels were thought to be in charge of governing the elements of the world; see J. Bonsirven, "Judaïsme palestinien au temps de Jésus-Christ," *Dictionnaire de la Bible: Supplément* 4 (Paris, 1949), col. 116.

The Jewish Kaddish *and the Christian Our Father*

KADDISH

At the base of all liturgical prayer or, even more simply, of all Christian prayer is the Our Father. But at the base of the Christian Our Father is the Jewish *Kaddish*. Therefore, by way of conclusion to the Jewish tradition and introduction to the New Testament, we give here the Jewish *Kaddish* and the Christian Our Father.

The *Kaddish* (Aramaic for "sanctification") concluded the synagogal office and was therefore familiar to Jesus from his childhood. It occurs in five principal forms, which are meant for different uses.[29] The first two petitions inspired the first two petitions of the Lord's Prayer.[30]

May his great name be magnified and sanctified
in the world that he created according to his good pleasure!
May he make his reign prevail
during your life and during your days,
and during the life of the entire house of Israel
at this very moment and very soon.
    And let them say: Amen!

May the name of the Lord — blessed be he! —
be blessed, praised, glorified, extolled,
exalted, honored, magnified, and hymned!
It is above and beyond
any blessing, hymn, praise, consolation
that men utter in this world.
    And let them say: Amen!

OUR FATHER

The Our Father has come to us in two traditions, the Matthean and the Lukan. The two are irreducible, that is, they cannot be traced back to a single Hebrew or Aramaic original. Back-translations into Aramaic, whether of the Matthean text (C. F. Burney) or of the Lukan text (C. C. Torrey) reveal that each text has a finely crafted rhythmical movement of its own. It is therefore highly

---

29. See Idelsohn, pp. 84–88; Ellbogen, pp. 94–98.
30. On the Jewish roots of the Our Father, see Strack-Billerbeck, 1:408–22; A. Hamman, *La prière* 1. *La Nouveau Testament* (Tournai, 1969), pp. 97–100. Our translation follows the text as given in Staerk, pp. 30–31. A fuller translation is given in Bonsirven, *Textes rabbiniques*, p. 3.

probable that two oral traditions, both stemming from the teaching of Jesus, existed separately before being recorded in the Gospels. It is possible that the Matthean text represents the Galilean tradition, and the Lukan text the tradition of Antioch.[31]

Even if the quest of the very words that Jesus used in teaching represents the supreme longing of the exegete, we must not let ourselves be hypnotized by the letter. Even in the Lord's Prayer, the spirit is more important than the words. And according to this spirit, every Christian prayer should be a child's invocation of its Father: "Abba!" Joachim Jeremias explains: "'*Abbā* was a children's word, used in everyday talk, an expression of courtesy. It would have seemed disrespectful, indeed unthinkable, to the sensibilities of Jesus' contemporaries to address God with this familiar word. Jesus dared to use '*Abbā* as a form of address to God. . . . It expresses the heart of Jesus' relationship to God. He spoke to God as a child to its father, confidently and securely and yet at the same time reverently and obediently."[32]

Even in the most hieratic prayers, even during the most solemn liturgies, we should always bear in mind that the most important title is this "Abba, Father," which the Christian, as child of heaven, speaks to his Father.

Matthew 6:9-13	Luke 11:2-4
Our Father	Father,
who art in heaven,	
hallowed be thy name.	hallowed be thy name.
Thy kingdom come,	Thy kingdom come.
thy will be done,	
on earth as it is in heaven.	
Give us this day	Give us each day
our daily bread;	our daily bread;
and forgive us our debts,	and forgive us our sins,
as we also have forgiven	for we ourselves forgive
our debtors;	every one who is indebted to us;
and lead us not into temptation,	and lead us not into temptation.
but deliver us from evil.	

---

31. See J. De Fraine, "Oraison dominicale," *Dictionnaire de la Bible: Supplément* 6 (Paris, 1969), col. 792. On the Our Father, see J. Carmignac, *Recherches sur le "Notre Père"* (Paris, 1969), with bibliography on pp. 469–553. We may mention especially E. Lohmeyer, *The Lord's Prayer*, tr. J. Bowden (London, 1965); H. Schürmann, *Praying with Christ: The "Our Father" for Today*, tr. W. M. Ducey and A. Simon (New York, 1964).

32. J. Jeremias, *New Testament Theology: The Proclamation of Jesus*, tr. J. Bowden (New York, 1971), p. 67.

For thine
is the kingdom and the power and the
   glory,
for ever. Amen. [33]

---

33. This doxology is not part of the primitive text of Matthew. It is, however, very old (it is attested by the *Didache*), and it is certainly consonant with the biblical tradition (see, for example, 1 Chr. 29:10-11) and the Jewish tradition as well: the Mishnah speaks of sealing a prayer with a doxology (*Berakoth* 1, 4; see Danby, pp. 2–3). Analyzing the data of textual criticism, Carmignac writes: "This doxology is a very ancient liturgical creation (first or second century), inserted into Matthew's Gospel by a copyist of the Antioch area in about the third century" (p. 333). Lohmeyer reaches the same conclusion: "Thus we may term the doxology a gift of the Syrian Church, whence it came into general Church use" (p. 231).

2

The Account of the Institution of the Eucharist

THE SUPPER OF THE LORD

THE TRADITION OF THE COMMUNITY

The text of the institution of the Supper[1] is attested by the synoptic writers, Mark, Matthew, and Luke, and by Paul in the First Epistle to the Corinthians. If we compare the four accounts, we observe that Matthew agrees with Mark, and Luke with Paul. This means that the primitive community knew the narrative in two versions. One is that of Matthew and Mark; it comes from a Palestinian milieu, and its very idiom points to a Semitic original. The other version is that of Luke and Paul; it attests the usages of the Church of Antioch. Its Greek is of a better quality; but then Antiochene circles would quickly realize the necessity of an authentically Greek text for their liturgical celebrations.

Each tradition contains elements that bring it very close to the original; at the same time, however, it is impossible to determine which is the older text. Even the text of Mark, whose Gospel ordinarily gives us the earliest traditions, shows an editor's hand at work in the joining of verse 24 to verse 23. For if we take the text as it stands, we might think that the Twelve first drank the consecrated cup (v. 23) and only then learned that it contained the blood of the covenant (v. 24); yet this surely does not reflect the real sequence of events at the Supper. Consequently, we are led to think that the explanatory verse on the blood of the covenant (v. 24) was introduced into the narrative at a different redactional stage than verse 23.

Paul himself, as is well known, refers to a "tradition": "For I received from the Lord what I also delivered to you" (1 Cor. 11:23a). Paul was living in Corinth from the end of the year 50 to the middle of the year 52 (Acts 18:1-18). The text relating to the Eucharist dates, therefore, from the very first years of Christianity.

This is the text that the primitive community used for its celebrations and that would be taken over by all the anaphoras; it was to form the nucleus of the Eucharistic celebration of all later Christian generations. No analysis can determine its origin in all the detail we would like; there are locked doors here that conceal inner gardens from our view. But this is because the key to a full understanding of the text must be sought elsewhere than in exegesis, namely, in the hands of the community. The community is bent on celebrating the Eucharist rather than on describing it in writing; it lives the Eucharist and only secondarily

---

1. The best analysis of the institution is provided by J. Jeremias, *The Eucharistic Words of Jesus*, tr. N. Perrin (London, 1966). See also my book *It's the Lord's Supper: The Eucharist of Christians*, tr. E. Bonin (New York, 1976), pp. 5–46.

turns to analyzing the structure of the celebration. The community is first, not the text, while the text is entirely at the service of the community.

As They Were Eating, Jesus . . .

Note the liturgical character of the introductory formulas of Matthew and Mark: "As they were eating, Jesus took bread. . . ." In the narrative of the passion, into which the text of the institution is inserted, the mention of the meal is quite unnecessary, since it merely repeats Mt. 26:21 and Mk. 14:18. On the contrary, it is wholly in place in a liturgical celebration, where it emphasizes the bond that links the Eucharist to the Passover meal and to its whole theological context. The festive meal of Jesus with his disciples is a part of the long series of communion meals that began at Mount Sinai, where "they . . . ate and drank" (Ex. 24:11). In that same series were the countless covenant meals in the course of Israel's history, the meals Jesus took with his followers before and after his resurrection, and the celebrations of the breaking of bread in the early community. The final link in that long chain will be the eternal banquet of heaven.

Paul, for his part, speaks with even greater solemnity of "the Lord Jesus." This formula is part of the professions of faith current in the primitive community; thus, one who confesses that Jesus is "Lord" will be saved (Rom. 10:9; 1 Cor. 12:3). The mention of "the night when he was betrayed" calls to mind the figure of the Servant of Yahweh, who was delivered up in accordance with the providential plan of God (Is. 53:6, 12).

The New Covenant

The statement "This cup is the new covenant in my blood" recalls Ex. 24:8: "Behold the blood of the covenant which the Lord has made with you." According to Matthew and Mark, the blood of Jesus is poured out for "many," that is, for all. It is well known that the underlying Semitic expression, which the Greek translates as "many," can have either an exclusive sense ("many," therefore not "all") or an inclusive sense ("many," that is, "all"). The same Semitic usage occurs in the logion in Mk. 10:45 and Mt. 20:28: The Son of Man came "to give his life as a ransom for many," that is, for all.[2] Taken together, these formulas again suggest the identification of Jesus with Isaiah's Servant of Yahweh:

Matthew	Isaiah
This is my blood	I have given you
of the *covenant*,	as a *covenant* to the people (42:6).
which is poured out for *many*	Yet he bore
for the forgiveness of *sins*.	the *sin* of *many* (53:12).

---

2. Some other examples: "Many are called," that is, all are called, "but few are chosen" (Mt. 22:14); "If many [i.e., all men] died through one man's [Adam's] trespass, much more have the grace of God and the free gift in the grace of that one man Jesus Christ abounded for many [i.e., for all mankind]" (Rom. 5:15).

In the blood of his sacrifice, Jesus, Servant of Yahweh, seals the new covenant (Jer. 31:31-34) that God makes with the entire human race.

TRADITION OF MATTHEW AND MARK

Matthew 26:26-29	Mark 14:22-25
26 Now as they were eating Jesus took bread, and blessed, and broke it, and gave it to the disciples, and said, "Take, eat; this is my body."	22 And as they were eating, he took bread, and blessed, and broke it, and gave it to them, and said, "Take; this is my body."
27 And he took a cup, and when he had given thanks, he gave it to them,	23 And he took a cup, and when he had given thanks, he gave it to them, and they all drank of it.
saying, "Drink it, all of you," 28 for this is my blood of the covenant, which is poured out for many for the forgiveness of sins.	24 And he said to them, "This is my blood of the covenant, which is poured out for many.
29 I tell you I shall not drink again of this fruit of the vine until the day when I drink it new with you in my Father's kingdom."	25 Truly, I say to you, I shall not drink again of the fruit of the vine until that day when I drink it new in the kingdom of God."

TRADITION OF LUKE AND PAUL

Luke 22:15-18

15 And he said to them: "I have earnestly desired to eat
   this passover with you before I suffer;
16 for I tell you I shall not eat it until it is fulfilled
   in the kingdom of God."
17 And he took a cup, and when he had given thanks he said,
   "Take this and divide it among yourselves;
18 for I tell you that from now on I shall not drink of the fruit
   of the vine until the kingdom of God comes."

Luke 22:19-20	1 Corinthians 11:23-26
	23 The Lord Jesus on the night when he was betrayed took bread,
19 And he took bread, and when he had given thanks he broke it and gave it to them, saying, "This is my body which is given for you. Do this in remembrance of me."	24 and when he had given thanks, he broke it, and said: "This is my body which is for you. Do this in remembrance of me."
20 And likewise the cup	25 In the same way also the cup,
after supper, saying, "This cup which is poured out for you is the new covenant in my blood.	after supper, saying, "This cup is the new covenant in my blood. Do this, as often as you drink it, in remembrance of me.
18 For I tell you that from now on I shall not drink of the fruit of the vine until	26 For as often as you eat this bread and drink the cup, you proclaim the Lord's death until
the kingdom of God comes."	he comes."

Do This in Remembrance of Me

The Eucharist celebrated by the Christian community is the memorial of the passion and resurrection of the Lord, of the entirety of the mysteries that go to make up his "passover" or passage from this world to the glory of the Father. The formula "in remembrance of me" seems to echo a prayer that was recited after the blessing of the third cup: "Our God and God of our fathers . . . *remember* the Messiah, the Son of David, your Servant . . ." (Passover Haggadah). The apostles, then, were to celebrate the Eucharist in order that God might remember Jesus Messiah, the Son of David (cf. Ps. 132:1), that is, that he might establish in the triumphant fullness proper to eschatological times the kingdom that Jesus has inaugurated. This idea is clearly brought out in the eucharistic prayer of the *Didache*: "Lord, remember your Church and deliver it from all evil; make it perfect in your love and gather it from the four winds, this sanctified Church, into your kingdom which you have prepared for it."[3]

---

3. *Didache* 10, 5.

3

Doxologies, Blessings, and Hymns of the New Testament

doxology - acclaims & celebrates glory of God
blessing - gives thanks to God and blesses God's name

DOXOLOGIES AND BLESSINGS

You are a chosen race,
a royal priesthood, a holy nation,
a people God has won for himself
that you might declare his praises.

1 Pet. 2:9

The highest forms of Christian prayer are the *doxology*, which acclaims and celebrates the glory (*doxa*) of God, and the *blessing*, which gives thanks (*eucharistein*) to him and blesses (*eulogein*) his name.[1] Before the transcendent God who dwells in inaccessible light, before the wonderful saving deeds by which God has manifested himself among his people, and before the mystery of Jesus who makes the inaccessible Godhead dwell amid human poverty, man can only say over and over again: "God, you are blessed eternally!" He is well aware that God "is exalted above all blessing and praise" (Neh. 9:5) and that he, man, can neither add to nor detract from the infinite riches of the Lord. But he is also mindful that his special greatness as a man consists precisely in acknowledging and acclaiming the greatness of God and opening himself to the inflooding power of this glory by a wholehearted "Amen!"

In so doing, man responds at the deepest level to his supernatural vocation. He becomes the living "praise of glory" (cf. Eph. 1:6, 12) that he has been predestined to be from all eternity, and he anticipates, in a measure, his future state in eternity. He makes his earthly life an apprenticeship for his life in heaven.

Consequently, the formula "Blessed be God," which is found throughout the Bible, captures man's essential response in his dialogue with God. It condenses into a couple of words the fundamental attitude with which the people of the Old Testament awaited the Messiah. So true is this that the mind and heart of Israel

---

1. It is an accepted fact that in the language of the Bible, *eulogein* (bless) and *eucharistein* (give thanks) are almost synonyms, and that the two often translate the same Hebrew or Aramaic word; compare, for example, the *eulogēsas* of Mt. 26:26 and Mk. 14:22 with the *eucharistēsas* of Lk. 22:19. On this point, see J. Beyer, "eulogeō," *TDNT* 2:762, and J.-P. Audet, *La Didachè: Instructions des apôtres* (Paris, 1958), pp. 377–91.

found its fullest expression in the *Shemone Esre*, or "Eighteen Blessings,"[2] in which the constant refrain is "Blessed be Yahweh!" and which every Israelite was bound to recite three times daily.

The blessing and the doxology are also regarded as the highest kind of prayer by the faithful of the New Testament. They accepted Christ and acknowledged and acclaimed in him the God of Abraham, Isaac, and Jacob, the Father of our Lord Jesus Christ.

> Blessed be the God and Father
> of our Lord Jesus Christ! (2 Cor. 1:3-4).

Above all, these two forms are the essential ones Jesus himself used. He used them in his "Hymn of Jubilation," when he was filled with joy by the Holy Spirit and said:

> I bless you, Father,
> Lord of heaven and earth. . . .
> Yes, Father,
> for such was your good pleasure in your sight (Lk. 10:21-22).

He recalled this "Yes, Father" amid his tears in Gethsemane: "Abba! Father! . . . Not what I want, but what you want" (Mk. 14:36).

The New Testament writings have preserved a good number of blessings and doxologies for us. Some are brief acclamations, cries of praise that burst out in the midst of a passage and lift the reader on sudden wings toward the "God who is blessed forever":

> God delivered the pagans, in the lusts of their hearts, to an impurity that degraded their own bodies, for they exchanged the truth for a lie, and they adored and served the creature in preference to the creator — *he is blessed forever!*[3]

Other blessings are developed into full-blown hymns, such as the magnificent six-part blessing that opens the Epistle to the Ephesians.[4] Others have a cultic ring to them, such as the doxologies in the First Epistle to Timothy;[5] these may have been used in the liturgy of the synagogue and then absorbed into the prayer and liturgy of the primitive community. Most of the blessings follow the Old Testament pattern and include a remembrance (*anamnesis*) of the "wonderful deeds of God." Thus they lead directly over into the celebration of the Eucharist, which is the Christian community's supreme act of thanksgiving and supreme memorial of God's saving actions.[6]

---

2. On the *Shemone Esre*, see Chapter 1, above.
3. Rom. 1:24-25. See also Rom. 9:5; 2 Cor. 11:31.
4. Eph. 1:3-14; this will be cited further on.
5. 1 Tim. 1:17 and 6:15-16; these too will be cited further on.
6. See Deiss, pp. 48–51.

The variety and rich content of these prayers are evidence that they represent the very heart of a Christian's adoration. In addition, their theological value does not depend on their literary form or the length of their formulas, but on the dynamic power with which they sweep the soul onward to the eternal glory in which God reigns.[7]

Hymn of Jubilation

At that same hour,[8] Jesus trembled with joy in the Holy Spirit and he said:

I bless you, Father,
Lord of heaven and earth,
for having hid this from the wise and the clever
and for having revealed it to the little ones![9]
Yes, Father,
for such was your good pleasure in your sight![10]

Everything has been handed over to me by my Father.[11]
And no one knows who the Son is
but the Father,
or who the Father is
but the Son
and the one to whom the Son wills to reveal it.

(Lk. 10:21-22)

Messianic Acclamations

Hosanna to the Son of David!
Blessed be he who comes in the name of the Lord!

---

7. To the doxologies mentioned add: Rom. 1:25; 9:5; Gal. 1:5; 2 Cor. 11:31, as well as 1 Pet. 1:3-9 and 1 Cor. 15:57, both of which will be cited below, and the hymns of the Apocalypse.

8. Lk. 10:21-22 puts the Hymn of Jubilation after the sending of the seventy-two disciples and their return. Mt. 11:25-27 gives it in a different context, after the section on John the Baptist (11:2-19). The beginning of the prayer is inspired by the Jewish *Shemone Esre*; see n. 32, p. 18.

9. The thanksgiving of Jesus recalls the prayer of Daniel (2:23), who thanks God for the "wisdom and strength" given him so that he might understand the "mystery" (2:19). The young men in the Book of Daniel were favored with the gift of revelation, while the wise men, that is, the Babylonian soothsayers, were without it. So too the "babes," that is, the disciples, receive access through Jesus to the mysteries of the kingdom, while these last remain hidden from "those outside" (Mk 4:11), namely, the scribes and Pharisees, who think they can retain a profitable monopoly on knowledge of God.

10. This "Yes, Father" is the highest expression of Jesus' religious piety toward his Father, a piety compounded of love for the Father and an adoring acceptance of his good pleasure. Jesus will repeat the words in Gethsemane.

11. Cf. Dan. 7:14; Mt. 28:18.

Hosanna in the highest heaven![12]

(Mt. 21:9)

Hosanna!
Blessed be he who comes in the name of the Lord!
Blessed be the kingdom of our father David
that is coming!
Hosanna in the highest heaven!

(Mk. 11:9-10)

Blessed be he who comes, the King,
in the name of the Lord!
In heaven, peace,
and glory in the highest heaven!

(Lk. 19:38)

O ABYSS OF THE WISDOM OF GOD!

O abyss of the riches
of the wisdom and knowledge of God!

How fathomless are his judgments,
how incomprehensible his ways!

For who has ever known the thoughts of the Lord?
Who has ever been his counselor?[13]

Who first made a gift to him
and requires to be repaid?

For from him, through him, and for him
all things are.

To him the glory forever!

(Rom. 11:33-36)

---

12. All three of the synoptic evangelists record the acclamation of the crowds as they welcome Jesus at his entry into Jerusalem on Palm Sunday. The basic text comes from Ps. 118:25-26, a psalm which, in the time of Jesus, was read as messianic and eschatological; see Deiss, pp. 62–63. A pilgrim was welcomed into the Temple with the words (according to the Hebrew text): "Blessed in the name of the Lord be he who enters." The Septuagint changed the meaning slightly, so that the Christian community later understood it as meaning "Blessed be he who comes [Christ] in the name of the Lord [God]." *Hosanna* is an approximate transliteration of a Hebrew expression meaning "Save, then!" Use had weakened the meaning to the point where it had become a simple acclamation.

13. Is. 40:13. The love of God that enriches man's poverty is essentially a prevenient love: "He first loved us" (1 Jn. 4:19; cf. 4:10). Man can only respond to the call of God; he cannot elicit that call. He offers to God only what God has first given him.

THE MYSTERY WRAPPED IN SILENCE FROM ETERNITY

To him who has power to strengthen you
in accordance with my gospel[14]
and the message of Jesus Christ,

A mystery wrapped in silence from eternity,
but manifested today
through the Scriptures which foretell it
according to the command of the eternal God,

A mystery made known to all the nations
to bring them to obey the faith, —

To the God who alone is wise,
through Jesus Christ,

To him glory forever and ever! Amen.

(Rom. 16:25-27)

TO THE GOD OF ALL CONSOLATION

Blessed be the God and Father
of our Lord Jesus Christ,
the Father of mercies
and the God of all consolation.

It is he who consoles us
in all our afflictions,
so that we ourselves may be able to console
those who are afflicted,
thanks to the consolation we receive from God.

(2 Cor. 1:3-4)

GOD WILL SATISFY ALL YOUR NEEDS

God will satisfy all your needs,
according to his riches, with glory
in Christ Jesus.

To God, our Father,
glory forever and ever! Amen.

(Phil. 4:19-20)

---

14. The gospel Paul preaches is a revelation of the "mystery" which has been kept hidden for long ages and which Jesus came to reveal. The "mystery" is God's plan according to which the pagans are called to share with the people of the promise the salvation Christ has brought (Eph. 3:1-7; Col. 1:25-29; see also Tit. 1:2-3 and 2 Tim. 1:9-10).

BLESSED BE GOD THE FATHER!

Blessed be the God and Father[15]
of our Lord Jesus Christ,
who has filled us with every spiritual blessing
in the heavens, in Christ.

He chose us in him
from before the creation of the world,
that we might be holy and spotless
in his presence, in love.[16]

He decreed in advance
that we should be adoptive sons
to him, through Jesus Christ,
in accordance with the good pleasure of his will,
for the praise of the glory of his grace
with which he graced us in the Beloved.[17]

It is in him that we have
redemption through his blood,
the forgiveness of our sins,
according to the riches of the grace
which the Father has lavishly given us
in all wisdom and understanding.[18]

He has made known to us the mystery of his will,
according to the good pleasure
which he decreed in advance in him,
that it might be realized in the fullness of time:
to bring the entire universe, both heaven and earth,
under a single head, in Christ.[19]

It is in Christ too
that we have been chosen,

---

15. The hymn that opens the Epistle to the Ephesians is a theological contemplation of the history of salvation. This history has its origin in God the Father, who is its creative source; it is accomplished in Christ and is sealed in us by the Spirit, who is the pledge of our inheritance. The hymn comprises six blessings that spell out the one blessing the Father has bestowed on us from eternity. This jubilant cry to "the praise of his glory" develops and expands in a majestic and seemingly endless sentence (the Greek original has only a single main clause for the entire eleven verses), in which Paul seeks in vain to put order into a thought that is too rich and full of jubilation to fit into the mold of classical rhetoric.

16. First blessing: election in Christ from all eternity.
17. Second blessing: divine sonship given to adopted children in the one Son.
18. Third blessing: redemption through the blood Christ shed on the cross.
19. Fourth blessing: revelation of the "mystery"; see note 14, above.

that we have been predestined
according to the plan of him who does everything
just as he wills,
so that those who in advance have hoped in Christ
might exist for the praise of his glory.[20]

It is in him too that you have heard
the word of truth,
the good news of your salvation.
It is in him too that you have believed,
that you have been marked with the seal
of the Spirit of the promise,
the Holy Spirit, pledge of our inheritance,
who prepares the redemption
of the people whom God won for himself
for the praise of his glory.[21]

(Eph. 1:3-14)

IN THE CHURCH AND CHRIST JESUS

To him whose power, acting in us,
can do infinitely more than we ask
and infinitely more than we can imagine,

To him the glory
in the Church and Christ Jesus,[22]
for all generations and all the ages! Amen.

(Eph. 3:20-21)

TO THE KING OF THE AGES

To the king of the ages,
the one God,
immortal[23] and invisible,

---

20. Fifth blessing: the election of Israel, the people to whom a blessed hope was given.
21. Sixth blessing: the call of the nations to share in the salvation promised to Israel.
22. This doxology is especially important in the theological perspective of the Epistle to the Ephesians, since it is *in Christ Jesus* that the Father calls believers to salvation, and it is in Christ Jesus that the faithful glorify the Father and lift up their thanksgiving to him. But they also glorify God *in the Church*, which is, as it were, the prolongation in time and space of the mystery of Christ, and the temple of the Lord in which the Father's glory is celebrated.
23. Literally: "incorruptible." "Incorruptibility" (2 Tim. 1:10) is for practical purposes equivalent to "immortality" (1 Tim. 6:16; see next hymn). These two fragments of hymns in the First Epistle to Timothy doubtless have their origin in the Jewish liturgy as celebrated in the Diaspora. They stand in direct opposition to the deification of the emperors and the idolatrous worship given to them. The hymns betray their typically Jewish origin when they state that no one has ever seen God, but fail to add that this God has revealed himself in Jesus Christ (Jn. 1:18).

honor and glory
forever and ever! Amen.

(1 Tim. 1:17)

To the Blessed and Only Sovereign

To the blessed and only Sovereign,
to the King of kings and Lord of lords,
to him who alone possesses immortality,
who dwells in inaccessible light,
whom no man has seen or can see:
to him honor and power forever! Amen.

(1 Tim. 6:15-16)

In Everything Let God Be Glorified

In everything let God be glorified
through Jesus Christ.
To him glory and power
forever and ever! Amen.

(1 Pet. 4:11)

The God of All Grace

The God of all grace,
who has called you to his eternal glory
in Christ Jesus,
after brief sufferings
will himself restore you,
steady you, strengthen you,
make you unshakable.

To him the power
forever and ever. Amen.

(1 Pet. 5:10-11)

Grow in Grace

Grow in the grace and knowledge
of our Lord and Savior Jesus Christ.

To him glory now
and to the day of eternity. Amen.

(2 Pet. 3:18)

To Him Who Can Keep You from Every Fall

To him who can keep you from every fall
and make you appear in the presence of his glory
without reproach and filled with joy,

To the only God, our Savior,
through Jesus Christ, our Lord,

Glory, majesty, strength, and power,
from before all time,
now and forever! Amen.

(Jude 24-25)

CHRISTOLOGICAL HYMNS

Let every tongue proclaim
that Jesus Christ is Lord,
to the glory of God the Father!

Phil. 2:11

In his letter to Emperor Trajan, Pliny the Younger singles out as characteristic of Christians the worship they pay to Christ as God: "It is their custom to assemble before dawn on a set day and to sing hymns to Christ as to a god."[24]

Most of these very early Christological hymns have doubtless left no trace in the New Testament writings. We may think of them as having taken the form of triumphant litanies celebrating the mystery of Christ, after the manner of the hymn in 1 Tim. 3:16 (which we shall cite below). They were spontaneous compositions, born of the jubilation the Spirit gives, and immediately disappearing as the prayer that formed them moved on. They were meant to build up the community, and not to have a permanent existence.

The Christological hymns that escaped the destroying hand of time and have come down to us due to the action of the Spirit who inspired the Scriptures are all theological contemplations of the mystery of Jesus. They hardly mention the historical conditions under which the Savior lived his life, unlike certain professions of faith that we find in the literature of the apostolic age. Here is an example of such professions, from St. Ignatius of Antioch:

> He is of the house of David,
> he is son of Mary.
> Truly he was born,
> he ate and he drank.
> Truly he was persecuted under Pontius Pilate,
> truly he was crucified,
> in the presence of heaven, earth, and hell.
> Truly he was raised from the dead.[25]

In the apostolic age, which had had no direct contact with the events of redemption, it was important to proclaim, in opposition to docetism, then just beginning, the reality of the incarnation, the entry of Jesus into human history, his birth from the house of David, his baptism by John, and his passion under Pontius Pilate and Herod.

For the faithful of the primitive community, however, such an emphasis on the humanness of Jesus was not required, for these people had seen him with their

---

24. *Epistularum liber* X, 96, 7.
25. *Ad Trallenses* 9.

38

own eyes and touched him with their own hands (1 Jn. 1:1-3). The human condition of the Savior was so evident to them that it had appalled them; at the end, it seemed to be almost an "annihilation" (see Phil. 2:7). For they had seen the crucified Jesus writhing on the cross; they had touched his gibbet; they had been devastated by his death cries. Consequently, their faith moved beyond the human side of Jesus and focused more on the divinity that was invisible to the eye but had nevertheless brought Jesus from his tomb at the resurrection. They proclaimed that Jesus, who had experienced the condition of a slave, was now sovereignly exalted; that he who had shown himself in the lowliness of the flesh was now raised up to glory; that he who had been put to death for our sins was now seated at the right hand of God.[26]

JESUS CHRIST IS LORD!

Have among you the sentiments that those in Christ Jesus ought to have.[27]
> He who was of a divine condition
> did not cling greedily
> to the rank that made him equal to God.
>
> But he annihilated himself,
> taking the condition of a slave,
> making himself like men.
>
> Taken as a man because of his appearance,
> he humbled himself,
> obedient unto death,
> even a death on a cross.
>
> Therefore God has sovereignly exalted him
> and given him the name
> which is above every name,

---

26. Cf. Phil. 2:5-11; 1 Tim. 3:16; 1 Pet. 3:18, 22. Especially in these three hymns we can see the original pattern followed in the proclamation of the Christian message (the *kerygma*), as exemplified in the five discourses of Peter in the Acts of the Apostles (2:14-29; 3:12-26; 4:9-12; 5:29-32; 10:34-43).

27. As part of an exhortation, Paul here cites an early hymn with which the Philippians were probably already familiar. Its vocabulary is archaic, and the hymn may have been used in the celebration either of the Eucharist (E. Lohmeyer) or, more probably, of baptism (E. Käsemann). Paul enriched the text especially with allusions to the Servant of Yahweh as depicted in Is. 52:13–53:12; see A. Feuillet, "L'hymn christologique de l'Epître aux Philippiens," *Revue biblique* 72 (1965), pp. 352–80, 481–507. See also E. Käsemann, "Kritische Analyse von Phil. 2, 5-11," in his *Exegetische Versuche und Besinnungen* 1 (Göttingen, 1960), pp. 51–95 (in French: *Essais exégétiques*, tr. D. Appia [Neuchâtel, 1972], pp. 63–110).

so that at the name of Jesus
every knee might bend
in heaven, on earth, and in hell,[28]

and that every tongue might proclaim:
"Jesus Christ is Lord,"
to the glory of God the Father.[29]

(Phil. 2:5-11)

To Christ, First-Born of All Creation

With joy[30] we give thanks to the Father who grants us a share in the lot of the saints in the light; who rescues us from the rule of darkness and sets us in the kingdom of the Son he loves, in whom we have deliverance and the forgiveness of sins.

He is the image of the invisible God,
the first-born of all creation,
for it is in him that everything was created
in the heavens and on the earth,

the visible and invisible world,
Thrones and Dominations, Principalities and Powers.
It is through him and for him that everything was created.
He is before every creature
and all holds together in him.

He is also the Head of the Body, the Church.
He is the beginning,
the first-born from among the dead,
so that in all things he might have primacy.

For in him God was pleased
to make all fullness dwell,

---

28. This list corresponds to the cosmology of antiquity; it emphasizes the universality of the sovereignty of the Lord Jesus.

29. "Jesus Christ is Lord": A formula in the profession of faith used by the primitive community; cf. Rom. 10:9; 1 Cor. 12:3.

30. A paschal hymn celebrating Christ as first-born of all creation (cf. Prov. 8:22) and first-born from the dead. It is for this universal reconciliation which extends beyond man to include the world of the angels and transfigures even the cosmos, that Christians give thanks (*eucharistountes*, v. 12) with joy. This hymnic text is an example of "eucharistic" prayers used in the primitive community; see C. Masson, *L'Epître de saint Paul aux Colossiens* (Commentaire du Nouveau Testament 10; Neuchâtel, 1950), p. 107.

On the hymn, see E. Lohse, *Die Briefe an die Kolosser und Philemon* (Göttingen, 1968), pp. 77–103; A. Feuillet, *Le Christ, Sagesse de Dieu* (Paris, 1966), pp. 163–273.

and through him to reconcile
every creature with himself.

He made peace by the blood of his cross
with his creatures on earth and in heaven.

(Col. 1:11-20)

THE MYSTERY OF GODLINESS

It is great, the mystery of godliness: [31]
(Christ) manifested in the flesh,
vindicated by the Spirit,

contemplated by the angels,
proclaimed among the pagans,

believed in the world,
exalted in glory.

(1 Tim. 3:16)

CHRIST SUFFERED FOR YOU!

Christ suffered for you,[32]
leaving you an example
so that you might follow in his footsteps.

He committed no sin
nor did his mouth speak any lie.

When insulted, he did not return the insult;
when mistreated, he did not threaten,
but put himself in the just Judge's hands.

---

31. This hymn to Christ in 1 Tim. 3:16 is "the heart of the letter" (C. Spicq), "the high point of the entire letter" (J. Jeremias). It celebrates the "epiphany" of Christ in the flesh (Tit. 2:11; 3:4), that is, his incarnation, his glorification by the Spirit in the mystery of his resurrection (Rom. 1:4), and the acknowledgment of his sovereignty by angels and men (Phil. 2:5-11). See C. Spicq, *Les épîtres pastorales* (Paris, 1969), pp. 468–75; J. Jeremias, in *Das Neue Testament deutsch* 9 (Göttingen, 1963), pp. 23–25; P. Dornier, *Les épîtres pastorales* (Paris, 1969), pp. 68–71.

The acclamation that the faithful address to Christ, "Great indeed . . . is the mystery of our religion," is set over against the acclamation addressed to Artemis by the pagans of Ephesus: "Great is Diana of the Ephesians!" (Acts 19:28, 34).

32. This hymn is inspired by the fourth Servant Song of Isaiah (ch. 53, especially vv. 4-5, 9, 11-12) and sees in Jesus the model of the believer who is unjustly persecuted; see M.-E. Boismard, *Quatre hymnes baptismales dans la première épître de Pierre* (Lectio divina 30; Paris, 1961), pp. 111–32.

It was our sins that he bore
in his body, on the wood,
in order that, rescued from our sins,
we might live for uprightness.
His wounds brought us healing.

For you were like straying sheep.
But, see, now you have returned
to the shepherd and guardian of your souls.

(1 Pet. 2:22-25)

THE LORDSHIP OF JESUS

Christ died once for sins,[33]
the righteous one for the unrighteous,
in order to lead us to God.

Put to death according to the flesh,
he was given life by the Spirit. . . .

Having ascended to heaven,
he is seated at God's right hand.

To him are the Angels subject,
and the Powers and Dominations.

(1 Pet. 3:18-22)

JESUS CHRIST, THE FAITHFUL WITNESS

Jesus Christ, the faithful witness,
the first-born from among the dead,[34]
the ruler of the kings of earth!

He loves us,
he has washed us of our sins in his blood,
he has made us a kingdom of priests[35]

---

33. This hymn evidently resembles the hymn on "the mystery of godliness" in 1 Tim. 3:16. The verses we have omitted here (vv. 19-20) are catechetical expansions. It is possible that 1 Pet. 1:20 ("destined before the foundation of the world but . . . made manifest at the end of the times") belongs to the original structure of this hymn; see Boismard, pp. 57–109.

34. Cf. Col. 1:18; 1 Cor. 15:20. The resurrection of Jesus, which is first in time, is also the cause and origin of our own resurrection.

35. Cf. Ex. 19:6; 1 Pet. 2:9; Rev. 5:10; 20:6. The entire Church, although in different degrees, shares in the royal priesthood of Jesus. See L. Cerfaux, "*Regale Sacerdotium*," in *Recueil Lucien Cerfaux* 2 (Gembloux, 1954), pp. 283–315; and Vatican II, *Dogmatic Constitution on the Church*, no. 10.

for his God and Father:
to him glory and power
forever and ever! Amen.

See, he is coming, accompanied by the clouds.
All will see him with their own eyes,
even they who pierced him.
On his account all the races on earth will lament.[36]
    Yes. Amen.

"I am the Alpha and the Omega,"[37]
says the Lord God,
he who is, who was, and who is coming,
    the Almighty.

                    (Apoc. 1:5-8)

Hymn to the Incarnate Word

In the beginning was the Word,[38]   Inclusion
and the Word was with God,
and the Word was God.
He was in the beginning with God.
Through him everything was made,
and without him nothing was made.
What was made in him was life,
and the life was the light of men.
And the light shone in the darkness,
and the darkness did not overcome it.

A man appeared who was sent by God;

---

36. In the description of the glorious coming of the Son of Man, the cloud plays a role because it is part of the regular scenario of a theophany. The images are borrowed from the repertory of images in the apocalypse of the synoptic Gospels: Mt. 24:30 = Dan. 7:13-14 and Zech. 12:12-14.

37. That is, the beginning and the end.

38. On the Prologue, see especially M.-E. Boismard, *St. John's Prologue*, tr. Carisbrooke Dominicans (Westminster, Md., 1957); A. Feuillet, *Le Prologue du Quatrième Evangile* (Paris, 1968); R. Schnackenburg, *The Gospel according to St. John*, 1, tr. K. Smyth (New York, 1968), pp. 221–81.

The Prologue is composed according to the Semitic pattern known as inclusion; the pattern here is: A, B, C, D — D', C', B', A' (see Boismard, pp. 76–79). John contemplates the Word as existing in God (A), his role in creation (B), the testimony of John (C), the coming of the Word into the world (D), and the power he gives believers to become children of God. John then considers the Word once again as pitching his tent among us (D'), the testimony of John (C'), the new creation in grace and truth (B'), and the Word in the bosom of the Father (A'). John emphasizes the importance of the gift of divine adoption by placing it at the very center of the Prologue.

his name was John.
He came as a witness,
to give testimony to the light,
so that all might believe through him.
He was not the light,
but he came to give testimony to the light.

The Word was the true light
that enlightens every man,
by coming into the world.
He was in the world,
and the world did not know him.
He came to his own,
and his own did not receive him.

But to all who did receive him,
he gave power to become children of God,
to those who believe in his name,
who are born not of flesh or of blood,
or from a carnal will,
but who are born of God.

And the Word became flesh,
and he pitched his tent among us.
And we have contemplated his glory,[39]
the glory which he has from the Father as the only Son,
full of grace and truth.

John bears witness to him; he proclaims:
"See the one of whom I said:
'He who comes after me
is ranked before me,
for he was before me.'"

Yes, of his fullness we have all received,
and grace upon grace.
For the law was given by Moses,

---

39. In the old covenant, God's presence among his people was symbolized by the bright cloud that covered the Tent of Meeting. "Then the cloud covered *the tent* of meeting, and *the glory* of the Lord filled the tabernacle. And Moses was not able to enter *the tent* of meeting, because the cloud abode upon it, and *the glory* of the Lord filled the tabernacle" (Ex. 40:34-35). In the new covenant, God's presence is made real by the Word who pitches *his tent* among men and manifests *his glory*.

but grace and truth have come through Jesus Christ.
No one has ever seen God;
The only Son, who is in the bosom of the Father,
it is he who has revealed him.[40]

(Jn. 1:1-18)

COME, LORD JESUS!

I, Jesus, have sent my angel,
to bear witness to this revelation on the Churches.

"I am the shoot and posterity of David,
the radiant morning star."

The Spirit and the Bride say: "Come!"
Let him who hears say: "Come!"

Let him who is thirsty come!
Let him who wishes
take the water of life without charge. . . .

He who testifies to this revelation says:
"Yes, I am coming soon."

Amen! Come, Lord Jesus!

(Apoc. 22:16-20)

---

40. John takes various literary elements from the theophany at Sinai and the giving of the covenant, and applies them to the incarnate Word. Moses had pleaded: "I pray thee, show me thy glory" (Ex. 33:18); John tells us: "We have beheld his glory." God had defined himself as "the Lord, the Lord, a God merciful and gracious, slow to anger, and abounding in steadfast love and faithfulness" (Ex. 34:6); here the transcendent God, whom no one has ever seen, has revealed himself through the Son, as the Word, who is himself God, comes to dwell among men. Finally, Moses had received the law, inscribed on stone tablets; now the new law, rich in grace and truth, comes to us in the person of Jesus Christ.

It is possible that verses 17-18 (from "For the law was given . . ." to the end) were added to the original hymn at a later redactional stage. On this point, see R. Schnackenburg, *op. cit.*, pp. 276–77.

PROFESSIONS OF FAITH AND BAPTISMAL HYMNS

One Lord,
one faith,
one baptism,
one God and Father.

Eph. 4:5

The believer whom God calls to messianic salvation responds to the proclamation of the good news by professing his faith.

The New Testament writings have preserved the memory of these professions of faith, some of which may have been used in the baptismal liturgy.[41] The simplest were doubtless limited to an assertion of the lordship of the risen Christ: "Jesus is Lord!" (1 Cor. 12:3). By these words, the neophyte was ratifying the baptismal formula that had been pronounced over him and that contained an "invocation" of the name of Jesus.[42]

Other, more solemn formulas of faith may have amounted to Christological hymns similar to the one on the "mystery of godliness" (1 Tim. 3:16), which we have already seen.

These hymns, which enjoy the incomparable dignity of being God's words, are like mirrors that reflect the faith of the primitive Church. The richness of their theology bears witness to the richness of that faith itself. They celebrate baptism as a sharing in the death and resurrection of the Lord; as man's being made righteous in the name of the Lord and the Spirit of God; as an entry into the unity of the Body which is the Church, wherein we acknowledge but one Father, one Lord, one Spirit, one faith, one enlightenment by the light of Christ, one bath in which we are regenerated and renewed by the Spirit.

JESUS IS LORD

If you proclaim with your mouth
that Jesus is Lord,
and if you believe in your heart
that God raised him from the dead,
    you will be saved.

For we believe "with the heart"

---

41. On this point, see J. Schmitt, *Jésus ressuscité dans la prédication apostolique* (Paris, 1949), pp. 62–84; Boismard, *Quatre hymnes baptismales.* . . .

42. In Acts 22:16, Ananias says to Saul: "*Be baptized*, and wash away your sins, *calling on his name.*"

in order to obtain justification,
and we profess "with the mouth"
    in order to attain to salvation.

(Rom. 10:9-10)

ONE GOD, THE FATHER

There is only one God, the Father,
from whom all things come
and for whom we were created.

And there is only one Lord, Jesus Christ,
through whom all things exist
and through whom we were created.

(1 Cor. 8:6)

ONE GOD AND FATHER

Endeavor to preserve unity of spirit
through the bonds of peace.

One body,[43] one Spirit,[44]   *source of unity*
as well as one hope
to which you have been called,

One Lord,
one faith, one baptism,
one God and Father of all,
who is above all, through all, and in all.

(Eph. 4:3-6)

AWAKEN, SLEEPER!

Awaken, sleeper!
Rise from the dead,
and Christ will enlighten you.[45]

(Eph. 5:14)

---

43. That is, the Church, the Body of Christ into which all the faithful are incorporated (cf. 1 Cor. 6:15; Rom. 6:12-13).

44. The Spirit is the source of unity in the Church, which is gathered by the Holy Spirit (see the opening prayer for the Wednesday of the Seventh Week of Easter). He is "the soul of the Body of Christ," says Pope Leo XIII, encyclical *Divinum illud munus* (May 9, 1897), in *ASS* 29 (1896–97), p. 650. See also Pius XII, encyclical *Mystici Corporis Christi* (June 29, 1943), and Vatican II, *Dogmatic Constitution on the Church*, no. 7, which refers to both of the papal texts. On the whole subject, see S. Tromp, "L'Esprit Saint âme de l'Eglise," *Dictionnaire de spiritualité* 4 (1961), cols. 1296–1302.

45. According to K. Staab and J. Freundorfer, *Das Neue Testament* 7 (Regensburg,

He is the sun of resurrection,
born before the morning star.
He gives life by his rays.[46]

REMEMBER JESUS CHRIST

Remember Jesus Christ, risen from the dead, born of the race of David according to my gospel. . . . This saying is certain:

If we are dead with him,
we will live with him.

If we suffer with him,
we will reign with him.

If we deny him,
he will also deny us.

If we are unfaithful,
he remains faithful,
for he cannot deny himself.

(2 Tim. 2:8-13)

REBORN FOR A LIVING HOPE

Blessed be the God and Father[47]
of our Lord Jesus Christ!
In accordance with his great mercy
he has given us rebirth.

For a living hope,
through the resurrection of Jesus Christ
from the dead,

For an incorruptible inheritance,

1950), this text is doubtless part "of an early Christian hymn that must in turn have been part of the baptismal liturgy. It becomes fully intelligible if we take it as an exhortation to the neophyte, calling his attention to the great event that has taken place in the sacrament: Baptism is an awakening from sleep, a resurrection from the dead, an entry into the light of Christ" (p. 122).

46. This second stanza is cited by Clement of Alexandria, *Protrepticus* IX, 84, 2 *(PG* 8:196A-B).

47. A baptismal hymn, the text of which resembles Tit. 3:4-7. The last two lines of the third stanza ("for you whom . . . faith") are doubtless a later addition; they break the original rhythm that is built on an enumeration: "for a living hope . . . for an inheritance . . . for a salvation."

undefiled and unfading,
which is stored up in the heavens —
for you whom God's power protects
by means of faith —,

For a salvation that will be manifested
in the last times.

(1 Pet. 1:3-5)

DIDACTIC AND HORTATORY HYMNS

> Instruct one another in all wisdom,
> exhort one another,
> sing to God with all your heart.
>
> Col. 3:16

In one of his descriptions of life in the primitive community that are given in the Book of the Acts of the Apostles, Luke writes: "They devoted themselves to the teaching of the apostles, to communion with the brethren, to the breaking of bread, and to the prayers" (Acts 2:42).

The primitive Church was thus built up not only in the Eucharistic celebration of the breaking of bread and in the sharing of a common praise of and prayer to Christ; it was also built upon the teaching given by the apostles. Unity of mind and heart[48] presupposed a unity of doctrine. This teaching supplied food to souls. It made the Church grow by rooting it in the mystery of Jesus and inspiring it to reach outward in the mystery of brotherly love.[49]

The apostles were not the only ones who taught. When speaking of the differentiation among the various members of Christ's Body, Paul writes: "As for you, you are the body of Christ, and each of you is a member of it. And there are those whom God has appointed to be in the Church, first, apostles, second, prophets, third, teachers — *didaskaloi*" (1 Cor. 12:27-28).[50]

Paul thus distinguishes between apostles, prophets, and teachers. The apostles are the appointed witnesses to the life of Jesus and especially to his resurrection.[51] The prophets are witnesses appointed by the Spirit, whose "revelations" they transmit;[52] along with the apostles, they form the foundation of the Church (see Eph. 2:20).[52a] The teachers, finally, provide their brethren with ordinary teaching as the community may need it; the teaching in question could be either doctrinal (didactic) or moral (parenetic or hortatory).

This distribution of functions was not fixed. The Spirit, who was present to help the Church, enlarged the professorial body (if we may so term it) that constituted the teaching Church; with the sovereign freedom that is his, he invested with charismatic functions those whom he wished. He raised up one man to teach, another to proclaim a revelation, a third to speak in mysterious tongues, a fourth to interpret them, and a fifth to sing inspired songs.[53] Some communities were espe-

---

48. "The company of those who believed were of one heart and soul" (Acts 4:32).

49. See Acts 2:44-45; 4:32-35.

50. See also Eph. 3:5; 4:11.

51. See Acts 1:22; 3:15.

52. See 1 Thess. 5:19-20; Acts 11:27-28; Apoc. 1:1; 10:7; 22:6.

52a. On this subject, see J. Delorme (ed.), *Le ministère et les ministres selon le Nouveau Testament* (Paris, 1974).

53. 1 Cor. 14:26: "When you assemble, each one can have a hymn, a teaching, a revelation." See also Rom. 12:6-8 and 1 Cor. 12:4-11.

cially fervent, and Paul realized that there could be disturbances in this school that was being run by the Holy Spirit. He wrote: "Strive earnestly to be prophets, do not prevent speaking in tongues; but let everything be done in a decent and orderly manner" (1 Cor. 14:39-40).

Even in the absence of the charismatic gifts, Paul wants the brethren to instruct one another: "Let the word of Christ dwell abundantly in you. Instruct one another in all wisdom, exhort one another, sing to God with all your heart, in a spirit of gratitude, by means of psalms, hymns, and inspired canticles" (Col. 3:16).

We shall here present some of these hymns that may have belonged to the repertory of the primitive community.

HYMN TO THE LOVE OF CHRIST

> Who will separate us from the love of Christ?
> Tribulation, distress, persecution, hunger,
> nakedness, dangers, the sword?
> For it is written:
> "For your sake, we are being slain all day long,
> we are regarded as sheep for the slaughter."[54]
> But in all this we win the victory,
> thanks to him who has loved us.
>
> Yes, I am sure of it: neither death nor life,
> nor angels nor principalities, nor present nor future,
> nor powers nor height nor depth,[55]
> nor any other creature —
> nothing will be able to separate us from the love of God
> which is in Christ Jesus our Lord.

(Rom. 8:35-39)

THE DAY IS NEAR AT HAND

> The hour has come
> for you to wake from sleep.
>
> For salvation is now nearer to us
> than when we first believed.
>
> Night is almost over,
> day is near at hand.

---

54. Ps. 44:23. Love for Christ is exercised under constant threat of persecution; death is not far from the life of the believer.

55. These terms probably refer to powers hostile to God, that is, "the spirits of evil who dwell in the heavenly spaces" (Eph. 6:12) as well as the powers of death that dwell in the depths of Sheol.

Let us therefore put aside the works of darkness
and put on the armor of light.

(Rom. 13:11-12)

UNITY IN DIVERSITY

There is a variety of spiritual gifts,
but it is the same Spirit.

There is a variety of ministries,
but it is the same Lord.

There is a variety of activities,
but it is the same God
who does everything in all.

To each is given the manifestation of the Spirit
for the common good.[56]

(1 Cor. 12:4-8)

HYMN TO LOVE[57]

I may speak with the tongues of angels and of men,
but if I lack love,
I am only a noisy gong
or a clanging cymbal.

I may possess the gift of prophecy,
know all the mysteries and everything that is to be known,
have all faith,
to the point that I can move mountains,[58]
but if I lack love,
I am nothing.

---

56. The unity of the members of the ecclesial community does not require uniformity or the elimination of individuality. It does, however, require the development and integration of the members' personal gifts into the unity of the Mystical Body "for the common good." This diversity in unity reflects as in a mirror the infinite riches of the trinitarian Unity. Each believer, in accordance with the particular gift given to him, fashions his own features that will shine throughout eternity and thus add to the beauty of the Church as a whole. St. Thomas Aquinas explains that "the beauty and perfection of the Church arises from the diversity of degrees within it" (*Summa theologiae*, I-II, q. 112, a. 4).

57. The hymn to love has also been called "the Song of Songs of Christian love" (E. B. Allo, *Première Epître aux Corinthiens* [Paris, 1956], p. 341). The hymn has three parts: (1) the first asserts the unqualified superiority of love over the charisms and the other virtues; (2) the second shows the universal influence of love, especially in relations with the neighbor; (3) the third treats of love's abiding existence.

58. Allusion to Mk. 11:23; Mt. 17:20; 21:21; Lk. 17:6.

I may distribute all my goods to the poor,
deliver my body to the flames,
but if I lack love,
it does me no good.

Love is patient,[59]
love serves,
love is not jealous,
it does not boast, is not swelled up (with pride).

Love does nothing dishonorable,
it does not pursue its own interest,
it is not irritable,
it does not keep an account of evil.

It does not rejoice at injustice,
but finds joy in the truth.
It excuses everything, it believes everything,
it hopes for everything, it puts up with everything.

Love will never pass away.
Prophecies? They will disappear.
The gift of tongues? It will cease.
Knowledge? It will disappear.

For we know only partially,
and our prophecies are only partial.
But when what is perfect comes,
what is imperfect will disappear.

When I was a child, I spoke as a child,
I thought as a child, I reasoned as a child.
But when I became a man,
I put an end to the things of childhood.

We now see
as in a mirror, confusedly,
but then we will see face to face.
I now know only partially,
but then I shall know face to face.

---

59. Charity is "the mother and root of all the virtues" (St. Thomas Aquinas, *Summa theologiae*, I-II, q. 62, a. 4) and confers on them as it were the radiance of its own splendor. Just as God is Love and all his other perfections are enriched by this love, so the life of the believer is a life of love and all his other virtues are as it were attracted and drawn into the sphere of influence of love.

Now, faith, hope, and love,
all three abide.
But the greatest of all is love.

(1 Cor. 13:1-13)

GOD WHO SAID

God who said:
"From the womb of darkness
let the light shine forth!"
has now made his light
shine in our hearts,
so that the knowledge of the glory of God
that is on the face of Christ
may be resplendent there.[60]

(2 Cor. 4:6)

LIGHT AND DARKNESS[61]

Do not be misyoked
with unbelievers.[62]

What sharing can there be between justice and iniquity?
What communion between light and darkness?
What agreement between Christ and Belial?[63]
What association between believer and unbeliever?
What understanding between God's temple and idols?

For we are the temple of the living God,
as God has said:
"I will dwell in their midst,
I will walk there, I will be their God
and they will be my people."[64]

(2 Cor. 6:14-16)

---

60. The revelation of the mystery of Jesus is like a new act of creation in which the Father makes his divine light shine in the hearts of believers.

61. As the reader may know, the scriptural theme of light and darkness played an important role in the theology of the Qumran community. This fragment of a hymn may have originally belonged to Jewish literature and only later taken over for Christian use. Christ is the true Light of the world; his followers are "sons of light and sons of the day" (1 Thess. 5:5) and stand in opposition to the angel of darkness.

62. The image is borrowed from Dt. 22:10.

63. In Jewish literature, "Beliar" or "Belial" is a name for the devil.

64. Lev. 26:12; Jer. 32:38.

The Paschal Life of the Christian

You have been raised up with Christ.
Therefore seek the things that are above,
where Christ now is,
sitting at the right hand of God.

Think of the things that are above,
not of earthly things.
For you are dead henceforth
and your life is hidden with Christ in God.

When Christ, who is your life,
shall be revealed,
you too shall be revealed
together with him, in glory.

(Col. 3:1-4)

Song for a Christian Pilgrim

You have come
to the mountain of God,
to the city of the living God,
to the heavenly Jerusalem,

to countless angels,
to a solemn feast,
to the assembly of the first-born[65]
who are enrolled in heaven,

to a God who judges the universe,
to the spirits of the just who have been made perfect,
to Jesus, mediator of a new covenant.

(Heb. 12:22-24)

Hymn to Christian Humility and Vigilance

Clothe yourselves all in humility,[66]
each toward the others,

---

65. The angels are doubtless meant here. According to Job 38:6-7, God "laid its [the world's] cornerstone, when the morning stars sang together and all the sons of God shouted for joy."

66. This hymn on Christian humility and watchfulness is very likely inspired by an exhortation to the candidates for baptism (cf. Boismard, *Quatre hymnes* . . . , pp. 133–63). The text has several points of contact with James 4:6-10 and with the Qumran literature. It cites Prov. 3:34 and Ps. 55:23.

for God resists the proud
but gives grace to the humble.

Humble yourselves, therefore,
under the mighty hand of God,
so that he may raise you up in (his) time.

All your anxieties
cast upon him,
for he takes care of you.

Be sober, keep watch!
For your enemy, like a roaring lion,
prowls about, seeking to devour you.

Resist him,
remain firm in faith!

(1 Pet. 5:5-9)

CANTICLES FROM THE LUKAN INFANCY NARRATIVE

> And all the people
> sang the praises of God.
>
> Lk. 18:43

Luke is the evangelist of messianic joy.[67] He delights in showing that the Lord's coming unseals the wellsprings of joy in the people, who, at the sight of the messianic miracles, praise and glorify God:

> They were giving glory to God . . . and were saying: "We have seen wonderful things today" (5:26).

> The whole crowd rejoiced at the wonderful things he did (13:17).

> At that very moment, the blind man regained his sight, and he followed Jesus, giving glory to God. And all the people, when they saw it, sang the praises of God (18:43).

> The entire multitude of the disciples was filled with joy and began to praise God in a loud voice for all the miracles they had seen (19:37).

This joy is especially apparent in the narrative of Jesus' childhood. It pours down from heaven to earth at the annunciations to Zechariah (1:14) and Mary (1:28), at the birth of John the Baptist (1:58), and at the birth of Jesus (2:10). To emphasize it even more, Luke records in his narrative four canticles that are, as it were, the climactic moments in the joyous celebration and enthusiastic liturgy that marks the dawn of salvation. The four are: the canticle of Zechariah (the *Benedictus*), the canticle of Mary (the *Magnificat*), the canticle of the angels at Bethlehem (the *Gloria in excelsis Deo*), and the canticle of Simeon (the *Nunc dimittis*).

It is to be noted that these canticles, especially the *Magnificat* and *Benedictus*, borrow their formulas from the Old Testament. This fact is extremely important for our understanding of the evangelist's message, for we know that the Lukan infancy narrative (1:5–2:52) is structured according to the literary genre of midrash.[68]

---

67. See L. Deiss, *Synopse de Matthieu, Marc et Luc, avec les parallèles de Jean* 1 (Paris, 1964), nos. 44–45.

68. The Hebrew root of the word *midrash* means "to search, scrutinize." The literary genre of midrash may be defined as a reflection and meditation on Scripture with a view to bringing out the theological meaning and moral applications. As a typical example we may cite chapters 10–19 of the Book of Wisdom, which offer a theological reflection on history from the beginning of time to the Exodus.

On Luke's use of midrash, see R. Laurentin, *Structure et théologie de Luc I–II* (Paris, 1957), pp. 93–119.

Benedictus – Canticle of Zechariah
Magnificat – Canticle of Mary
Gloria in Excelsis Deo – Canticle of Angels @ Bethlehem
Nunc Dimittis – Canticle of Simeon

Meditating on the ancient texts of Scripture, Luke collates them with the totally new situation which the coming of Jesus into this world brings about. Thus does he perceive, with the light of the Holy Spirit, the continuity between the marvels of past history and the incarnation of Christ, while at the same time centering attention on the transcendency of God's Word, which ceaselessly affirms its eternal presence above and beyond the particular circumstances of its utterance in time.[69]

When Mary sings the *Magnificat*, the whole Old Testament joins with her in welcoming the Messiah and singing the praises of the redemption he brings. If we bear in mind that Israel is itself the firstfruits of the nations, then we can go a step further and assert that Mary's song contains the praise of all mankind for Jesus, the Savior and Brother of every human being.

We should also note the clearly Christological accent in these songs of thanksgiving. Mary is shaken by joy in God her *Savior*, that is, in Jesus (1:47); Zechariah celebrates the *saving* power that God is exercising in the house of David in order to *save* it from its enemies (1:68, 71); the angels at Bethlehem sing of the *Savior*, that is, Jesus, who has been born there (2:11); and as Simeon holds the infant Jesus in his arms, he says that his eyes have seen *salvation* (2:30). These allusions were evident in the Hebrew (or Aramaic) original, in which the words "Jesus," "Savior," and "salvation" all have the same root.[70] They have disappeared, however, in Luke's Greek translation, and they cannot be recaptured in English. The understanding and piety of the reader must restore the allusions and so find in these songs the full biblical richness that Luke endeavors so fervently and joyously to pass on to us.

THE CANTICLE OF MARY[71]

> My soul exalts the Lord,
> and my spirit trembles with joy in God my Savior!

---

69. L. Deiss, *Mary, Daughter of Sion*, tr. B. T. Blair (Collegeville, Minn., 1972), p. 51 (translation slightly modified).

70. See R. Laurentin, "Traces d'allusions étymologiques en Luc I–II," *Biblica* 37 (1956), pp. 444–47.

71. We can distinguish within the *Magnificat* a song of thanksgiving (first part), a song of the poor, to whom Yahweh has given seven marvelous blessings (second part), and a song of the fulfillment of the covenant (third part). The canticle is marked by a high degree of literary elegance. It was doubtless composed in Old Testamental or Jewish-Christian communities for use in liturgical celebrations. It takes the form of a linked series of texts from the Old Testament (on the ecclesial significance of these texts, see Deiss, *Mary, Daughter of Sion*, pp. 112–44).

Our Lady's thanksgiving quite naturally finds expression in formulas created by Old Testament piety; its originality is thus not to be found in the texts themselves but in the situation in which she uses them. Mary rejoices in God her *Savior*, that is, in *Jesus* whom she carries within herself. When the faithful repeat Mary's canticle, they prolong her praise

[handwritten margin note: song of poor]

For he has gazed on his lowly servant-maid:
see, henceforth all generations
will call me blessed.
For the Mighty One has done wonderful things for me,
holy is his name.

[handwritten margin note: blessing]

His mercy extends from generation to generation
toward those who fear him.
He displays the strength of his arm,
he scatters the proud of heart,
he overthrows the mighty from their thrones,
he raises up the lowly.
The hungry he fills with good things,
but the rich he sends empty-handed away.

[handwritten margin note: Fulfillment of covenant]

He helps Israel, his child,
being mindful of his mercy,
as he promised our fathers,
on behalf of Abraham and his race forever.

(Lk. 1:46-55)

The Canticle of Zechariah

[handwritten margin note: old hymn]

Blessed be the Lord, the God of Israel![72]
He visits and rescues his people,
he raises up a mighty power for salvation
in the house of David, his servant,
as he foretold
by the mouth of the saints of old, his prophets.

He saves us from our enemies
and from the grasp of all who hate us.
He shows mercy to our fathers,

---

of Christ and assert that the salvation given to Mary is a prophecy of their own salvation (see H. Schürmann, *Das Lukas-Evangelium* [Freiburg, 1969], p. 70). They also sing of her as Mother of the Messiah, and thus they fulfill the prophecy that "all generations will call me blessed."

On the structure of the *Magnificat*, see L. Monloubou, *La prière selon saint Luc* (Lectio divina 89; Paris, 1976), pp. 219–39.

72. Like the *Magnificat*, the *Benedictus* is a cento of biblical texts, and in this form may have antedated the infancy narrative. Its insertion into Luke's text means that the coming of Jesus is the answer to the long-standing hope of Israel. The first part of the canticle is doubtless an old eschatological hymn; the second is a genethliacon, or birthday ode. The style is unpolished and abrupt; the many biblical citations give the text a high degree of compactness but slow the lyric movement somewhat.

he is mindful of his holy covenant,
of the oath sworn to our father, Abraham,
to grant us that we would be rescued
from the hand of our enemies
and serve him without fear
in justice and holiness before him,
throughout our days!

And you, little child,
will be called a prophet of the Most High,
for you will walk before the face of the Lord,
to prepare his paths,
to give knowledge of salvation to his people
in forgiveness of sins,
through the mercy of the heart of our God,

the rising Sun who comes to visit us,
a light upon those who sit
in darkness and the shadow of death,
a guide for our feet on the road of peace.

(Lk. 1:68-79)

The Canticle of the Angels at Bethlehem

Glory to God in the highest heaven
and peace on earth to the men he loves![73]

(Lk. 2:14)

The Canticle of Simeon

Now let your servant go,
Master, according to your word, in peace!

---

73. The final words, in literal translation, would be "men of his good will." The Qumran literature has the expression "sons of his good will" in *Hymns* IV, 32–33; see J. Carmignac and P. Guilbert, *Les textes de Qumrân* 1 (Paris, 1961), p. 210. The Vulgate translation, "men of good will," does not convey the sense of Luke's words.

Peace is a messianic blessing brought by the Child who is born at Bethlehem, and is essentially a result of the divine good will. Man's good will can only receive what God gives.

On the basis of variants supplied by textual criticism, the Canticle of the Angels may be read as follows:

Glory to God in the highest heaven
and on earth, peace
to men, (God's) good will.

For my eyes have seen your salvation,[74]
which you have prepared in the sight of the peoples,

a light to enlighten the nations,[75]
and the glory of your people, Israel.

---

74. In seeing *Jesus* (= Savior), Simeon sees the *salvation* of God.

75. Jesus is identified with the Isaian Servant of Yahweh; the Servant is a "light to the nations" (Is. 42:6; 49:6).

HYMNS OF THE APOCALYPSE

The Apocalypse contains the prophetic revelation of what "must come soon," [76] the manifestation of the "mystery of God, according to the good news which he gave of it to his servants, the prophets" (Apoc. 10:7). The imminent event that stands at the door of history is the definitive establishment of the kingdom of God and the lordship of Christ. The Apocalypse is thus a vast song of hope; it brings to the Church the invincible certainty, based on the testimony of Jesus himself, "the faithful witness" (1:5), of the eschatological victory.

This song of hope was meant, first of all, for the first generations of Christians. It strengthened them in their trials, sustained them amid torments, and confirmed them in their trust in Christ. It is difficult for us to imagine the challenge to faith that was created by the historical situation in which the Church found itself after the Lord's death. A storm of violent hatred burst upon the faithful and threatened to discourage them utterly. Jesus had indeed been enthroned as Lord and Christ through his resurrection from the dead, but the persecutions of Nero and Domitian meant the continual slaying of the faithful "for the word of God and for the testimony they had given" (6:9). The exalted Christ had sent the Spirit of Pentecost, whose outpouring was to signal "the last days," [77] but Rome did not on that account stop spreading and imposing on everyone the idolatrous worship of its divinized emperors. Christ reigned in heaven, but the faithful were suffering terribly on earth. He was the Lord of history, but, in the world's eyes, history had already crushed the Lord of history.

The Apocalypse is a response to this critical situation of great suffering. Let the faithful take heart: Jesus will soon return; his second coming is at hand! [78] Persecutions will last only a little while, since they represent the final combats to be fought, and victory is imminent. Babylon the great, "mother of the loathsome prostitutes of the earth . . . who gorged herself on the blood of the saints and martyrs of Jesus" (17:5-6) must drain the cup of wrath. The Beast, with all its worshipers and false prophets, will be thrown alive "into the pool of fire and burning sulphur" (19:20),[79] while the elect who have risen above their torments, "thanks to the witness of their martyrs" (12:11), will sit at the marriage supper of the Lamb and will reign for all eternity (19:1-9).

The Apocalypse is thus first and foremost the book of Christian hope. The enthusiastically optimistic teaching that the author addressed to his contemporaries applies to our age as well and will apply to all Christian ages to come. For two thousand years Christians have been carrying on their struggle, and for two thousand years their hope has been alive.

---

76. Dan. 2:28, as cited in Apoc. 1:1; 4:1; 22:6.
77. Jl. 3:1-5, as cited in Acts 2:17-21.
78. See Apoc. 1:3, 7; 22:10, 12, 20.
79. The image symbolizes eternal death; see 20:14.

In using the hymns of the Apocalypse, which are songs of glory and triumph for the moments of intense struggle, the believer expresses once again his confidence in Jesus:

The victory that has overcome the world is our faith (1 Jn. 5:4). ✳

THE CELEBRATION OF THE FATHER IN THE LITURGY OF HEAVEN

Behold, a throne was set up in heaven and Someone was seated on the throne.[80] And he who sits there is like a vision of jasper and carnelian. Around the throne, a rainbow, like a vision of emerald.

Around the throne, too, are twenty-four thrones, and on these thrones sit twenty-four Elders,[81] clad in white robes, with golden crowns on their heads. And from the throne come flashes of lightning, voices, and claps of thunder. Before the throne burn seven fiery torches, which are the seven spirits of God. Also before the throne there is as it were a sea of glass that is like crystal.

In the midst of the throne and all around the throne are four Living Creatures,[82] who have eyes everywhere. The first Living Creature is like a lion, the second is like a young bull, the third has as it were a human face, the fourth is like an eagle in full flight. The four Living Creatures each have six wings, with eyes all around and within. And they never cease to sing day and night:

Holy, holy, holy is the Lord,[83]   Isaiah 6:3
God, the Almighty,
he who was, who is, and who is coming![84]   I am who I am

And each time that the Living Creatures give glory, honor, and thanksgiving to him who sits on the throne and who lives forever and ever, the twenty-four Elders prostrate themselves before him who sits on the throne, adore him who lives forever and ever, and lay their crowns before the throne, saying:

You are worthy, Lord our God,

---

80. The prophetic vision of the Apocalypse begins with contemplation of the liturgy in heaven at which God — the One whose name the devout Jew feared to utter — sits enthroned as sovereign Lord and holds sway over time and history.

81. The twenty-four elders symbolize either the angels who compose God's court or, more probably, important personages of the Old Testament who compose as it were the court of time and history. Note that the liturgical celebration in heaven is not the celebration of a solitary God but a vast festival that links heaven and earth in a common joy.

82. The four living creatures seem to represent the four angels who are regarded as governing the world.

83. This doxology is inspired by Is. 6:3. Recall that the Christian liturgy has introduced the threefold *Holy* in the Eucharistic Prayer and sings it in union with all the angels, thus uniting the liturgy on earth to the liturgy in heaven.

84. The formula "who was and is and is to come" is a stereotyped expression (Apoc. 1:4; 4:8) inspired by the divine name "I am who I am" (Ex. 3:14) and emphasizing the eternity of God.

to receive glory, honor, and power!
For it is you who create the universe,
it is by your will that it exists and was created!

(Apoc. 4:2-11)

CANTICLE TO THE LAMB

The four Living Creatures and the twenty-four Elders prostrated themselves before the Lamb, each holding a harp and golden cups overflowing with perfumes, which are the prayers of the saints. And they sang a new song:

You are worthy to take the book[85]
and open its seals.

For you were sacrificed
and you ransomed for God, with your blood,
men of every tribe, tongue, people, and nation.

You made of them for our God
a kingdom of priests.
They shall reign upon the earth.

Behold, I then heard the voice of a multitude of angels around the throne and around the Living Creatures and the Elders. Their number was myriads of myriads and thousands of thousands. They were crying in a loud voice:

Worthy is the Lamb who was sacrificed
to receive power, riches, wisdom,
strength, honor, glory and praise.[86]

And every creature in heaven, on earth, and under the earth, on the sea and in the sea, I heard crying:

To him who sits on the throne of the Lamb
praise, honor, glory, and power
forever and ever!

And the four living Creatures answered: "Amen!" And the Elders prostrated themselves and adored.

(Apoc. 5:8-14)

THE CANTICLE OF THE ELECT IN HEAVEN

Behold, an immense crowd appeared which no one could count, from all nations, tribes, peoples, and tongues. They stood before the throne and before the

---

85. The book of divine decrees.
86. The doxology contains seven terms (as in 7:12). The author thus emphasizes the fullness of glory that belongs to the risen Christ, the Passover Lamb.

Lamb, clad in white robes and holding palms in their hands. And they cried with a mighty voice:

> Salvation to our God
> who sits upon the throne,
> and to the Lamb!

And all the angels who surrounded the throne, the Living Creatures, and the Elders, prostrated themselves before the throne with their faces to the ground, in order to adore God. They sang:

> Amen!
> Praise, glory, and wisdom,
> thanksgiving and honor,
> power and strength, to our God
> forever and ever!
> Amen!
>
> (Apoc. 7:9-12)

THE CANTICLE OF THE TWENTY-FOUR ELDERS

The twenty-four Elders who sit before God on their thrones fell to the ground face down. They adored God, saying:

> We give you thanks, O Lord God,
> O Almighty One, you "who are and who were,"
> for you have taken your great power
> and have established your reign!
>
> The nations were enraged,
> but your wrath came.
>
> It is time to judge the dead,
> time to reward your servants,
>   the prophets and the saints,
> those who fear your name,
>   both small and great,
> time to destroy the destroyers of the earth!
>
> (Apoc. 11:17-18)

THE ESCHATOLOGICAL BATTLE

A battle began in heaven. Michael[87] and his angels were warring against the Dragon. The Dragon and his angels fought, but they were overcome, and they had no place any longer in heaven. He was cast down, that great Dragon, the ancient

---

87. In the biblical tradition (Dan. 12:1), Michael is the champion and protector of the people of God.

Serpent, he who is called Devil and Satan, he who beguiles the whole inhabited world — he was cast down to earth, and his angels were cast down with him. Then I heard a mighty voice from heaven that shouted:

> See, victory and power,
> the reign of our God
> and the empire of his Christ have come!

> He is overcome, the Accuser[88] of our brethren,
> who accused them before our God
>   day and night!

> They have conquered him through the blood of the Lamb
> and the testimony of their martyrdom,
> for they held life in contempt to the point of dying.

> Rejoice then, O heavens
> and you who dwell in them!
> Woe to earth and sea!

> For the Devil has descended among you,
> filled with a great wrath,
> for he knows that his days are numbered.

(Apoc. 12:7-12)

THE CANTICLE OF MOSES AND THE LAMB

Those who have triumphed over the Beast and his image and the number of his name,[89] accompany themselves on the harps of God and sing the canticle of Moses,[90] the servant of God, and the canticle of the Lamb. They say:

> Great and wonderful are your works,
>   O Lord God, O Almighty One!

> Just and true are your ways,
>   O King of the nations!

> Who would not fear you, Lord,

---

88. The word "accuser" translates the Hebrew "Satan," which likewise means "accuser" (see Zech. 3:1).

89. The beast symbolizes the Roman empire, which was persecuting Christians. More generally, it represents all powers that oppose the establishment of Christ's reign. The number of the beast (666 according to Apoc. 13:15) doubtless stands for the emperor Nero, according to the gematria of the time.

90. The "Canticle of Moses" (Ex. 15:1-18; Dt. 32:1-43) is the supreme canticle of deliverance. We should remember that from the viewpoint of the Bible, the Exodus is the great type of messianic and eschatological liberation.

who would not give glory to your name?
> For you alone are holy.

And all the nations will come
and prostrate themselves before you,
> for your judgments have been revealed!

(Apoc. 15:2-4)

LAMENT OVER BABYLON[91]

I then saw an angel descend from heaven. He possessed great authority, and the earth was filled with the radiance of his glory. And he cried with a mighty voice:

> She is fallen, she is fallen,
> Babylon the great!
> She has become a lair of demons,
> a refuge for every unclean spirit,
> a refuge for every unclean and disgusting beast!

> For all the nations have drunk
> the wine of her prostitution,
> and the kings of the earth have fornicated with her,
> and the traders of the earth have enriched themselves
> with the wealth of her lustfulness. . . .

> She said in her heart:
> "I sit on a queen's throne,
> I shall never be widowed,
> I shall never know mourning!"

> See, then, why in a single day
> the plagues shall rain upon her:
> pestilence, mourning, and famine,
> and she will be consumed by fire.

> Ah, yes! he is mighty,
> the Lord God who has judged her!

They will sob, they will lament over her, the kings of the earth who shared her life of debauchery and pleasure, when they see the smoke of her burning. They will stand far off for fear of her torments and will say:

---

91. The fall of Babylon the great is paired with the exaltation of the new Jerusalem that descends from heaven, beautiful as a bride (Apoc. 21:5). In the language of the prophets, "prostitution" meant, from Hosea on, infidelity to the covenant (cf. Ezek. 16 and 23).
The triple lament of the kings of earth is inspired by Jer. 50–51 and Ezek. 26–28.

Alas! Alas! mighty city,
Babylon, O powerful city!
For a single hour was enough
for your judgment to come upon you! . . .

Alas! Alas! mighty city,
clothed in linen, purple, and scarlet,
all bedecked with gold, precious stones, and pearls!
For a single hour was enough
to lay waste such great wealth! . . .

Alas! Alas! mighty city,
her wealth enriched all those
who had ships upon the sea.
For a single hour was enough
to lay her waste!

Rejoice because of her, O heaven,
and you, the saints, apostles, and prophets!
For in condemning her
God has vindicated you.

A mighty angel then took a stone like a great millstone and hurled it into the sea, saying: "So shall Babylon, that mighty city, be hurled headlong and cast down. Never shall she be seen again.

The song of harpers and musicians,
of flute-players and of trumpeters
shall never be heard in you again.

And the craftsmen of every kind
shall never be seen in you again.

And the song of the millstone
shall never be heard in you again.

And the light of the lamp
shall never shine in you again.

And the voice of bridegroom and bride
shall never be heard in you again.

(Apoc. 18:1-23)

THE SONG OF VICTORY

I heard as it were the mighty voice of a countless throng in heaven, and it cried:

Alleluia![92]
Salvation, glory, and power to our God!
Yes, true and just are all his judgments.
For he has judged the great Harlot
who corrupted the earth with her prostitution.
He has avenged on her the blood of his servants.

Once more they cried:

Alleluia!
Her smoke goes up forever and ever![93]   *smoke as sign of God's wrath*

Then the twenty-four Elders and the four Living Creatures prostrated themselves and adored God who sits on the throne. They said:

Amen! Alleluia! . . .
Praise our God, all you his servants,
you who fear him, small and great.

Then I heard as it were the voice of a vast throng, the voice of many waters, the voice of mighty thunder:

Alleluia! For he reigns,
the Lord our God, the Almighty.
Let us rejoice and exult and give him glory,
for, behold, the marriage of the Lamb![94]
His Bride is ready;
it was granted to her to clothe herself in linen bright and pure.   *idea of covenant*
This linen is the good works of the saints."

And the angel said to me: "Write: Happy they who are invited to the marriage feast of the Lamb!"[95]

(Apoc. 19:1-9)

---

92. This victory is the only passage in the New Testament that contains the triumphal acclamation "Alleluia" (= "Praise God"). The author thus emphasizes the intensity of the joy with which the victory of God and the Lamb is welcomed. The first Alleluia defends the divine judgment to which the martyrs appeal who were slain for the word of God and for the witness they gave (Apoc. 6:11). The second Alleluia, ratified by an "Amen," associates the elect of the Old Testament (the twenty-four Elders) and the angelic world (the four Living Creatures) with this defense and praise. Finally, in the third Alleluia the vast throng of the redeemed celebrates the establishment of God's kingdom.

93. The smoke of burning Babylon (Apoc. 14:11; Is. 34:10) rises to heaven as a sign of God's wrath that has struck it (Apoc. 18:8-9).

94. The metaphor of the wedding expresses the idea of the covenant which, like a marriage contract, binds Israel to its God in fidelity and love (cf. Hos. 1–3; Is. 50:1; 54:5-6; Jer. 2:2; 3:6-13; Ezek. 16 and 23). The New Testament has transferred the image to the union of the Church with Christ (Eph. 5:27; 2 Cor. 11:2; Apoc. 21:2).

95. Compare the beatitude in Lk. 14:15: "Blessed is he who shall eat bread in the kingdom of God!" The image of a banquet is traditional in biblical literature as a symbol of messianic and eschatological joy (cf. Is. 25:6; Mt. 8:11; 22:2-10; Apoc. 3:20).

4

The Didache

THE DIDACHE

In 1875, Philotheos Bryennios, at that time the Greek metropolitan of Nicomedia, discovered a Greek parchment manuscript in the Monastery of the Holy Sepulcher at Constantinople. In addition to the *Letter of Barnabas* and the two *Letters of Clement*, the manuscript contained the text of the *Didache*, or *Teaching of the Lord to the nations, given through the twelve apostles*.

This was an extremely important discovery, and the interest it aroused at the time can only be compared to the interest aroused in our own time by the discovery of the manuscripts of Qumran and the Judean desert. For the *Didache* sheds a very vivid light on the period immediately following the apostolic age. It makes a unique contribution to our knowledge of the early Church and its initial legislation. In addition, it served as an archetypal model for all later collections of apostolic constitutions and canons.

The text of the *Didache* has been continually studied since Bryennios first published it in 1883, and yet no scholarly consensus has been reached as to the date of its composition. Internal analysis and comparison with other versions seem to show that documents of diverse origin and date have been combined in this short text. The compilation may have been made during the second century or even toward the end of the first. Some passages, moreover, may have been written even earlier, during the years from 50 to 70; they would thus be contemporary with the formation of the Pauline corpus and the collecting of the first evangelical logia.

The document seems to have originated in the communities of Antioch in Syria and to have been composed for the sake of the Christian communities whose members had been pagans.

THE EUCHARISTIC PRAYER

If we keep in mind that the word "eucharist" means "thanksgiving," this prayer of the *Didache* may be called the oldest "eucharistic" prayer in the Christian tradition.

It surely originated in the atmosphere of Jewish worship, and specifically in the world of Jewish blessings for community meals. But its relationship to the Christian Eucharist in the strict sense of the term remains disputed.

The least that can be said is this: The prayer, it seems sure, served as a mealtime prayer for the faithful who gathered for the agape meals (cf. 1 Cor. 11:17-22), meals that may have preceded the Eucharist proper.

The most that can be claimed is that it served as a eucharistic prayer for the celebration of the Lord's Supper (the prayer by which the bread and wine were consecrated). It is true, of course, that the account of institution is lacking in this prayer. But the necessary reference to the Lord's Last Supper can be established without repeating the words of institution; it can also, and in a more simple way, be established by the act of celebration itself as it imitates what the Lord did at the Last Supper.[1]

It seems that this second interpretation, which may at first sight seem "maximalist" and therefore highly vulnerable to critical assault, is the one that best explains both the text of the *Didache* and its links with the Jewish tradition. In an analysis of these links T.-J. Talley reaches this circumspect conclusion: "It does not appear improbable that *Didache* 10 is, or is meant to seem, a careful adaptation of the *Birkat ha-mazon* to the requirements of the Lord's Supper, which has become *zebah todah*: the eucharistic sacrifice."[1a]

Whatever the position taken on this point, the prayer can be considered the golden link connecting Jewish prayer with the Christian Eucharist.

With regard to the eucharist, give thanks in this manner:

> First, for the cup:
> "We thank you, our Father,
> for the holy vine of David your servant[2]
> which you have revealed to us through Jesus your Child.[3]
> Glory be yours through all ages!"

---

1. As a eucharistic prayer in the proper sense, yet lacking the account of institution, this prayer would resemble the anaphora of Addai and Mari (to be given later in this book). On this point, see A. Vööbus, *Liturgical Traditions in the Didache* (Stockholm, 1968), p. 94. — On the various interpretations of the "eucharistic" prayer in the *Didache*, see W. Rordorf, "The *Didache*," in R. Johanny (ed.), *The Eucharist of the Early Christians*, tr. M. J. O'Connell (New York, 1978), pp. 1–23. For an analysis of the *Didache*, see J.-P. Audet, *La Didaché: Instructions des apôtres* (Paris, 1958); S. Giet, *L'énigme de la Didaché* (Paris, 1970); W. Rordorf and A. Tuilier, *La Doctrine des Douze Apôtres (Didaché)* (SC 248; Paris, 1978).

1a. T.-J. Talley, "De la Berakah à l'Eucharistie: Une question à réexaminer," *La Maison-Dieu*, no. 125 (1976), p. 28.

2. The mysterious expression "the holy vine of David" is prophetic in style and seems to refer here to the entirety of salvation, especially the establishment of the new covenant that was sealed by the suffering of the cross and the glory of the resurrection. In his sermon at Antioch in Pisidia, Paul speaks along these lines: "We bring you the good news that what God promised to the fathers, this he has fulfilled to us their children by raising Jesus; as also it is written in the second psalm, 'Thou art my Son, today I have begotten thee' [2:7]. And as for the fact that he raised him from the dead, no more to return to corruption, he spoke in this way, 'I will give you the holy and sure blessings of David' [Is. 55:3]" (Acts 13:32-34).

3. The term "child" as applied to Jesus is characteristic of the very earliest Christian texts. The Greek word *pais* can in fact be interpreted either as "child" or as "servant." The

Then for the bread broken:
"We thank you, our Father,
for the life and knowledge
which you have revealed to us through Jesus your Child.
       Glory be yours through all ages!

Just as the bread broken
was first scattered on the hills,
then was gathered and became one,
so let your Church be gathered
from the ends of the earth into your kingdom,
for yours is glory and power through all ages."

Let no one eat or drink of your eucharist
except those baptized in the name of the Lord.
For it is of this that the Lord was speaking when he said,
"Do not give what is holy to dogs." [4]

When your hunger has been satisfied, give thanks thus:
"We thank you, holy Father,
for your holy name
which you have made to dwell in our hearts,
and for the knowledge and faith and immortality
which you have revealed to us through Jesus your Child.
       Glory be yours through all ages!

All-powerful Master, you created all things
for your name's sake,
and you have given food and drink to the children of men
for their enjoyment

---

primitive community, meditating on the texts about the "Servant of Yahweh" in the songs of Is. 42:1-9, 49:1-6, 50:4-11, and especially 52:13–53:12, saw in them the prophetic announcement of the vocation of Jesus, "thy holy servant" (Acts 4:27-30; cf. 3:26; Mt. 8:17 = Is. 53:4; Mt. 12:18-21 = Is. 42:1-4; Lk. 22:37 = Is. 53:12).

It was all the easier to apply these texts to Jesus because the Hebrew word for "servant," *ebed*, could also mean "child, son." As such, it was most appropriate for expressing the mystery of *Jesus*, who is *Servant* of God in his messianic and redemptive role, but also the beloved *Son* of the Father by reason of his divine origin. He is the *Servant* who was brought low by the suffering of his passion, but he was also "designated *Son of God* in power . . . by his resurrection from the dead" (Rom. 1:4). In addition, the fact that the figure of the Servant of God in Israel was both individual and collective suggested the ecclesial dimension of the vocation of Jesus, who carries the entire community of the faithful with him in his passion and resurrection. The term "child" as applied to Jesus in the earliest Christian texts is associated with this entire range of history and theology.

    4. Mt. 7:6.

so that they may thank you.
On us, moreover, you have graciously bestowed
a spiritual food and drink
that lead to eternal life,
    through Jesus your Child.

Above all, we thank you
because you are almighty.
    Glory be yours through all ages!
    Amen.

Lord, remember your Church
and deliver it from all evil;
make it perfect in your love
and gather it from the four winds,
this sanctified Church,[5]
into your kingdom which you have prepared for it,
    for power and glory are yours through all ages!

May the Lord come[6] and this world pass away!
    Amen.

Hosanna to the house of David!
If anyone is holy, let him come!
If anyone is not, let him repent!
    Marana tha![7]
    Amen."
        (*Didache* 9–10)

The Lord's Day

The day "of the Lord" is set aside for the celebration of the supper "of the Lord"; from the very beginning, Sunday, which is the memorial day of the resur-

---

5. Throughout this prayer the word "Church" has the meaning it had in the Old Testament, namely, the assembly of the children of Israel who are gathered together by the word of God to celebrate the covenant (see Dt. 23:2-4, 9). Similarly in the new covenant, the Lord gathers the Church from the four winds by calling all the faithful into the eternal kingdom of Jesus.

6. "May the Lord come!" (see Apoc. 22:20) in the Coptic version; a variant has, "May grace come!"

7. An Aramaic expression which had passed into the idiom of the liturgy and which means, "Lord, come!" (1 Cor. 16:22; cf. Apoc. 22:20; Rom. 13:12; Phil. 4:5; Jas. 5:8; 1 Pet. 4:7). It is possible to read the words as *Mar anatha*, which would mean, "The Lord is coming."

rection, has been linked to the celebration of the Eucharist. And with the mention of the Eucharistic meal is connected the prayer of thanksgiving and the communal confession of sins. The Church of the *Didache* is thus a Church that intensifies its unity through the acknowledgment of its sins, prayer of thanksgiving, and the Eucharistic meal.

Come together on the Lord's day,
break bread and give thanks,
having first confessed your sins
so that your sacrifice may be pure.
Anyone who has a quarrel with his fellow
should not gather with you
until he has been reconciled,[8]
lest your sacrifice be profaned.

For this is the sacrifice of which the Lord says:
"In every place and at every time
offer me a pure sacrifice,
for I am a great king, says the Lord,
and my name is marvelous among the nations."[9]

(*Didache* 14)

---

8. See Mt. 5:23-24.
9. Mal. 1:11, 14.

5

Clement of Rome
Letter to the Corinthians

(about 95–98)

CLEMENT OF ROME

The oldest list we have of the bishops of Rome is supplied by Irenaeus,[1] who gives Clement as the third successor of Peter, after Linus and Anacletus. According to Tertullian, Clement was ordained by Peter himself.[2]

Eusebius dates Clement's pontificate as beginning in the twelfth year of the reign of Domitian (81–96) and ending in the third year of the reign of Trajan (98–117).[3] According to this calculation, Clement occupied the chair of Peter from 92 to 101.

LETTER TO THE CORINTHIANS

Toward the end of the reign of Domitian or at the beginning of the reign of Nerva (therefore about 95–96) "the Church of God sojourning at Rome" wrote a letter to "the Church of God sojourning at Corinth." A schism had just broken out there. A few "rash and arrogant" (1, 1) ringleaders had roused the community against its elders and stripped the latter of "the service they were exercising blamelessly and honorably" (44, 6). In short, a kind of palace revolution within the holy Church of Christ! And all these scandalous goings-on took place in public, where Jews and pagans could see and gloat (47, 7)!

Clement was obliged to intervene. He did so with gentleness and love, but also as a man who meant to be obeyed.

Thus the quarrelsome Corinthians (they had been quarrelsome in Paul's day, too! See 1 Cor. 1:10-13) elicited for us the letter of St. Clement of Rome, the oldest piece of non-canonical Christian literature for which the name and position of the author can be historically determined. The letter has also been called the first manifestation of the Roman primacy. Not only does the Church of Rome not excuse herself for intervening in the internal affairs of a sister Church; she even excuses herself for not intervening sooner! But her intervention takes the form of an appeal for unity and charity.

THE SANCTUS, HYMN OF UNITY

Let God be the object of our pride and confidence. Let us submit to his will.

---

1. *Adversus Haereses* III, 3, 5 (*PG* 7/1:849–50).
2. *De praescriptione haereticorum* 32 (*CCL* 1:213).
3. *Historia ecclesiastica* III, 15, 34 (*SC* 31:120).

Let us contemplate the entire multitude of his angels and consider how they stand ready and serve his will. For the Scripture says:

> Ten thousand times ten thousand stood near him,
> and thousands upon thousands served him,
> and they cried out,
> "Holy, holy, holy is the Lord of hosts!
> All of creation is filled with his glory!"[4]

We too, then, should assemble in oneness of mind and cry out to him perseveringly, as with a single mouth, that we might share in his great and glorious promises. For it is said: "Eye has not seen nor ear heard nor has the heart of man imagined what the Lord has prepared for those who wait for him."[5]

(34, 5-8)

JESUS CHRIST, OUR HIGH PRIEST

> Jesus Christ [is] the high priest of our offerings,
> our protector and helper in our weakness.
> Through him we fix our gaze on the heavenly heights.
> Through him we see as in a mirror
> the pure and lofty face of God.
> Through him the eyes of our heart have been opened.
> Through him our foolish and darkened mind
> grows up again into the light.
> Through him the Master willed
> that we should taste immortal knowledge.

(36, 1-2)

The Great Prayer

Clement ends his letter with the "Great Prayer," one of the jewels of early Christian literature. This hieratic text, woven of biblical reminiscences, was doubtless, at least in part, a liturgical prayer of the Church of Rome. Like such Jewish prayers as the *Birkat ha-mazon* and the *Shemone Esre*, it combines thanksgiving with petition. It thus anticipates later liturgical compositions that will add the account of institution and the anamnesis and thereby create the great Eucharistic Prayers.

> May the Creator of the universe
> guard the elect

---

4. See Is. 6:3; Dan. 7:10; Apoc. 4:8; 5:11.
5. Is. 64:3; 1 Cor. 2:9.

who have been numbered throughout the world
through his beloved Child, Jesus Christ.

Through him you have called us
from darkness to light,
from ignorance to full knowledge of your glorious name
and to a hope in your name,
which is the origin of all creation.

You opened the eyes of our hearts
that they might know you
who alone are the Most High in the heavenly heights,
the Holy One who rests among the saints.

You cast down the insolence of the proud,
you frustrate the plans of the nations,
you raise up the humble and abase the proud.

You enrich and you reduce to poverty,
you slay, you save and give life,
sole benefactor of spirits and God of all flesh.

You gaze into the abysses,
you watch over the deeds of men,
helper of men in peril,
savior of the hopeless,
Creator and overseer of every spirit!

You multiply the peoples of the world
and from among them all you choose
those who love you
through Jesus Christ, your beloved Child.
Through him you have taught us,
sanctified us and glorified us.

We pray you, Master,
be our help and protection.

Save the afflicted among us,
have mercy on the lowly.

Raise up the fallen,
show yourself to those in need.

Heal the sick
and bring back those who have strayed.

Fill the hungry,
give freedom to our prisoners.

Raise up the weak,
console the fainthearted.

Let all peoples acknowledge
that you alone are God,
and Jesus Christ is your Child,
that we are your people,
the sheep to whom you give pasture.

Through your works
you have made known the eternal constitution of the world.
Lord, you have created the world.
You are faithful from age to age,
just in your judgments,
wonderful in power and magnificence,
wise in creating
and prudent in solidly founding what exists,
good in all things visible,
faithful to those who trust in you,
merciful and compassionate.

Forgive us all our sins and iniquities,
our failures and faults.
Do not reckon up every sin
of your servants and handmaids,
but cleanse us with your cleansing truth.

Guide our steps on the right path
that we may walk in holiness of heart
and may do
what is good and pleasing in your eyes
and the eyes of those who direct us.

Yes, Master, make your face shine upon us
so that we may enjoy blessings in peace,
be sheltered by your mighty hand
and liberated from all sin by your uplifted arm
and rescued from those who hate us without cause.

Grant concord and peace
to us and all who dwell on earth,
as you gave them to our fathers
when they called to you
in holiness, faith, and truth.

Make us obedient
to your almighty and glorious name,
and to those who rule
and direct us on earth.

It is you, Master,
who gave them kingly authority
by your marvelous and indescribable power,
that we might acknowledge
the glory and honor you have given them
and might be submissive to them
and in no way oppose your will.
Lord, grant them health,
peace, concord, and stability
that they may without offense
exercise the rule you have given them.

It is you, Master, heavenly King of the ages,
who give the children of men
glory, honor, and authority over earthly things.

Lord, guide their counsels
in accord with what is good and pleasing to you.
Let them exercise in peace, gentleness, and piety
the authority you have given them,
and thus win your favor.
You alone have power to answer our prayer
and bestow even greater blessings upon us.

We praise you through Jesus Christ,
the high priest and guardian of our souls.
Through him be glory and majesty yours
now and from generation to generation
and through all ages. Amen.

(59-61)

6

The Witness of Saint Justin

(about 150)

SAINT JUSTIN

THE MAN

Justin was born at Flavia Neapolis, a pagan Roman city in the heart of Galilee. The city was built on the site of ancient Shechem, not far from the well of Jacob. Although Justin lived so close to the well where Jesus had promised the Samaritan woman the living water that slakes thirst forever and leaps up for eternal life, he was ignorant of Christ. His soul thirsting for God, he set out to search the world for the truth.

He entrusted himself first of all to a Stoic. It was his first disappointment, for this self-styled teacher "knew nothing of God and did not even think knowledge of him to be necessary."

Justin tried his luck next with a Peripatetic. But this disciple of Aristotle was not a great-souled man like his master, and from him the truth was not to be gotten for free. So when he began by asking for his fees, the disheartened Justin told him the lesson was over.

He also entrusted himself to a Pythagorean, but the latter required the prior study of music, astronomy, and geometry. Justin was in a hurry; he wanted to get to the heart of things.

Meanwhile a Platonist came along. Justin attached himself to him, thinking that this man surely had the truth. This was his final disappointment, though, for he finally met Christ, and was dazzled and spellbound:

> A fire was suddenly kindled in my soul. I fell in love with the prophets and these men who had loved Christ; I reflected on all their words and found that this philosophy alone was true and profitable.
>
> That is how and why I became a philosopher. And I wish that everyone felt the same way that I do.[1]

At the same time that he met Christ, Justin also met Christians. The life of the disciples seemed to him worthy of their Master, and their splendid scorn for death completely refuted the spiteful accusations spread against them:

> In the days when the teachings of Plato were my delight, I myself used to hear the accusations leveled against Christians. But when I saw how fearless

---

1. *Dialogus cum Tryphone* 8 (PG 6:492CD).

they were in the face of death and of every possible terror, I realized they could not possibly be living vicious, pleasure-seeking lives. For if a man loves pleasure and debauchery, if his delight is to eat human flesh, will he seek out death, which deprives you of all these pleasures? Will he not endeavor to preserve his present life at any cost and to elude the magistrates rather than to inform on himself and be handed over to death?[2]

After his conversion, which in all probability occurred at Ephesus about 130, he once again set out on his journey as a wandering philosopher. He came to Rome during the reign of Antoninus Pius (138–161) and opened a Christian school there. He died a martyr between 156 and 166.

How moving are these words he wrote before dying! They form the most beautiful possible signature to his work:

> No one believes in Socrates to the point of dying for what he taught. . . . But for the sake of Christ not only philosophers and scholars but even workmen and uneducated people have scorned fame, fear, and death![3]

HIS WORK

Of the extensive writings of Justin, we still possess the two *Apologies* and the *Dialogue with Trypho the Jew*.

The two *Apologies* were written at Rome around 150 (Justin tells us therein that Christ had been born 150 years earlier). The dedication of the work is splendid in its nobility and boldness: "To the Emperor Antoninus Pius . . . and to his son Verissimus [Marcus Aurelius] . . . to the sacred Senate and the entire Roman people, on behalf of the men of every race who are unjustly hated and persecuted, I who am one of them, Justin, son of Priscus, son of Baccheius, a native of Flavia Neapolis in Palestinian Syria, address this discourse and petition." *I, who am one of them* — what mad frankness! Justin knows that Christians are being martyred and that merely to bear the name of Christian is considered a crime. He does not care. He does not take the precaution to send the emperor an anonymous letter, but cries his faith aloud.

It is in the course of thus proclaiming his faith that he gives us the texts that are of special interest to us: those describing Christian initiation, the celebration of the Eucharist, and the celebration of the Lord's Day. Through these texts that are eighteen centuries old, we feel the liturgy of the second century come to life again.

Christian Initiation

We shall now describe the way in which we are renewed by Christ and

---

2. *Apologia II* 12 (*PG* 6:464AB).
3. *Apologia II* 10 (*PG* 6:461AB).

consecrated to God. If we were to omit this, we would seem deficient in our explanation.

First of all, those who believe in the truth of our teachings and discourses promise that they can live in accordance with it. Then they are taught to pray and, while fasting, to ask God for the forgiveness of their past sins. We, for our part, pray and fast with them.[4]

Next, we bring them to a place where there is water, and they are reborn in the same way as we ourselves were reborn before them. That is to say, they are cleansed with water in the name of God the Father and Master of the universe, and of our Savior Jesus Christ, and of the Holy Spirit. For Christ said: "Unless you are born again, you shall not enter the kingdom of heaven."[5] But, as is evident to everyone, those who have once been born cannot return to their mothers' wombs. This is why Isaiah the prophet, whom we mentioned earlier, teaches us how sinners are to flee their sins and repent. He speaks as follows:

> Wash and purify yourselves,
> remove the evil from your souls,
> learn to do good.
> Be just to the orphan
> and protect the widow.
> Then come and let us talk together, says the Lord:
> Even though your sins be like purple,
> they shall become white as wool,
> and though they be scarlet,
> they shall become white as snow.
> But if you do not obey,
> the sword shall devour you.
> The mouth of the Lord has spoken.[6]

Such is the teaching the apostles have handed on to us in this matter. . . .

Upon the person who wishes to be reborn and who repents of his sins, we invoke the name of God the Father and Master of the universe. . . .

We call this washing an "enlightenment," because those who are taught as we have described have their minds enlightened.

(We also invoke) upon the person who is enlightened and cleansed the name of Jesus Christ, who was crucified under Pontius Pilate, and the name of the Holy Spirit, who through the prophets foretold the entire story of Jesus.

(Apologia I, 61)

---

4. The preparation of neophytes for baptism included, on the one hand, teaching on the Christian faith (*Apologia I*, 61) and morality (*Apologia I*, 61 and 66), and, on the other hand, the practice of prayer and fasting. A prebaptismal fast is attested by the interpolation in *Didache* 7, 4; see J.-P. Audet, p. 233.

5. Free citation of Jn. 3:5.

6. Free citation of Is. 1:16-20.

The Celebration of the Eucharist

THE COMMUNAL PRAYERS

After we have thus cleansed the person who believes and has joined our ranks, we lead him in to where those we call "brothers" are assembled.

We offer prayers in common for ourselves, for him who has just been enlightened, and for all men everywhere. It is our desire, now that we have come to know the truth, to be found worthy of doing good deeds and obeying the commandments, and thus to obtain eternal salvation.

THE KISS OF PEACE

When we finish praying, we greet one another with a kiss.

ANAPHORA

Then bread and a cup of wine mixed with water are brought to him who presides over the brethren.

He takes them and offers prayers glorifying the Father of the universe through the name of the Son and of the Holy Spirit, and he utters a lengthy eucharist[7] because the Father has judged us worthy of these gifts.

When the prayers and eucharist are finished, all the people present give their assent with an "Amen!" "Amen" in Hebrew means "So be it!"

(Apologia I, 65)

COMMUNION

When the president has finished his eucharist and the people have all signified their assent, those whom we call "deacons" distribute the bread and the wine and water over which the eucharist has been spoken, to each of those present; they also carry them to those who are absent.

This food we call "eucharist,"[8] and no one may share it unless he believes that our teaching is true, and has been cleansed in the bath of forgiveness for sin and of rebirth, and lives as Christ taught. For we do not receive these things as if they were ordinary food and drink. But, just as Jesus Christ our Savior was made flesh through the word of God and took on flesh and blood for our salvation, so too (we have been taught) through the word of prayer that comes from him, the food over which the eucharist has been spoken becomes the flesh and blood of the incarnate Jesus, in order to nourish and transform our flesh and blood.

For, in the memoirs which the apostles composed and which we call "gospels," they have told us that they were commissioned thus: Jesus took bread and, having given thanks, said: "Do this in memory of me; this is my body." And in a

---

7. That is, a thanksgiving.

8. This is the first example of the word "eucharist" being used not simply for the prayer of thanksgiving but also for the bread over which the prayer of thanksgiving has been said.

like manner he took the cup and, having given thanks, said: "This is my blood." And he gave these to the apostles alone.

(Apologia I, 65-66)

The Liturgy of the Lord's Day

A COMMUNITY OF LOVE AND PRAYER

Those of us who have any resources come to the aid of all who are in need, and we are always assisting one another.

For all that we eat we thank the Maker of the universe through his Son Jesus Christ and the Holy Spirit.

THE CELEBRATION OF THE LORD'S DAY

On the day named after the sun,[9] all who live in city or countryside assemble.

The memoirs of the apostles or the writings of the prophets are read for as long as time allows.[10]

When the lector has finished, the president addresses us and exhorts us to imitate the splendid things we have heard.

Then we all stand and pray.[11]

As we said earlier, when we have finished praying, bread, wine, and water are brought up. The president then prays and gives thanks according to his ability,[12] and the people give their assent with an "Amen!" Next, the gifts over which

---

9. That is, "Sunday" in English and the other Germanic languages, but "the Lord's [day]" in French and the Romance languages (*dimanche, domenica, domingo*).

10. The Mass as described by Justin already contains the essential components of the Christian celebration: reading of the word of God, homily of the celebrant, common prayer, and Eucharist.

It is of interest to note the necessary link between Eucharist and word of God. The community to which Justin belonged, like the community described in the Acts of the Apostles, was built up on "the apostles' teaching and . . . the breaking of bread" (Acts 2:42). See L. Deiss, *God's Word and God's People*, tr. M. J. O'Connell (Collegeville, 1976), pp. 253–72.

11. In the early Church the normal posture for prayer was standing. This was more than an attitude of respect for God, more even than a simple inheritance from the Jewish tradition. It was, before all else, an expression of the holy freedom the Lord had given his followers by his resurrection. It was also a sign of expectation of the Lord's coming (see Lk. 21:36); this expectation was especially keen on Sunday, the day that was a kind of anticipation of the eternal Day of God. Basil the Great says in his *De Sancto Spiritu* (ed. B. Pruche, SC 17bis; Paris, 1968): "We pray standing on the first day of the week [Sunday]. . . . We do so because we are risen with Christ and must seek the things that are above [Col. 3:1]; therefore on the day consecrated to the resurrection, by standing when we pray we call to mind the grace given to us. But we also stand because Sunday is a kind of image of the world to come" (p. 484).

12. The celebrant freely improvises the prayer of the anaphora, but in doing so he follows a basic schema.

the thanksgiving has been spoken are distributed, and everyone shares in them, while they are also sent via the deacons to the absent brethren.

The wealthy who are willing make contributions, each as he pleases, and the collection is deposited with the president, who aids orphans and widows, those who are in want because of sickness or some other reason, those in prison, and visiting strangers — in short, he takes care of all in need.

It is on Sunday that we all assemble, because Sunday is the first day: the day on which God transformed darkness and matter and created the world, and the day on which Jesus Christ our Savior rose from the dead. He was crucified on the eve of Saturn's day,[13] and on the day after, that is, on the day of the sun, he appeared to his apostles and disciples and taught them what we have now offered for your examination.

(*Apologia I*, 67)

---

13. That is, Friday, the eve of "Saturn's day," our present "Saturday."

7

The Homily On the Pasch
of Melito of Sardis

(second half of second century)

MELITO OF SARDIS

THE MAN

There exists a very short account of Melito, bishop of Sardis in Lydia, that gives us a few rather general facts about him. The notice is in the letter that Polycrates of Ephesus wrote to Pope St. Victor (189–199). The letter itself has been preserved by Eusebius of Caesarea in his *History of the Church*. Polycrates places Melito among "the great luminaries [who] lie at rest in Asia and will rise again on the day of the Lord's coming."[1] He calls him "Melito the eunuch," that is, the celibate, and claims that he "lived entirely in the Holy Spirit."[2]

Melito's literary activity was carried on in the second half of the second century. Eusebius cites the beginning of the treatise *On the Pasch*, where Melito writes: "Under Servillius Paulus [=Sergius Paulus], proconsul of Asia, at the time when Sagaris was martyred, there was a great debate at Laodicea regarding Easter, which, as it happened, was being celebrated just at that time."[3] We know that this Sergius Paulus governed the province of Asia from 164 to 166.

It seems that Melito was closely involved in the controversy just mentioned, which had to do with the correct date for the liturgical celebration of Easter. Some Eastern Churches followed Jewish custom and celebrated the Christian Passover on the fourteenth of Nisan, that is, on the fourteenth day after the appearance of the new spring moon, no matter what day of the week the fourteenth might be. This custom was meant to bring out the fact that the Pasch, or Easter, was the memorial not only of the Lord's resurrection but of his passion as well, and that the two mysteries were inseparably linked in the rich unity of the paschal mystery. The other Churches, however, celebrated Easter on the Sunday after the fourteenth of Nisan. Here the emphasis was on the Christian newness that the resurrection had brought to Sunday, the day which Christians from apostolic times on called the "day of the Lord."[4]

We have no very sure knowledge of how this first Easter controversy turned out. It seems likely that Melito and his colleagues won the day, since toward the end of the second century all the Churches of Asia were following the quartodeci-

---

1. Eusebius of Caesarea, *Historia ecclesiastica* V, 24, 2 (SC 41:67).
2. *Ibid.*, V, 24, 7 (SC 41:68).
3. *Ibid.*, IV, 26, 3 (SC 31:209).
4. See Apoc. 1:10.

man practice (that is, celebrating Easter on the fourteenth of Nisan). Melito could argue from the antiquity of this practice to its legitimacy, "in accordance with the rule of faith."[5]

Unfortunately for the quartodecimans — if "unfortunately" be the right word — the Montanist and Novatian heretics adopted the same custom. This was enough to compromise the custom in orthodox eyes and to give it the smell of heresy. In consequence, it gradually lost ground, especially since the great sees of Rome and Alexandria firmly opted for the practice of celebrating Easter on Sunday. In the end, the Council of Nicaea in 325 rejected the quartodeciman practice and prescribed that Easter should be celebrated on the Sunday after the fourteenth of Nisan. By this time Melito, the "great luminary of Asia," had been dead for a century and a half.

THE WORK

Melito's literary activity was extensive. Eusebius, who had access to the catalogue of the very rich library at Caesarea, tells us that Melito wrote two books *On the Pasch* and treatises *On Christian Life and the Prophets, On the Church, On the Lord's Day, On Man's Faith, On Creation, On the Obedience of Faith, On the Senses, On Soul and Body, On Hospitality, On Baptism, On Truth, On Faith and the Birth of Christ, On Prophecy, The Key, On the Devil, On St. John's Apocalypse,* and *On God Incarnate.*[6]

We should give special mention to an *Apologia,* or *Defense,* written about 170 and addressed to Emperor Marcus Aurelius. Eusebius has preserved a few fragments of this in his *History of the Church.*[7] In them Melito shows himself as the first promoter of a certain solidarity between the empire and the Christian religion.

Another work calling for special mention is the six books of *Extracts from the Law and Prophets Dealing with Our Savior and with Our Faith in Its Entirety.* The preface to this work contains the earliest list we have of the canonical books of the Old Testament.[8] Melito had gone on a pilgrimage to Palestine, and he writes to a friend, Onesimus:

> I went to the East and reached the very place where the Scriptures were preached and fulfilled. There I learned just which books make up the Old Testament; I drew up a list of them and send it now to you. Here are the names: Five books of Moses: *Genesis, Exodus, Numbers, Leviticus, Deuteronomy; Jesus Nave* [=Joshua], *Judges, Ruth;* four books of *Kings* and two of *Paralipomena;* the *Psalms* of David, the *Proverbs* or *Wisdom* of Solomon; *Ecclesiastes, Canticle of Canticles, Job;* prophets: *Isaiah, Jeremiah,* the twelve in one book, *Daniel, Ezekiel, Esdras.*

---

5. Eusebius, *Historia ecclesiastica* V, 24, 6 (SC 41:68).
6. *Ibid.,* IV, 26, 3-14 (SC 31:208-11).
7. *Ibid.,* IV, 26, 5-11 (SC 31:209-11).
8. *Ibid.,* IV, 26, 14 (SC 31:211).

The homily *On the Pasch* was doubtless the work of Melito that was most definitely meant for a popular audience. This masterpiece of ancient rhythmical prose shared the general fate of early Christian literature; from the fourth century on it was not copied and recopied, and so was forgotten. In 1855, W. Cureton published a first extract from the homily in Syriac.[9] Then, in 1940, C. Bonner published an almost complete Greek text, which in turn enabled scholars to identify other fragments, in Greek, Coptic, and Syriac, which belonged to the homily and filled in the lacunae in the Greek text.[10] When we add the third-century copy in the Bodmer Library collection (published in 1960[11]), we may claim to possess, or at least to be able to reconstruct, the original text.

This is a literary work that needs no recommendation. It speaks for itself — or rather, it sings and cries and shouts of the new mystery of the eternal Pasch, and does so in a wild succession of fiery images that are sustained by a rhythm as of a mighty wind.

Homily on the Pasch

NEW AND OLD, MORTAL AND IMMORTAL . . .

We have just read from the Scriptures the story of the Exodus of the Hebrews. Then we explained the words of the mystery: how the lamb was sacrificed, how the people were saved. Understand, then, beloved:

> The mystery of the Pasch
> is new and old,
> eternal and temporal,
> corruptible and incorruptible,
> mortal and immortal.
>
> Old according to the Law,
> new according to the Word;
> temporal according to the world,
> eternal by grace;
> corruptible by the immolation of the lamb,
> incorruptible by the life of the Lord;
> mortal by his burial in the earth,
> immortal by his resurrection from the dead.

---

9. W. Cureton, *Spicilegium Syriacum* (London, 1855), pp. 49–50, 54–56.
10. *The Homily on the Passion by Melito of Sardis*, ed. C. Bonner (Studies and Documents 12; London and Philadelphia, 1940).
11. M. Testuz, *Papyrus Bodmer XIII: Méliton de Sardes, Homélie sur la Pâque* (Cologne–Geneva, 1960). Our translation is based on the Greek text of Bodmer Papyrus XIII, which we have compared with the Greek text published by B. Lohse in his *Die Passa-Homilie des Bischofs Meliton von Sardes* (Textus Minores 24; Leiden, 1958).

The Law is old,
but the Word is new.
The figure is temporal,
but grace is eternal.
The lamb is corruptible,
but the Lord is incorruptible,
who had no bone broken as a lamb
but who rose from the dead as God. . . .

For the figure has passed away,
the reality has been revealed:
in the lamb's place God has come,
in the sheep's place, the Man.
In the Man is the Christ
        who contains all things.

For the sacrifice of the Lamb
and the celebration of the Pasch
and the letter of the Law
have been fulfilled in Christ.
Through him was made
everything in the old Law
        and, still more, everything in the new Law.

For the Law has become the Word,
the old has become new
— it goes forth from Zion and from Jerusalem [12] —
and the commandment has become grace,
and the figure has become the reality,
and the lamb has become the Son,
and the sheep has become a Man,
        and the Man has become God.

Born as Son,
led like a lamb, [13]
sacrificed like a sheep,
buried as a man,
he rises from the dead as God,
being by nature both God and man.

He is all things:

---

12. Allusion to Is. 2:3: "Out of Zion shall go forth the law, and the word of the Lord from Jerusalem."
13. Allusion to Is. 53:7: "Like a lamb that is led to the slaughter."

when he judges, he is law,
when he teaches, Word,
when he saves, grace,
when he begets, father,
when he is begotten, son,
when he suffers, lamb,
when he is buried, man,
when he rises, God.

Such is Jesus Christ!
To him be glory forever! Amen.

(1-10)

THE DEATH OF THE FIRST-BORN IN EGYPT

Pharaoh wore Egypt like a mourning garment.
Such was the robe woven for the tyrant's body,
such the garment the angel of justice threw about the
    hard-hearted Pharaoh:
mourning that pierces, darkness that thickens,
    and no more children. . . .[14]
Swift and insatiable the death of the first-born! . . .

If you listen to the story of this astounding tragedy, amazement will seize you.
For here is what enveloped the Egyptians:

a vast night
and a thick darkness,
and groping death,
and the exterminating angel,
and the lower world that swallows up their first-born.

But listen to something even more astounding and terrifying: in the darkness
that was almost palpable, insatiable death was hiding. The anguished Egyptians
were groping in the darkness, and groping death was seizing the first-born of the
Egyptians at the angel's command!
If anyone, then, was groping about in the darkness, the angel snatched him
away. If a first-born touched a hidden body, terror filled his soul and he uttered a
frightful wail:

"Whom is my hand grasping?
Whom does my soul fear?
What darkness surrounds my body?
If it be my father, help me!

---

14. A line is missing; the text is doubtless corrupt.

>If it be my mother, comfort me!
>If it be my brother, speak to me?
>If it be a friend, support me!
>If it be an enemy, depart,
>for I am a first-born!"

But before the first-born falls silent, unending silence has enveloped him. It whispers to him: "First-born, you belong to me; I, the silence of death, am fated to be yours! . . ."

>One blow and he is dead
>who was the fruit,
>the first-born of the Egyptians,
>the first one sown,
>the first one brought to birth,
>desired and coddled:
>he has been smashed to the ground.

>(20, 22-26)

THE DEATH OF THE LAMB BROUGHT LIFE TO THE PEOPLE

>O unutterable mystery!
>The sacrifice of the lamb was the salvation of the people,
>the death of the lamb brought life to the people,
>its blood intimidated the angel!

>Tell me, angel, what intimidated you:
>the sacrifice of the lamb or the life of the Lord,
>the death of the lamb or the prefiguration of the Lord,
>the blood of the lamb or the Spirit of the Lord?

>Show me what intimidated you.[15]
>You saw the mystery of the Lord
>in the lot of the lamb,
>and the life of the Lord
>in the sacrifice of the lamb,
>and the figure of the Lord
>in the death of the lamb.
>That is why you did not strike Israel
>but deprived only Egypt of her children.

>(31-33)

THE GOSPEL IS THE EXPLANATION OF THE LAW

The gospel is the explanation and fulfillment of the Law, and the Church is the place where the Law comes true.

---

15. Translation uncertain.

The figure was precious before the reality came,
and the parable marvelous before it was explained.
That is, the people were precious
before the Church was established,
and the Law was marvelous
before the light of the gospel shone.

But when the Church was built
and the gospel was revealed,
then the figure was emptied out,
for it passed its power on to the reality,
and the Law was fulfilled,
for it passed its power on to the gospel. . . .

For precious of old was the sacrifice of the law,
but now it has lost its value
because of the Lord's life.

Precious was the death of the lamb,
but now it has lost its value
because of the salvation of the Lord.

Precious was the blood of the lamb,
but now it has lost its value
because of the Spirit of the Lord.

Precious was the lamb that remained silent,[16]
but now it has lost its value
because of the sinless Son.

Precious was the earthly temple,
but now it has lost its value
because of Christ who is above.

Precious was the earthly Jerusalem,
but now it has lost its value,
because of the Jerusalem that is above.

Precious was the inheritance strictly (reserved),
but now it has lost its value
because of the grace generously (poured out).

For no longer is there a single place nor the tiniest enclosure where the glory

---

16. See note 20, below.

of God has not been established, but his grace has been poured out to the very ends of the earth, and there the almighty God has built his tabernacle, through Jesus Christ.

To him be glory forever! Amen.

(40-42, 44-45)

IF YOU WISH TO SEE THE MYSTERY OF THE LORD. . . .

The Lord had foreordained an image of his suffering in the persons of the patriarchs and the prophets and the entire people. . . .

> If you wish to see the mystery of the Lord,
> consider Abel, who was likewise killed,
> Isaac, who was likewise fettered,
> Joseph, who was likewise sold,
> David, who was likewise persecuted,
> the prophets, who likewise suffered
> because of Christ.

> Consider, finally, the lamb
> that was sacrificed in the land of Egypt
> and saved Israel by its blood. . . .

Many other predictions were made by the prophets in regard to the mystery of the Pasch, that is, in regard to Jesus Christ.

To him be glory forever! Amen.

(57, 59, 65)

FROM DEATH TO LIFE

> Through his body which was subject to suffering
> he put an end to the sufferings of the flesh,
> and through his Spirit who cannot die
> he slew the death that slays men.

> Like a sheep he was led away,
> like a lamb he was sacrificed,
> he who delivered us
> from slavery to the world,
> as from another Egypt,
> and who liberated us
> from slavery to the devil,
> as from the hand of Pharaoh,
> and who impressed upon our souls
> the seal of his own blood. [17]

---

17. Textual variant: "who impresses on our soul the seal of his own Spirit and on the members of (our) body the seal of his own blood."

It is he who covered death with shame
and threw the devil into mourning
as Moses did Pharaoh.

It is he who struck down iniquity
and deprived injustice of its children
as Moses did Egypt.

It is he who led us out
from slavery to freedom,
from darkness to light,
from death to life,
from tyranny to eternal kingship.[18]

He is the Pasch of our salvation.
It is he who endured many sufferings
in many men.

It is he who was slain in Abel;
in Isaac he was fettered,
in Jacob he was a hireling,
in Joseph he was sold,
in Moses he was exposed to die,
in David he was persecuted,
in the prophets he was scorned.

It is he who took flesh in the Virgin;
he was hung on the tree,
he was buried in the earth,
he was wakened from among the dead,
he was exalted to the heights of heaven.[19]

He is the silent Lamb,[20]
he is the Lamb slain,
who was born of Mary, the noble Lamb.

It is he who was taken from the flock
and led to sacrifice;
at evening he was sacrificed

---

18. Addition: "who makes of us a new priesthood and an eternal chosen people."
19. Textual variant for these two lines: "and who raised man from the depths of the tomb (to exalt him) to the heights of heaven."
20. Allusion to the Servant of Yahweh in Is. 53:7: "Like a lamb that is led to the slaughter, and like a sheep that before its shearers is dumb, so he opened not his mouth."

> and in the night he was buried;
> he was not broken on the tree[21]
> and in the earth suffered no corruption;
> he rose from the dead,
> he rose from the depths of the tomb.

(66-71)

COMPLAINT OF CHRIST ABOUT ISRAEL

He was put to death. . . . Where was he put to death? In the midst of Jerusalem. Why?

> Because he had cured their lame,
> because he had cleansed their lepers,
> because he had restored sight to their blind,
> because he had raised their dead.

That is why he suffered. Therefore it is written in the Law and the prophets:

> They returned me evil for good,
> and my life has become barren.[22]
> They have plotted evil against me,[23]
> saying: "Let us load the just man with chains,
> for he is a stumbling block to us."[24]

O Israel, why have you committed this unheard-of crime? You have dishonored him who honored you; you have deprived of glory him who glorified you; you have denied him who acknowledged you as his own; you have rejected the proclamation of him who proclaimed you; you put to death him who gave you life! Why did you do this, O Israel? Was it not for you that it was written: "You shall not shed innocent blood, lest you die a wretched death"?

> "Yes," says Israel. "It is I who put the Lord to death."
> "Why?"
> "Because he had to suffer!"
> "You are mistaken, Israel, when you make clever play of the Lord's

sacrifice!

> "He had to suffer,
>   but not at your hands!
> [He had to be scorned,
>   but not by you!"

---

21. Allusion to Ex. 12:46: "You shall not break a bone of it," which is cited in the passion narrative of John (19:36).
22. Words fairly close to Ps. 35:12.
23. Ps. 41:8.
24. Wis. 2:12.

> He had to be judged,
>> but not by you!][25]
> He had to be hanged (on the cross),
>> but not by you! . . .

> You were not moved to reverence for him
>> by the withered hand of the paralytic[26]
>> that he made whole,
>> or by the eyes of the blind
>> that his hand reopened,
>> or by the bodies of the paralytics
>> that his voice restored to health.

> You were not moved to fear
>> by this even stranger sign:
>> the dead man whom he called back from the tomb
>> where he had lain for four days.

No, you took no account of these (miracles), but in order to immolate the Lord as evening came, you prepared for him

> sharp nails
> and false witnesses
> and ropes and whips
> and vinegar and gall
> and sword and pain,
> as for a bandit who had shed blood.

You scourged his body, you set upon his head a crown of thorns, you bound his kindly hands that had shaped you from the dust,[27] you gave a drink of gall to the noble mouth that had fed you with life, and you put your Savior to death during the great feast!"

(72-79)

CHRIST, FIRST-BORN OF GOD

> Did you not know, O Israel,
>> that he is the first-born of God,[28]
>> begotten before the morning star?[29]
>> He made the light shine
>> and the day be radiant. . . .

---

25. The bracketed lines do not seem to belong to the primitive text.
26. Literally: "a withered hand restored healthy to the body." An allusion to the cure of the man with the withered hand: Mt. 12:9-13; Mk. 3:1-5; Lk. 6:6-10.
27. Allusion to Gen. 2:7: "The Lord God formed man of dust from the ground."
28. Col. 1:15.
29. Ps. 110:3, according to the Septuagint.

It is he who chose you
and led you on your road
from Adam to Noah,
from Noah to Abraham,
from Abraham to Isaac and Jacob
and to the twelve patriarchs.

It is he who guided you in Egypt
and protected you and fed you there.
It is he who lighted your way
with the column (of fire)
and who shaded you with the cloud.
He parted the Red Sea
and brought you across it
and scattered your enemies.

It is he who gave you the manna from heaven;
[he gave you (water) from the rock to drink,
gave you the Law on Horeb
and an inheritance on earth.][30]
He sent you the prophets
and raised up your kings.

It is he who drew close to you,
who cared for the suffering in your midst
and raised the dead.

(82-86)

WHO WILL DISPUTE WITH ME?

He has risen from the dead and cries:
"Who will dispute with me?
Let him come before me!
It is I who have freed the condemned man,
it is I who gave life to the dead,
it is I who raised the buried!
What man shall gainsay me?

It is I, says Christ,
I who have destroyed death,
and triumphed over the enemy
and trodden hell under foot,
and chained the strong men,[31]

---

30. The bracketed lines are probably additions to the primitive text.
31. Allusion to Mt. 12:29 (Mk. 3:27; Lk. 11:21-22): Jesus comes to chain the strong man, that is, the devil.

and brought man to the heights of heaven:
It is I! says Christ.

Come then, all you races of men
whom sin has saturated,
and receive the forgiveness of sin.
For it is I who am your forgiveness,
I, the saving Pasch,
I, the Lamb sacrificed for you,
I, your purification,[32] I, your life,
I, your resurrection, I, your light,
I, your salvation, I, your King!

It is I who bring you
to the heights of heaven;
it is I who shall raise you up here on earth.
I will show you the eternal Father,
I will raise you with my right hand!

(101-103)

SUCH IS HE WHO MADE HEAVEN AND EARTH

Such is he who made heaven and earth,
who in the beginning fashioned man,
who was foretold by the Law and the prophets,
who took flesh in the Virgin,

who was hanged on the tree,
who was buried in the earth,
who was awakened from among the dead,
who ascended to the heights of heaven,

who sits at the Father's right hand,
who has power to judge and save all men,
through whom the Father created all things
from the beginning to eternity!

He is the Alpha and the Omega,
he is the beginning and the end,[33]
beginning that cannot be expressed
and end that is beyond our understanding!

---

32. Literally "purifying water" or "bath" (of baptism, as in Eph. 5:26 and Tit. 3:5).
33. A borrowing from Apoc. 22:13: "I am the Alpha and the Omega, the first and the last, the beginning and the end." See also Apoc. 1:8 and 21:6.

He is the Christ,
he is the King,
he is Jesus,
the leader and the Lord!

He is risen from among the dead,
he sits at the Father's right hand,
he possesses the Father and is possessed by the Father.
To him be glory and power forever!
    Amen.

Melito, On the Pasch. — Peace to him who wrote (this homily) and to him who reads it and to those who love the Lord in simplicity of heart!

(104-105)

8

Clement of Alexandria

(about 150–220?)

CLEMENT OF ALEXANDRIA

Titus Flavius Clemens was born about 150, perhaps at Athens. He received a good literary formation and then traveled the world in search of the truth from "blessed and truly eminent teachers."[1] The great good fortune of his life, as he tells it, was to meet one of these men at Alexandria. He speaks of him in a tone of wonder:

> I came across a final one of these teachers (but he was the first of them all for greatness!), and when I had tracked him down in Egypt, where he was hiding, I stayed there. He was a real Sicilian bee: he gathered honey from the flowers of the field that he discovered in the prophets and apostles, and then he caused the souls of his hearers to give birth to pure knowledge.[2]

Alexandria had about a million inhabitants at this period. Situated as it was at the crossroads of East and West, it was the most important mercantile city of the empire ("ships of Alexandria" are mentioned in the Acts of the Apostles 27:6 and 28:11). While Athens had sunk into an intellectual lethargy and Rome had gotten mired down in Eastern cults, Alexandria had also become a capital for the life of the mind. Stoics and Platonists, poets and rhetoricians of every possible persuasion used to consort at the vast library, which was the pride of the city.

The city could be equally proud of its biblical past. For it was in Alexandrian circles that the Hebrew Bible had been translated into Greek, while here too the Book of Wisdom and various Greek pseudepigrapha had been composed. Apollos, "a man well versed in the Scriptures," as Luke attests (Acts 18:24), had also been born here. The presence of numerous Jewish ghettos in the various sections of the city emphasized the city's biblical past; it also led at times to confrontations with the pagan populace, and some of these in turn developed into pogroms.[3]

Clement had come to Alexandria as a disciple, but he soon became a teacher himself and directed a Christian school. Since the city was overflowing with liter-

---

1. *Stromata* I, 1, 11.

2. *Ibid.* See M. Caster, in *Clément d'Alexandrie: Les Stromates, Livre I (SC* 30; Paris, 1951), p. 51. It is possible that the teacher in question was Pantaenus, but the texts do not enable us to infer this with certainty.

3. See, for example, the testimony of Philo of Alexandria († about 45–50) in his *Legatio ad Caium*. See A. Pelletier, *Legatio ad Caium* (Les oeuvres de Philon d'Alexandrie 32; Paris, 1972), pp. 148–64.

ary groups and with university courses of every kind, the opening of a new school created no excitement in the Egyptian metropolis. Besides, the Church of Alexandria, which legend tells us was founded by St. Mark himself, had its own well-known official catechetical school; this first drew attention when Pantaenus, a universally respected teacher, was its head, and it was to reach its peak of greatness when the genius of Origen made it celebrated. It is possible that Clement had an official teaching post in this school.[4] We know in any case that his reputation spread not only through his teaching at Alexandria but through his writings as well.[5]

In about 202, the persecution of Septimius Severus forced Clement to flee from Alexandria. We find him in Cappadocia in 211. He died before 220.[6]

At the end of the second century, Christianity might with some success have challenged pagan literature and culture. Clement preferred to have Christianity enter into dialogue with paganism. His view was that culture and faith should complement each other and not be enemies; poetry and the gospel can be united.

> Clement was both a Greek and a Christian, and he was each of these in a very sincere and ardent way. He wanted to integrate his religious ideal with his cultural ideal. Consequently, he was interested in more than simply the relations between the new faith and the truth contained in the old philosophies. He went much further, and sought to have all of life become Christian: literature, the arts, social and familial life, education, work, leisure. He was already attempting to formulate the principles of a culture that would be permeated by his faith and impregnated with his ideal. For this reason, he has an excellent claim to the title of Christian humanist, and indeed to being the first of a long line.[7]

---

4. On the word of Eusebius it has been commonly accepted that the direction of the catechetical school of Alexandria passed, in a master-disciple succession, from Pantaenus to Clement, then to Origen, and then to Heraclas (Eusebius, *Historia ecclesiastica* VI, 6); see G. Bardy *Eusèbe de Césarée: Histoire ecclésiastique* (SC 41; Paris, 1955) p. 94. Bardy sharply criticized this view and argued that the catechetical school began only with Origen and that Origen was perhaps not Clement's disciple. But Bardy's own position was in turn challenged by A. Méhat, *Etude sur les Stromates de Clément d'Alexandrie* (Patristica Sornoniensia 7; Paris, 1966), where there are good pages on the "catechetical school" (pp. 62–70). In the present state of research, no one has the right to misuse texts by presenting as certain various statements that are still hypotheses. By way of hypothesis, it may be claimed that the decidedly "ecclesiastical" character of Clement's writings suggests they were used in the context of a more or less official catechetical teaching.

5. Out of the mass of these writings, there have come down to us, in addition to a homily on Mk. 10:17-31 (*What Rich Man Can Be Saved?*) and various fragments (for example, the *Extracta Theodoti* [SC 23; Paris, 1948]), the following three works: The *Protrepticus*, or "Exhortation to the Greeks" (SC 2; Paris, 1949²), the *Paedagogus*, or "Teacher," in three books (SC 70, 108, and 158; Paris, 1960, 1965, and 1970), and the *Stromata*, or "Carpets," in eight books (Book I in SC 30; Paris, 1951).

6. According to P. Nautin, *Lettres et écrivains chrétiens* (Patristica 2; Paris, 1961), p. 141.

7. C. Mondésert, in *Clément d'Alexandrie: Le Protreptique* (SC 2; Paris, 1949²), pp. 18–19.

Clement was fully successful in his quest of the ideal that the *Letter to Diognetus* (written precisely at Alexandria[8] around 190–200) expresses in these words: "Let your knowledge be inseparable from your heart, and let the Word of truth become your life."[9] In his writings, some 1500 citations from the Old Testament and another 2000 from the New are very much at home with 360 from the classical authors. A man of brilliant and open mind, Clement was able to combine with an enthusiastic faith a profound sympathy for all the beauty that pagan man had created, and for all the ecstasies he had experienced.[10] Moreover, though Clement's Greek can be difficult, the music of his lines charms our ear even today.

It is not certain that the extracts we present here were used in the liturgy of the Church of Alexandria. What is certain, however, is that they nourished the devotion of the Christians of the day.[11] To this extent, they reflect, in some degree at least, the official liturgical prayer of the Alexandrian Church. We think them sufficiently beautiful to cite them here.

———————

SING, O WORD, HIS PRAISES

> Let us receive the light
> and we will receive God!
> Let us receive the light
> and become disciples of the Lord!
> For he promised the Father:
> "I will reveal your name to my brothers.
> In the midst of the congregation I will sing of you"
>
>   (Ps. 22:23)

> Sing, (O Word,) his praises[12]
> and reveal God, your Father, to me!
> Your words will save me
> and your song will teach me.
> Until now I was going astray

———————

8. See H.-I. Marrou, *A Diognète* (SC 35; Paris, 1951), p. 265.

9. *Ad Diognetum* XII, 7. On this subject see the excellent little book of A. Mandouze, *Intelligence et sainteté dans l'ancienne tradition chrétienne* (Paris, 1962).

10. It is quite to be expected that such an approach, at such an early period in the Church's history, would result in some inadequacies at the theological level. On these weaknesses in Clement's thought, see J. Lebreton, "Clément d'Alexandrie," *Dictionnaire de spiritualité* 2 (Paris, 1953), cols. 950–60. Clement bears witness in advance to his own orthodoxy when he writes: "As for ourselves, who are children, we protect ourselves against the winds of heresy, whose breath causes pride to swell; we refuse to lend credence to those who teach us differently than our fathers did; we reach perfection when we form the Church, with Christ as our Head" (*Paedagogus* I, 5, 18).

11. See A. Méhat, "Clément d'Alexandrie," in R. Johanny (ed.), *op. cit.*, pp. 101–27.

12. It is thought that this poem from the *Protrepticus* is in fact an early Christian hymn. See J. Lebreton, *Histoire du dogme de la Trinité* 2 (Paris, 1928[4]), p. 222.

in search of God.
But ever since you enlightened me,
Lord, you have taught me to find
him who is my God as well,
and I receive your own Father from you.
I become his heir with you,
for you have not been ashamed of your brother.[13]

(*Protrepticus* XI, 113)

PRAYER TO CHRIST THE TEACHER

Be favorable, O Teacher, to your little children,
O Father and Guide of Israel,
Son and Father at once, and Lord!
Grant us who follow your commandments
to perfect the likeness of your image in us,
and to experience, according to our strength,
the goodness of the God who judges without severity.

Grant us all our petitions.
(Grant us) to live in peace,
to establish ourselves in your city,
to cross, unbattered by the waves,
the storm-tossed waves of sin,
to be impelled over a calm sea
by the Holy Spirit, who is Wisdom ineffable.

Grant us to sing by night and day
and until the final day
a canticle of thanksgiving
to Father and Son, to Son and to Father,
to the (Son,) Teacher and Master,
with the Holy Spirit.

Everything belongs to the Only Son,
everything subsists in him,
through him everything is in unity,
through him eternity exists,
and we are his members.
To him, glory and eternity!

Everything belongs to the God of goodness,

---

13. An allusion to Heb. 2:11-12.

everything belongs to the God of beauty,
everything belongs to the God of wisdom,
everything belongs to the God of justice.
To him, glory now
and forever! Amen.

(*Paedagogus* III, 12, 101)

HYMN TO CHRIST THE TEACHER[14]

Bridle-bit of untamed colts,
Wing of birds that do not go astray,
sure Tiller of ships,
Shepherd of the King's lambs!

Gather your children
who live in simplicity.
Let them sing in holiness,
let them celebrate with sincerity,
with a mouth that knows no evil,
the Christ who guides his children!

O King of the saints,
O sovereign Word
of the Most High Father,
Prince of wisdom,
Support of toiling men,
eternal Joy of the human family,
O Jesus Savior,

Shepherd and Toiler,
Tiller and Bridle-bit,
Wing rising to heaven
from the assembly of the saints,
Fisher of men,
you, their Savior:
from the sea of evil

---

14. This hymn concludes Clement's *Paedagogus*. It "has perhaps preserved for us the prayer of praise used in the School of Alexandria" (B. Altaner and H. Chirat, *Précis de patrologie* [Paris, 1961], p. 287). The brilliant images, sometimes abrupt, often unexpected (but some are borrowed from Plato and would therefore be familiar to the students in the School of Alexandria), make it a typical example of the teaching of Clement, who seeks to draw the philosophy of the age within the orbit of the gospel. If we look beyond images and methods, we find, above all, a very lively and tender love for Christ, the Teacher of his children.

you pull the pure fish,
out of the hostile storm
you draw them to the life of blessedness.

O holy Shepherd, lead
your sheep of wisdom.[15]
O holy King, lead
your children unstained.
The footsteps of Christ
are a road to heaven.

O Word ever springing forth,
measureless Duration,
eternal Light,
Fountain of mercy,
Worker of virtue
so that the singers of God
can live a holy life!

O Christ Jesus, you are the heavenly milk
which a young wife gives us,[16]
full of the graces of your wisdom.
As for us, little children,
our still tender lips
seek to be nourished
by the spiritual milk,
by the dew of the Spirit,
until we are filled.

With sincere praises
let us celebrate with uprightness
the sovereign Christ.
He is the sacred price
for the teaching that gives life:
let us all sing together of him.
Let us be the true retinue
of the almighty Son.

---

15. Literally: "sheep who participate in reason," which may also be taken as meaning "sheep who participate in Reason," that is, in the Word, Christ. Throughout the *Paedagogus*, Clement plays on the ambiguity of the term in order to show that adherence to the Word is fully consonant with human reason.

16. Literally: "you are the heavenly milk pressed from the sweet breasts of a young wife." The reference is to the Church, the Bride of Christ (2 Cor. 11:2), who nourishes her children with the milk of her teaching (cf. 1 Pet. 2:2).

Choirs of peace,
scions of Christ,
people of wisdom,
let us all celebrate together
the God of peace.

     (*Paedagogus* III, Hymn)

9

The Apostolic Tradition
of Hippolytus of Rome
(about 215)

HIPPOLYTUS OF ROME

THE MAN

In 212 A.D., Origen, then a young man, journeyed to Rome in order to learn about "the very ancient Church of Rome," as he called it. He chanced to hear a sermon on the "praise of our Lord and Savior." The preacher's name was Hippolytus. He was a simple priest of the Roman Church, but the prestige of his vast learning, his undoubted talents as a writer, and his many personal relationships had made him a leader in the religious life of the time. His extensive knowledge of Greek philosophy and his astonishing familiarity with the Eastern mystery cults are reason to suppose that he was not Roman or Latin by birth, but hailed rather from the East.

At this time the theological debates on the Trinity had turned Rome into a doctrinal battlefield. The quarrels were fierce. The Monarchians laid a heavy emphasis on the unity of Trinity but were in danger of not emphasizing enough the trinity of Persons; the Anti-Monarchians brought out the distinction of Persons well enough but ran the risk in turn of casting doubt on the divine nature of the Word.

According to Photius, Hippolytus claimed to be a disciple of Irenaeus, meaning by this that he shared his master's zeal for the defense of traditional doctrine. He threw himself into the battle with all the weight of his learning and his fiery temperament. But, as sometimes happens in such situations, excessive zeal for the true faith can lead to extreme views.[1] Hippolytus felt obliged to attack Pope Zephyrinus (198–217), whom he accused of secretly favoring the Monarchian heresy.

As a matter of fact, Pope Zephyrinus had little knowledge of theological subtleties and little inclination to indulge in metaphysical worries; consequently, he made hardly any effort to get to the heart of the matter. He was a worthy man and had the wisdom of old men, which in this case meant repeating the formulas tradition had left to him, even if this meant he would be treated as an ignoramus.

---

1. See A. d'Alès, *La théologie de saint Hippolyte* (Paris, 1906). Hippolytus's doctrinal position on the Word is especially vulnerable to criticism and would normally lead to affirming the existence of two gods. It is quite understandable that Callistus should describe Hippolytus and his followers as "worshipers of two gods," despite the anger of the latter in the face of such an accusation (*Philosophoumena* 9, 12, 4 [*PG* 16:3383C]).

Hippolytus had no trouble in pointing out to him the ambiguity of certain state-ments.[2]

The situation was rather tense when the pope died. The Roman clergy then chose Callistus as his successor. This was in 218.

Callistus was a former slave with a rather stormy past, but he was also a confessor of the faith who had the good fortune to emerge alive from prison. He had been Zephyrinus's principal deacon, in charge of the temporal administration of the Church. His accession to the responsibility of the supreme pontificate could therefore only antagonize Hippolytus, who now directed to the new pope his old opposition to Zephyrinus.

The situation became still worse when Callistus felt obliged to ease the disci-pline of the Church in regard to penitents who had sinned seriously. Hippolytus considered such indulgence to be weakness. He finally chose the solution of despair and cut himself off from the Church. He had himself elected bishop of Rome by an influential group of clergy, founded a new church in opposition to the Roman community, and thus became the first antipope. He persevered in his schism even after Callistus had been replaced by Urban (223–230) and Urban in turn had made way for Pontian (230–235).

There seemed to be no way of resolving this painful situation. But religious persecution provided an unexpected solution, one that allowed both parties to win the victory, not at the level of theological discussion but at the level of the profes-sion of the faith. As soon as Emperor Maximus the Thracian (235–238) reached power, he issued an edict proscribing the leaders of the Churches for the crime of preaching the gospel. Pontian and Hippolytus, pope and antipope, both found themselves in the mines of Sardinia, the extermination camps of that age. Com-munion in suffering and wretchedness paved the way for communion in faith and love. Pontian abdicated on September 28, 235. Hippolytus did the same and thus

---

2. In the *Philosophoumena* 9, 12 (*PG* 16:3386AC), he wrote: "The first [Callistus] dared to legitimate acts of pleasure by saying that he would forgive everybody's sins. Anyone who had been led astray by another, so long as he was Christian in name, would receive forgiveness if he joined the school of Callistus. . . . In these cases he used to apply the words of the Apostle: 'Who are you to pass judgment on the servant of another?' (Rom. 14:4). He even held that the parable of the weeds, 'Let the weeds go on growing with the wheat' (Matthew 13:30), had been taught for this very reason, that is, for the sake of those who commit sins after their entry into the Church. He also claimed that the ark of Noah was a type of the Church, that ark which contained dogs, wolves, ravens, and all the animals clean and unclean; so too, he claimed, should it be in the Church."

Even when one allows for a measure of rhetorical exaggeration and personal polemical feeling, these accusations show the high idea Hippolytus had of the holiness of the Church. At the same time, however, they have not led history to condemn Callistus. The Pope may in fact have had excellent pastoral reasons for easing the penitential discipline. Besides, the Church remembers him without attaching any stigma to him, and history has never had to disavow him.

On the whole question, see A. d'Alès, *L'Edit de Calliste* (Paris, 1914), especially ch. 7, "The Witness of St. Hippolytus" (pp. 217–27).

returned to unity. Both died as martyrs on "death island." Pope Fabian (236–250) had the bodies of both men brought back to Rome. Their funerals were celebrated on the same day, August 13, 236 or 237.

So it is that each year on August 13 the Church lovingly celebrates the memory of St. Hippolytus, antipope and martyr, "whose courage urges our hearts on to an ever more solid faith."[3]

THE WORK

The list of Hippolytus's writings is extensive. Unfortunately, many of his works seem lost to us beyond recovery, buried under the debris of eighteen centuries of history, rotted away or burned in the ruins of ancient libraries. To time's forgetfulness has been added the forgetfulness of men. The fact is that Hippolytus wrote in Greek, and after his death people at Rome became less and less familiar with Greek. In addition, Hippolytus had been an antipope. Understandably, then, the Roman tradition did not trouble itself unduly over the loss of works that were of suspect orthodoxy and written in a language no longer used.

Among the writings that have survived are works of controversy, such as the *Philosophoumena* or *Refutation of All the Heresies* (written after 222), which remind us to some extent of the *Contra Haereses* of Irenaeus, and the *Demonstration Against the Jews*; dogmatic works, like the treatise *On the Antichrist* (about 202); exegetical writings, like the commentaries *On Daniel, On the Song of Songs, The Story of David and Goliath*, and *On the Psalms*. In the commentaries, he adopts, in moderation, the allegorical and typological methods of interpretation so dear to Origen. We also have some chronological treatises, such as the *Determination of the Date of Easter* (222) and, above all, the *Chronicle*, in which Hippolytus endeavors to moderate the anxious expectation of certain Christians who believed that the end of the world was at hand (Hippolytus calculated that the world was 5738 years old and would last until at least the year 6000).

We may mention also various homilies, such as those *On Easter, On the Heresy of Noetus*, and *On the Praise of the Lord, Our Savior*. Finally, we must call attention to the work that is of special interest to us here, the *Apostolic Tradition*.

A number of these works have come down to us in various translations: Latin, Syriac, Coptic, Arabic, Ethiopic, Armenian, Georgian, and Slavonic, showing the interest taken by the Christian Churches of the East in this Roman theologian. On the other hand, the number and variety of his writings are evidence of how hard this writer worked in behalf of the Christian faith. And just as men usually lend only to the rich, so they have attributed to him a number of works that are not his.

THE APOSTOLIC TRADITION

No work of Hippolytus roused as much interest in the theological world, and especially among liturgists, as the discovery and identification of the *Apostolic*

---

3. Secret of the Mass for August 13 (old Missal).

Tradition. It was compiled in 315 and is by far the richest source we now have for understanding the constitution of the Roman Church and its liturgy at the beginning of the third century. The discovery of the document was a genuine triumph of scientific scholarship.

In 1551, a statue of Hippolytus was dug up in a Roman cemetery, the Ager Veranus on the Via Appia, and on its pedestal a list of Hippolytus's writings was engraved. Among others, there was this title: (AP)OSTOLIKĒ PARADOSIS, or *Apostolic Tradition*, but what had happened to this work?

Since 1870 scholars had indeed had in hand a work known as the *Canons of Hippolytus*, in an Arabic translation from an earlier Coptic version. But critics distrusted this work as a whole because it appeared to be a compilation from various sources and hardly seemed identifiable with the *Apostolic Tradition*. On the other hand, they had shown an undeniable relationship between the *Canons of Hippolytus* and certain other documents, such as the *Apostolic Constitutions*, a Greek compilation of Syrian origin, dating from the end of the fourth century,[4] the *Testament of Our Lord*, also of Syrian origin and dating probably from the fifth century, and, above all, the *Egyptian Church Order*. These were the various sites where digging had to go on if the *Apostolic Tradition* was to be found. A long time was spent in inconclusive hypotheses. E. Schwartz was the first to suspect that the work being sought had survived in the *Egyptian Church Order*; he published his hypothesis in 1910.[5] Six years later, without having known of his predecessor's work, R. H. Connolly succeeded in proving conclusively that the *Egyptian Church Order* lay behind all the other compilations and was in fact identical with the *Apostolic Tradition* of Hippolytus.[6]

The original text had an eventful history before reaching us. Hippolytus wrote in Greek. This original is lost, but a Latin translation had been made of it, probably at the beginning of the fourth century; this translation was later found on a palimpsest in the Chapter Library at Verona. It is fragmentary, since a number of leaves are missing, but extremely faithful, allowing the original Greek to be glimpsed behind the errors and misinterpretations of the translator. To fill in the gaps in the Latin, we must have recourse to the other Eastern texts. The *Egyptian Church Order* is represented by translations into Coptic (first Sahidic, then Bohairic[7]), Arabic, and Ethiopic. These translations do not all possess the same value. The one closest to the original seems to be the one in the Sahidic dialect; the Arabic version is based on it, and probably the Ethiopic version as well. Comparison of

---

4. See below, pp. 215–39.

5. E. Schwartz, *Über die pseudoapostolischen Kirchenordnungen* (Schriften der wissenschaftlichen Gesellschaft in Strassburg 6; Strasbourg, 1910).

6. R. H. Connolly, *The So-called Egyptian Church Order and Derived Documents* (Texts and Studies 8/4; Cambridge, 1916).

7. *Sahidic* (saidi) is the dialect of Upper Egypt; *Bohairic* (beheri) is the dialect of Lower Egypt.

these various sources makes possible a conjectural restoration of the text and enables the scholar to translate it back into the original Greek.[8]

FIRST PART

THE LITURGY OF HOLY ORDERS

2–3. *The Bishop*

He is to be ordained bishop who has been chosen by the entire people[9] and who is of blameless life. When he has been nominated and accepted by all, let the people assemble on the Lord's Day with the presbytery[10] and the bishops who are at hand. The latter, with the consent of all, will impose hands on him. The priests attend in silence. All are to be silent and pray in their hearts for the descent of the Holy Spirit.

One of the bishops present shall, at the request of all, lay hands on the man receiving episcopal consecration and pray as follows:[11]

> God and Father of our Lord Jesus Christ,
> Father of mercies and of every consolation,[12]
> you who dwell in the highest heaven
> and lower your gaze to what is lowly,[13]
> you who know all things before they exist;
> who have assigned the boundaries of your Church
> by your word of grace;
> who from the beginning have predestined

---

8. The best edition is that of B. Botte, *La Tradition Apostolique de saint Hippolyte: Essai de reconstitution* (Liturgiewissenschaftliche Quellen und Forschungen 39; Münster, 1963). This edition will be the basis for our work here. Botte has also published an edition that omits the technical apparatus, in the *Sources chrétiennes* series (no. 11bis; Paris, 1968). [The numbers of the sections here are from Botte's edition.]

9. Hippolytus emphasizes the participation of the entire community in the designation of the future bishop; the latter is elected by all, is approved by all, and receives the laying on of hands with the consent and at the request of all.

10. The college of priests.

11. What follows is the "prayer of consecration"; it accompanies and explains the rite of the laying on of hands by which the episcopate is conferred. These splendid formulas develop the theme of the episcopal ministry so fully that they were often to be reintroduced as "prayers for the bishop" or even "prayers for the pope."

12. 2 Cor. 1:3.

13. Allusion to Ps. 113:5-6: "The Lord our God, who is seated on high, who looks far down upon the heavens and the earth."

the race of just men descended from Abraham;
who have appointed leaders and priests
and have not left your sanctuary without its liturgy,
and whose delight it has been, since the foundation of the world,
to be glorified by those you have chosen:

Pour out now the power that comes from you,
the sovereign Spirit[14] whom you gave
to your beloved Child Jesus Christ,[15]
and whom he handed on to the apostles
who built the Church, your sanctuary,
for the glory and ceaseless praise of your name.

Father, who know the heart,
grant that your servant whom you have chosen bishop
may feed your holy flock
and exercise your sovereign priesthood without blame,
serving you day and night.

May he always make you merciful to us
and offer you the gifts of your holy Church.
In virtue of the Spirit of high priesthood,
may he have the power to forgive sins
as you have commanded.

May he distribute offices according to your order;
may he loose from every bond in virtue of the power
you bestowed upon the apostles.[16]

May he please you
by his gentleness and purity of heart.
May he offer you a sweet fragrance
through your Child Jesus Christ, our Lord.

Through him, glory is yours, power and honor,
Father and Son, with the Holy Spirit,
in your holy Church,[17]
now and always for ever and ever!
        Amen.

---

14. A formula from Ps. 51:14 according to the LXX.

15. An archaizing formula found in the Greek text (see above n. 3, p. 74). The Latin text has "to your beloved Son Jesus Christ."

16. Allusion to Mt. 18:18 and Jn. 20:22-23.

17. "In your holy Church" is found only in the Ethiopian version, but the words are characteristic of the doxology in Hippolytus (see below, n. 30, p. 133).

4. The Anaphora

Immediately after the bishop has been consecrated and the kiss of peace given, the newly ordained bishop celebrates the Eucharist. He does so in union "with the entire presbytery."

We have the almost unbelievable good fortune to possess the anaphora[18] of this first episcopal Mass. The formulas Hippolytus gives us allow us to come in contact with the Mass as celebrated at Rome in 215. Of course, this anaphora does not represent the only type used in the Roman liturgy of the time, but it is the only one we have from that early period; it is also the earliest we have in all of Christian literature.

It is not Hippolytus's intention to make this text obligatory. He simply suggests it[19] and leaves intact both the right of the celebrant to improvise freely and the right of the Spirit to put other formulas of prayer on the lips and in the heart of the celebrant, who represents Christ to the community.

The reader will note the clearly Christological character of this anaphora. He will also note the absence of the *Sanctus*, which was soon to become traditional, and of any mention of the *mirabilia Dei*, the wonderful acts of God in creation and in the history of salvation. The exceptional conciseness of Hippolytus's formulas brings out magnificently the movement proper to the Eucharistic Prayer. The anaphora is resplendent in its antique simplicity, being as yet unencumbered by any of the developments with which later centuries will delight in adorning it and which, like a luxuriant but parasitic overgrowth, will often risk concealing the very beauty they were meant to enhance.

This ancient anaphora of Hippolytus, forgotten for centuries at Rome but still recited by Abyssinian priests, has now become the basis of the Second Eucharistic Prayer. As a result, the words of the Roman martyr still echo throughout the universal Church.

ACCLAMATION

When he has been consecrated bishop, all are to give him the kiss of peace and acclaim him with the words: "He has become worthy!"[20]

The deacons are then to present him with the oblation. Laying hands upon it, together with the entire presbytery, he is to say the thanksgiving:

—The Lord be with you!

---

18. In classical Greek, *anaphora* means the "offering" (literally, the "raising up") of a sacrifice to a god. In Christian liturgical language, it refers to the prayer of offering in the Eucharistic liturgy, a prayer comprising essentially the account of the institution of the Supper and the words of consecration.

19. *Apostolic Tradition* 9. Justin emphasizes the same freedom when he writes in *Apologia I*, 67: "The president then prays and gives thanks *according to his ability*."

20. Another possible translation: "greeting him because he is worthy" (Botte, p. 11).

(All respond:)
> And with your spirit!
> —Let us lift up our hearts.
> They are turned to the Lord.
> —Let us give thanks to the Lord!
> It is right and just![20a]

THANKSGIVING

> Let him continue thus:
> We give you thanks, O God,
> through your beloved Child Jesus Christ,
> whom you have sent us in the last days[21]
> as Savior, Redeemer, and Messenger of your will.
> He is your Word, inseparable from you,
> through whom you have created everything
> and in whom you find your delight.
>
> You sent him from heaven
> into the womb of a Virgin.
> He was conceived and became flesh,
> he manifested himself as your Son,
> born of the Spirit and the Virgin.[22]
>
> He did your will,
> and, to win for you a holy people,
> he stretched out his hands in suffering
> to rescue from suffering
> those who believe in you.

ACCOUNT OF INSTITUTION

> When he was about to surrender himself to voluntary suffering
> in order to destroy death,
> to break the devil's chains,
> to tread hell underfoot,
> to pour out his light upon the just,
> to establish the covenant
> and manifest his resurrection,[23]

20a. On the opening dialogue, see E. Lanne, "Liturgie eucharistique en Orient et en Occident (1er-4e siècles)," *Dictionnaire de spiritualité* 9 (1978), cols. 887–89.

21. That is, in the messianic age, which is regarded as the "final age" or "last days" in the history of salvation; see Acts 2:17.

22. There is an equivalent formula in Hippolytus's homily *On the Heresy of Noetus* 4 (*PG* 10:810B): "The flesh offered by the Word of the Father . . . who comes from the Spirit and the Virgin and is manifested as perfect Son of God."

23. These formulas seem to have undergone the influence of Irenaeus, who wrote in

he took bread,
he gave you thanks and said:
"Take, eat, this is my body
which is broken for you."
In like manner for the cup, he said:
"This is my blood
which is poured out for you.
When you do this,
do (it) in memory of me."

ANAMNESIS[24]

Remembering therefore your death
and your resurrection,
we offer you the bread and the wine,
we thank you for having judged us worthy
to stand before you and serve you.

EPICLESIS[25]

And we pray you
to send your Holy Spirit
on the offering of your holy Church,
to bring together in unity
all those who receive it.
May they be filled with the Holy Spirit
who strengthens their faith in the truth.
May we be able thus to praise and glorify you
through your Child Jesus Christ.

DOXOLOGY

Through him glory to you and honor,
to the Father and the Son, with the Holy Spirit,
in your holy Church,
now and for ever and ever!
    Amen.

---

his *Demonstration of Apostolic Preaching* 38: "God the Father then was full of mercy; he sent the word . . . (who) undid the chains of (our) prison. And his light appeared and dissipated the darkness of the prison and sanctified our birth and destroyed death, undoing those very bonds in which we had been chained. And he showed his resurrection, becoming himself the first-born from the dead." See L. M. Froidevaux, *Irénée de Lyon: Démonstration de la prédication apostolique* (SC 62; Paris, 1959), p. 92.

24. The *anamnesis* (Greek *anamnēsis*, "remembrance, memory, memorial") is the prayer that commemorates the mysteries of salvation contained in the celebration of the Eucharist. It is based on our Lord's words "Do this in remembrance of me."

25. The *epiclesis* (Greek *epiklēsis*, "invocation") is the prayer that invokes the descent of the Holy Spirit on the offerings.

Blessing of the Offerings of the Faithful

Immediately after the anaphora, Hippolytus proposes formulas of blessing for the offerings which the faithful present.

The insertion of these blessings at this point in the Eucharistic liturgy[26] seems to fit in with a very definite theological plan which we today would call a "theology of earthly realities." Irenaeus explains that when the Church offers the Eucharist, she is presenting God with the firstfruits of creation under the sign of bread and wine.[27] The offerings that the faithful now present for the bishop's blessing are brought under the influence of the Eucharist; they are sanctified by the extended action of the thanksgiving that has changed the oblations into the body and blood of Christ.[28]

---

5. The Offering of Oil

If someone offers oil, the bishop is to give thanks for it as he has for the bread, not in the same words but in the same spirit. Let him say:

> O God, by sanctifying this oil
> you give holiness
> to those who use and receive it.
> With it you anointed
> kings and priests and prophets.
> May it likewise now give
> solace to those who taste it
> and health to those who use it.

---

26. Hippolytus could just as well have placed these blessings in chapter 28, where he expressly treats of offerings. The Roman Canon in a similar way has kept a blessing of the offerings of the faithful, in the prayer *Per quem haec omnia* ("Through whom, O Lord, you constantly create . . ."), which precedes the final doxology. In his *The Mass of the Roman Rite: Its Origin and Development (Missarum Solemnia)*, 2, tr. F. A. Brunner (New York, 1955), J. A. Jungmann observes: "In the earlier stages of the Roman canon, and for that matter right on to the late Middle Ages and even after, a blessing of natural products was on occasion inserted in this spot" (p. 260).

27. *Adversus haereses* IV, 17, 5 (SC 100:591–93; PG 7:1023BC): "Christ urged his disciples to offer to God the firstfruits of his creatures, not as though he needed them but in order that the disciples might not themselves be barren of fruit or ungrateful. He did this when he took bread, which comes from creation, and gave thanks, saying, 'This is my body.' And likewise the cup, which comes from the creation to which we belong, he declared to be his blood and taught that it was the new oblation proper to the new covenant. This oblation the Church received from the apostles, and throughout the world she offers it to God, who gives us food, as the *firstfruits of his gift to us in the new covenant*" (italics added).

28. See Deiss, *It's the Lord's Supper*, pp. 135–36.

6. *The Offering of Cheese and Olives*

Again, if someone offers cheese and olives, let the bishop pray thus:

> Sanctify this curdled milk
> by uniting us to your love.[29]
> Grant too that this fruit of the olive tree
> may never lose its sweetness.
> It is a symbol of the abundance
> that you made flow from the tree (of the cross),
> to give life to those who hope in you.

Blessing for Other Offerings

In every blessing, say:

> Glory be yours, Father and Son,
> with the Holy Spirit,
> in the holy Church,[30]
> now and always
> and forever and ever!
>   Amen.

7. *Priests*

(PRAYER OF ORDINATION)

When the bishop ordains a priest, let him lay his hand on the head of the ordinand, while the other priests likewise touch him.[31] He is to pronounce prayers similar to those set down earlier, as we indicated for a bishop.

Let him pray thus:

> God and Father of our Lord Jesus Christ,

---

29. Literally, "make this coagulated milk holy by coagulating us to your love."

30. The mention of "in the (your) holy Church" in the doxology is characteristic of the liturgy of Hippolytus (cf. *Apostolic Tradition* 3, 4, 6, 8, 22, 23). It is found again in an apocryphal prayer attributed to St. Cyprian; see J. Lebreton, 2:623. The phrase is probably inspired by Eph. 3:21, but Hippolytus may have taken it directly from Irenaeus; see N. Maurice-Denis and R. Boulet, *Euchariste or la Messe dans ses variétés, son histoire et ses origines* (Paris, 1953), p. 375. Instead of expressing the equality of the Spirit with the Father and the Son, as the traditional Latin doxology does, it underlines the special relation that unites the Spirit to the first two Persons, as well as his role of sanctification "in the holy Church." The Church is thus the privileged place where the Spirit pours out the holiness of God.

31. The Roman ritual has kept this practice in ordination to the priesthood: after the bishop, all the priests present lay their hands on the ordinands.

look upon your servant here.
Grant him the Spirit of grace and counsel,
so that he may help and govern your people with a pure heart.

Thus did you look upon your chosen people
and order Moses to choose the elders:
you filled them with your Spirit
whom you had given to your servant.[32]

And now, Lord, grant that we may always preserve within us
the Spirit of your grace.
Make us worthy to serve you with faith,
in the simplicity of our hearts.

We praise you through your Child, Christ Jesus.
Through him, glory is yours and power,
Father and Son, with the Holy Spirit,
in the holy Church, now and for ever!
 Amen.

8. Deacons

(PRAYER OF ORDINATION)

When a deacon is to be ordained, he is to be chosen in accordance with what was said earlier. Let the bishop alone lay hands on him, as we have prescribed. . . . For a deacon is not ordained for the priesthood but for the service of the bishop, that he may carry out the bishop's orders. He is not a member of the council of the clergy, but takes care (of the sick) and brings needs to the bishop's attention. He does not receive the common spirit of the presbytery, in which the priests share, but the spirit that is given to him (so that he may work) under the authority of the bishop. This is why the bishop alone ordains a deacon, whereas all the priests lay their hands on a priest because the same Spirit is common to the ministry of all. The priest has power only to receive this Spirit and not to give him. That is why he does not ordain clerics. At the ordination of a priest, he simply makes the gesture of laying hands on the other, while the bishop does the ordaining.

Let the bishop say the following prayer over a deacon:

O God, who created the universe
and put it in order through your Word,
Father of our Lord Jesus Christ,
whom you sent to carry out your will

---

32. A reference to the seventy elders who assisted Moses at the concluding of the covenant (Ex. 24:1-11).

and reveal your plan to us:
grant the Spirit of grace and zeal
to your servant here.

You have chosen him to serve your Church
and bring into your sanctuary
the oblation of him whom you appointed
your high priest
to the glory of your name.

Let him serve you without reproach and in purity.
Let him thus reach a higher level,
and praise and glorify you
through your Son Jesus Christ, our Lord,
now and always
and for ever and ever. Amen.

9. *The Formulas for Liturgical Prayer*

. . . Let the bishop give thanks in the manner we indicated earlier. It is not necessary, however, that he repeat the same words we provided, as though he had to try to say them from memory in his thanksgiving to God.[33]

Let each one pray according to his ability. If he is capable of praying at length and offering a solemn prayer, well and good. But if he prays differently and pronounces a shorter and simpler prayer, he is not to be prevented, provided his prayer be sound and orthodox.

11. *The Reader*

When someone is ordained a reader, the bishop is to give him the book. He is not to lay hands on him.

12. *The Virgin*

With regard to virgins: there is to be no imposition of hands on a virgin, for it is her own decision alone that makes her a virgin.

---

33. Hippolytus bears witness to the bishop's freedom to improvise liturgical prayer on the basis of a typical schema, provided that the prayer was "orthodox." From the fourth century on, the rule was to use texts that had already been fixed by tradition. Exceptions lingered, however, in certain liturgies until the seventh century; see Jungmann, 1 (New York, 1951), p. 30, n. 10.

13. The Subdeacon

For subdeacons: there is no imposition of hands on a subdeacon, but he is simply appointed to serve the deacon.

14. Gifts of Healing

If anyone makes the claim: "I have received the gift of healing through a revelation," do not impose hands on him. The facts themselves will show whether or not he is speaking the truth.

SECOND PART

CHRISTIAN INITIATION

The second part of Hippolytus's *Apostolic Tradition* is concerned with the catechumenate and baptism.

The information given us here on the catechumenate as it existed in the Roman community at the beginning of the third century will certainly surprise the Church historian and even the ordinary Christian of our day. The Church was expanding rapidly, and yet nowhere do we find any trace of organized propagandistic activity. She displayed an intense missionary activity, and yet she had no missionaries, that is, no believers who devoted themselves specially to the task of evangelization. She continually faced and overcame the paganism that surrounded her, and yet she had no workers specially trained for this task.

The explanation of this missionary "miracle" is of course to be found first and foremost in the inherent dynamism of Christ's message and in the action of the Holy Spirit on souls. We must also take into account, however, the missionary witness that each Christian gave to the faith he had received. Reflecting on this marvelous expansion of Christianity during the first three centuries, A. von Harnack wrote:

> The most numerous and successful missionaries of the Christian religion were not the regular teachers but the Christians themselves, in virtue of their loyalty and courage. . . . It was characteristic of this religion that everyone who seriously confessed the faith proved of service to its propaganda. Christians are to "let their light shine, that pagans may see their good works and glorify the Father in heaven." If this dominated all their life, and if they lived according to the precepts of their religion, they could not be hidden at all; by their very mode of living they could not fail to preach their faith plainly and audibly.[34]

---

34. *The Mission and Expansion of Christianity in the First Three Centuries*, tr. J. Moffatt (New York, 1908), 1:366–68.

For this reason Hippolytus has no special name for priests or other members of the clergy whose task it would be to recruit catechumens, but he does speak readily of "those who introduce them." Each member of the community engaged in this apostolic task in virtue of his baptism, by which he was deputed to this mission.

We must likewise call attention to the severity shown in the choice of candidates for baptism. The Church evidently preferred to remain small in numbers rather than to diminish in quality. She excluded from the catechumenate not only those whose professions were manifestly opposed to the law of God, such as brothel-keepers and prostitutes, priests of idolatrous cults and wizards, sorcerers and fortunetellers, but all those as well whose professional activity was on the borderline of the sinful. In an age when paganism permeated the whole of social life, this borderline was rather broad and vague. Hippolytus excluded from the catechumenate the sculptors and painters who furnished a dying paganism with its idols; actors, since the theater of the time was highly immoral; the performers in the circus who turned human lives into a source of amusement; the gladiators who exposed themselves to butchery; the magistrates who had to organize the pagan festivals and orgies. Soldiers were accepted only with reserve, since they had to take oaths and the armies of the time were not exactly schools of virtue.

This primitive severity in regard to catechumens does honor to the Church. It was hostility not to sinners but only to their sin.

A. Catechumenate

15. Newcomers to the Faith

Those who are to be initiated into the new faith must first be brought to the catechists[35] to hear the word, before the people arrive.

They are to be asked the reason why they seek the faith.

Those who introduce them must testify regarding them, that it may be known whether they are capable of hearing the word. They are also to be asked about their state of life. Has the man a wife? Is he a slave? If he is slave of a believer, and if his master allows, let him hear the word. If his master does not give him a good character, he is to be sent away. If his master is a pagan, he is to be taught to please his master, lest he provide grounds for calumny. . . .

16. Trades and Professions

Inquiry is to be made regarding the trades and professions of those who are brought for instruction.

---

35. Literally, "teachers" (*doctores*).

If a man is a pander, that is, supports prostitutes, let him give it up or be sent away.

If he is a sculptor or painter, he is to be instructed not to make any more idols. Let him give it up or be sent away.

If he is an actor or gives performances in the theater, let him give it up or be sent away.

If he teaches children, it is preferable that he give it up.[36] But if he has no (other) trade, he is to be allowed to continue.

If he is a charioteer or a wrestler or attends wrestling matches, let him give it up or be sent away.

If he is a gladiator or teaches gladiators to fight, or is a beast-fighter,[37] or if he is an official who organizes gladiatorial games, let him give it up or be sent away.

If he is a priest of idols or a guardian of idols, let him give it up or be sent away.

A soldier in a position of authority is not to be allowed to impose a death sentence; if he is ordered to do so, let him not carry out the order; he is not to be allowed to take an oath. If he does not accept, he is to be sent away.

A man with the power of the sword or a civil magistrate who wears the purple must give it up or be sent away.

Catechumens or believers who wish to enlist as soldiers are to be sent away, for they have shown contempt for God.

A prostitute or a pederast or an effeminate man or one who has done something unspeakable is to be sent away, for he is defiled.

Wizards, too, are not to be admitted for testing.

The sorcerer, astrologer, fortuneteller, interpreter of dreams, coiner,[38] or amulet-maker must give it up or be sent away.

If a concubine be a slave and has raised her children and is united only to this man, she is to be admitted to instruction; otherwise she is to be sent away.

A man who has a concubine is to give her up and take a wife according to the law. If he refuses, he is to be sent away.

If we have omitted any category, the professions themselves will provide the information you need. For we all have the Spirit of God.[39]

17. The Length of the Instruction (Subsequent to the Examination) of Trades and Professions

The catechumens are to listen to the word for three years.

---

36. The instructor or teacher had to explain the myths to his pupils.

37. The "beast-fighter" (bestiarius) was a gladiator who fought with ferocious beasts.

38. The text is not certain, and the passage is corrupt. Botte (p. 39) suggests a falsifier of currency: "the 'cutter,' who trims the edges of pieces (of money)."

39. A golden rule: Every bishop has the Holy Spirit and can trust in him when deciding difficult cases for which no precedent exists.

If, however, a man is zealous and firmly perseveres in this undertaking, he is to be judged not by length of time but solely by his conduct.

18. The Prayer of Those Who Are Receiving Instruction

When the catechist has finished an instruction, the catechumens are to pray apart, separately from the faithful.[40] Women, be they catechumens or among the faithful, are to have their place apart for prayer, in the church. At the end of their prayer, the catechumens are not to exchange the kiss of peace, since their kiss is not yet holy. The faithful are to greet one another, the men the men and the women the women. The men are not to greet the women. . . .

19. The Imposition of Hands on the Catechumens

After the prayer, the catechist is to impose his hand on the catechumens. He is to pray and then dismiss them. He who teaches them, be he cleric or layman, is to do likewise.

BAPTISM OF BLOOD

If a catechumen is arrested for the name of the Lord, he is not to be left anxious about his testimony. For if he suffers violence and is put to death before receiving the forgiveness of his sins, he will nonetheless be justified, for he will have been baptized in his own blood.[41]

20. Rites Preparatory to Baptism

THE CHOICE OF CANDIDATES

When those to be baptized have been selected, their life is to be examined: Have they lived uprightly during their catechumenate? Have they respected widows, visited the sick, practiced all the good works?[42]

---

40. The "catechism lesson" was not merely instruction; it began with prayer and ended with a blessing which the catechist gave while laying his hands on the catechumens.

41. In his treatise *On Baptism* 16, 1-2, Tertullian attests the same belief for the African Church: "For us there is also a second washing, which is likewise unique, namely that of blood, concerning which the Lord says: 'I have a baptism in which to be baptized,' after he had already been baptized. He had come, as John wrote, 'through water and blood,' so that he might be baptized by water and glorified by blood. In like manner, so that he might call us through water and elect us through blood, he sent forth these two baptisms from the wound in his pierced side. . . . It is this [second] baptism that replaces the washing which has not been received, or restores it when it has been lost" (*PL* 1:1217AB; *CCL* 1:290–91). Elsewhere, speaking of martyrs, Tertullian writes: "Your whole key to paradise is your blood" (*De anima* 55, 5 [*PL* 2:745A; *CCL* 2:863]).

42. Note that the examination of the candidates is concerned here, not with the knowledge they have acquired, but with the life they have led.

THE GIVING OF THE GOSPEL

If those who introduced the candidates testify that they have been living in this way, let them hear the Gospel.

THE DAILY EXORCISMS

From the moment they have been chosen, they are to have hands laid on them daily in exorcism.

As the day of their baptism approaches, the bishop is to exorcise each of them, to find out if they are pure. If any one of them is not a good man or is not pure, he is to be rejected, for he has not heard the word with faith, since it is impossible that the stranger (the demon) should remain hidden in him. . . .[43]

FASTING AND PRAYER

Those who are to receive baptism must fast on the Friday and Saturday.

On Saturday, the bishop is to gather them all together in one place and bid them all pray and kneel.[44]

Let the bishop lay his hand on them and command all the foreign spirits to depart from them and never return to them again.

THE BAPTISMAL VIGIL

When he has finished the exorcism, let him breathe on their faces,[45] make the sign of the cross on their ears and nose, and then bid them stand. They are to pass the entire night in watching. They are to be given readings and instructions.

Those about to be baptized are to bring nothing with them, except what each person brings for the Eucharist. For it is fitting that he who has become worthy of it should himself bring the oblation at this time.

B. Baptism

21. The Giving of Holy Baptism

RUNNING WATER

At cockcrow a prayer is first said over the water.

---

43. The text is obscure. F. X. Funk, *Didascalia et Constitutiones apostolorum* (Paderborn, 1905), 2:108, proposes to read: *Quia impossibile est, alienum in aeternum occultum manere* — "because it is impossible for the stranger to remain hidden for ever."

44. Tertullian writes similarly: "Those who are about to enter upon baptism should pray with frequent prayers, fasts, genuflections, and vigils, and confess all their past sins, so that they may imitate the baptism of John, of whom we read: 'They were baptized as they confessed their sins'" (*De baptismo* 20, 1 [*PL* 1:1222BC; *CCL* 1:294; *SC* 35:94]).

45. The rite of exsufflation is a rite of exorcism intended to drive away the devil. It is distinguished from the rite of insufflation, which symbolizes the gift of the Holy Spirit and which Christ performed on his apostles (John 20:22).

The water is to be water flowing from a fountain, or running water. This rule is to be observed except when impossible. If the impossibility is permanent and the need pressing, use whatever water is available.

The candidates are to remove their clothes.

The children are to be baptized first. All of them who can, are to give answer for themselves. If they cannot, let their parents or someone in the family answer for them.[46]

First you are to baptize the men, then the women; the women will have unbound their hair and laid aside their jewels of gold and silver.

Let no one go down into the water with anything of the stranger.[47]

THE OIL OF THANKSGIVING AND THE OIL OF EXORCISM

At the hour set for baptism, the bishop will pronounce a prayer of thanksgiving over the oil and collect it in a vessel. This is the oil that is called the "oil of thanksgiving."

He will then take another oil and pronounce an exorcism over it; this oil is called the "oil of exorcism."

The deacon will carry the oil of exorcism and stand at the priest's left. Another deacon will take the oil of thanksgiving and stand at the priest's right.

RENUNCIATION OF SATAN

The priest will take aside each of those who are to receive baptism. He will order each to turn to the west and to make his abjuration in these words:

> I renounce you, Satan,
> and all your undertakings
> and all your works.

THE ANOINTING OF EXORCISM

After this abjuration, he anoints them with the oil of exorcism, saying: "Let every evil spirit depart from you!"

The person to be baptized lays aside his clothes. Then he is brought to the bishop or priest, who stands near the water of baptism. A deacon descends into the water with the one to be baptized.

THE TRIPLE IMMERSION

This last goes down into the water. The one doing the baptizing lays his hand on him and asks him:

> Do you believe in God,
> the Father almighty?

---

46. The text bears witness to the practice of infant baptism in the Church of Rome; see J. Jeremias, *Infant Baptism in the First Four Centuries*, tr. D. Cairns (Philadelphia, 1960), pp. 73–75.

47. This must mean anything that belongs to "the stranger," that is, the devil.

The one being baptized is to answer: "I believe."
Let him baptize him then a first time, keeping his hand on the person's head.
He then asks him:

> Do you believe in Christ Jesus, Son of God,
> born by the Holy Spirit of the Virgin Mary,
> who was crucified under Pontius Pilate,
> who died, was raised on the third day,
> living from among the dead,
> who ascended to the heavens,
> who sits at the right hand of the Father,
> who will come to judge the living and the dead?

When he has answered: "I believe," he is to baptize him a second time.
He is to ask him again:

> Do you believe in the Holy Spirit,
> in the holy Church,
> in the resurrection of the flesh?

The one being baptized is to answer: "I believe." Then he baptizes him a third time.[48]

THE ANOINTING WITH THE OIL OF THANKSGIVING

After this, he comes up again. The priest will then anoint him with the oil of thanksgiving.[49] He will say:

> I anoint you with the oil that has been sanctified
> in the name of Jesus Christ.

After drying themselves off, they will put their clothes on again and enter the church.

C. Confirmation

Here we have the first Roman ritual of confirmation. It includes a laying on of hands by the bishops, a prayer in supplicatory form, an anointing with the oil of thanksgiving, the signing of the forehead, and the kiss of peace.

---

48. Note that the *Apostolic Tradition* does not contain the traditional baptismal formula inherited from Mt. 28:19: "I baptize you in the name of the Father and of the Son and of the Holy Spirit." In Hippolytus's time, the triple question and the triple profession of faith in the Father, the Son, and the Spirit was the baptismal formula.

49. The "oil of thanksgiving" is the oil which has been sanctified (*quod sanctificatum est*) by a thanksgiving, that is, over which a blessing has been spoken (B. Botte). This anointing corresponds to the postbaptismal anointing with chrism in the present ritual. It signifies that the baptized person has become a *christian*, that is, a sharer in Christ, who is *par excellence* the "anointed one." Tertullian explains in his *De baptismo* 7: "When we come up from the bath, we are anointed with blessed oil according to the ancient practice. . . . They [priests] were called 'christs' from chrism, that is, anointing, which also gave the Lord his name" (*PL* 1:1206–1207; *CCL* 1:282; *SC* 35:76).

Confirmation was given immediately after baptism. In the East, as we know, the two sacraments of baptism and confirmation were given together, sometimes by the same rites. At Rome and in the West, they were administered in two different rites, as Hippolytus testifies and Pope Innocent I was later to approve,[50] but in one and the same ceremony.[51]

THE IMPOSITION OF HANDS

While imposing hands on them, the bishop will pronounce the following invocation:

> Lord God,
> who have given these men and women the dignity
> of meriting the forgiveness of sins
> through the bath of regeneration of the Holy Spirit,
> put your grace in them
> that they may serve you according to your will.
> For yours is the glory,
> Father and Son, with the Holy Spirit
> in the holy Church,
> now and for ever and ever!
>   Amen.

THE ANOINTING

With his hand he next pours the oil of thanksgiving. He spreads it on their heads, saying:

> I anoint you with the holy oil
> in the Lord, Father almighty,
> Christ Jesus and the Holy Spirit.

THE SEAL OF THE HOLY SPIRIT

He will then mark them with the sign[52] on the forehead, then give them a kiss, saying: "The Lord is with you."
The person marked with the sign will answer: "And with your spirit."
He is to do this for each one.

---

50. *Letter to Decentius*, March 19, 416 (*PL* 10:554; Mansi, *Sacrorum conciliorum nova et amplissima collectio* 3:1029BC).
51. It was only from the ninth century on that in the West the administration of confirmation was frequently separated from that of baptism. See R. Béraudy, "L'initiation chrétienne," in A. C. Martimort *et al.*, *L'Eglise en prière* (3rd ed.; Paris, 1965), p. 573.
52. The Latin text here has the verb *signare*. In Christian usage, *signare* means to mark with a seal. In the present context it refers to a rite symbolizing the spiritual seal that the Holy Spirit impresses on the soul.

From now on they will pray with the entire people. But they are not to pray with the faithful before receiving all this.

When they have prayed, let them offer the kiss of peace.

D. The Baptismal Mass and First Communion

THE OFFERING

The deacons then present the oblation to the bishop.

He gives thanks with regard to the bread, which represents the body of Christ; (he gives thanks) also with regard to the cup, in which the wine is mixed that represents the blood poured out for all those who believe in him. He also gives thanks with regard to the mingled milk and honey,[53] which represents the fulfillment of the promise God made to our fathers, a promise signified by the land flowing with milk and honey and fulfilled in the flesh of Christ which he gives us and by which believers are nourished like little children,[54] for the sweetness of his word changes the bitterness of our hearts into gentleness. Finally, he gives thanks with regard to the water for the oblation, to signify purification, so that the interior, spiritual man may receive the same effect as the body.

Let the bishop explain all this carefully to those who receive it.

COMMUNION

After breaking the bread, he distributes each piece, saying:

The bread of heaven
in Christ Jesus!

The person receiving it is to answer: "Amen."

If there are not enough priests present, let the deacons too present the cups. They are to stand in proper order and modestly, the first presenting the water, the second the milk, the third the wine.

Those who drink of them will taste each cup, while the one presenting it says:

In God, the Father almighty.

The person receiving it is to answer: "Amen."

And in the Lord Jesus.

(The person will say: "Amen.")

And in the Holy Spirit and the holy Church.

---

53. The custom of offering milk and honey to the newly baptized was still observed in Rome at the beginning of the sixth century, as we learn from John the Deacon in his *Letter to Senarius* 12 (PL 59:405–406).

54. An allusion to 1 Pet. 2:2: "Like newborn babes, long for the pure spiritual milk, that by it [i.e., by the Lord] you may grow up to salvation."

And the person will say: "Amen."

This is to be done for each of them.

When all this is finished, each person must hasten to do good works, please God, and live a good life. Let him devote himself to the Church, putting into practice what he has been taught and making progress in the service of God. . . .

22. *Communion*

On Sundays, the bishop, if possible, will himself distribute Communion to the entire people, while the deacons see to the breaking of the bread. The priests too will break the bread. When the deacon brings the bread to the priest, he will offer him the plate. The priest will then take the bread and distribute it to the people from his own hand.

On other days, Communion will be in accordance with the bishop's instructions.

23. *Fasting*

Widows and virgins are to fast often and pray for the Church. Priests as well as laity are to fast as they wish. The bishop can fast only when the entire people fasts, for it may be that someone wants to make an offering and the bishop cannot refuse it. At any rate, when he does accomplish the breaking of bread, he eats at meals.

24. *Gifts for the Sick*

. . . Let those who receive (the gifts) serve with zeal. He who has received (gifts) to bring to a widow or a sick person or someone who is working for the Church is to bring them on that same day. If he has not brought them on that day, he will bring them the next day, adding something of his own, because the bread of the poor has stayed in his possession.

THIRD PART

CHRISTIAN OBSERVANCES

The third part of the *Apostolic Tradition* deals with various observances of Christian life. The result is a vivid picture of the devotions practiced by the early Christians. Their piety, though it drew its vitality from the community celebration of the Eucharist, moved far beyond the context of the liturgical assembly and touched their whole life. In those years when persecution was intermittent and had not ceased for good, Christians were bent on joyously following the Lord's command: "Watch at all times, praying that you may have the strength . . . to stand before the Son of Man" (Lk. 21:36).

25. *The Bringing In of the Lamp for the Community Meal*
(The Lucernary)

On Saturday evening, when the vigil for Sunday began, the faithful were accustomed to gather for an evening of prayer; this service was called the Lucernary.[55] A lamp was lit to commemorate the risen Christ, who is the splendid reflection of the Father's glory and the light of the world, and also in expectation of the parousia. It is this ancient office, which had become a daily evening prayer for the entire Christian community, that Hippolytus describes.

————————————

When evening comes and the bishop has arrived, the deacon brings a lamp. Standing in the midst of the faithful, the bishop gives thanks; he begins with the greeting:

The Lord be with you!

And all the people answer:

And with your spirit!

—Let us give thanks to the Lord.

They will answer:

It is right and just.
His are greatness and magnificence
as well as glory.

He is not to say: "Let us lift up our hearts," because this is to be said at the moment of the offering.[56]

Then let him pray like this:

————————————

55. In Greek *lychnikon*. This term designates the evening office celebrated at the hour of the lighting of the lamps (*lychnia*). This celebration was taken over from biblical custom. It may be recalled that in the Tent of Meeting a lamp with pure oil was kept perpetually lit "before Yahweh" (Lev. 24:3-4) on the golden seven-branched lampstand (Ex. 25:31-40). St. John transfers this custom to the heavenly liturgy in his Apocalypse and therefore sees the glorified Christ surrounded by seven golden lampstands (Apoc. 1:12-13). This celebration of light had become part of the domestic liturgy, both Jewish (the lighting of the "Sabbath lamp") and Christian (the gathering at Troas where Paul presides at the breaking of bread in Acts 20:7-8).

There is an echo of the Lucernary in the Easter Vigil at the blessing of the paschal candle, in the rite of the baptismal candle, and in the practice of lighting candles before altars, ikons, and, at a latter date, the reserved Sacrament.

56. See above, p. 130.

We give you thanks, O God,
through your Son, Jesus Christ, our Lord,
for having enlightened us
by revealing to us the incorruptible light.
Having ended the course of this day
and reached the edge of night,
having been filled by the light of day
which you create for our joy,
we now possess, through your kindness,
the evening light.
Therefore do we praise you and glorify you
through your Son, Jesus Christ, our Lord.

Through him be glory yours, power and honor,
with the Holy Spirit, now and always
and for ever and ever. Amen.

Then all are to answer: "Amen."

After the meal they will rise for prayer. The children will sing psalms, as well as the virgins.[57]

26. *The Agape*[58]

At the meal, the faithful present receive a morsel of bread from the bishop's hand before they break their own bread. This morsel is a eulogy[59] and not a eucharist, as the body of the Lord is.

Before drinking, it is fitting that all should take a cup and give thanks over it. Then they may eat and drink in all purity. As for the catechumens, they are to be given an exorcised bread, and each is to offer a cup.

28. *We Must Eat with Moderation and According to Need*

When you eat and drink, do so with moderation and not to the point of

---

57. The traditional psalm for the Lucernary was Psalm 141, the second verse of which seemed especially appropriate: "Let my prayer be counted as incense before thee, and the lifting up of my hands as an evening sacrifice!" "Joyous Light" might be sung as a hymn (see p. 251).

58. *Agape* (Greek *agapē*, "love") is the Christian name for a fraternal meal that is liturgical in character, the kind of meal that had been customary in the Jewish religious brotherhoods. The purpose of the agape was to deepen the solidarity of the faithful and to be a help to the poor and the widowed. It is possible that in Paul's time the celebration of the Eucharist at Corinth was preceded by an agape (see 1 Cor. 11:17-34).

59. In liturgical language, *eulogy* (Greek *eulogein*, "to bless") means the loaves that were blessed and given to those who had offered them, or shared among those present.

drunkenness. Then no one can mock you, and your host will not be grieved by the disturbance you would cause. On the contrary, he will be glad of having been thought worthy enough for the saints to enter his house. "You," says (the Lord), "are the salt of the earth" (Mt. 5:13). . . .

When the bishop speaks, each person is to keep a modest silence in praise of him, until he asks another question. If in the absence of the bishop the faithful are at a meal at which a priest or a deacon is present, they shall likewise eat with moderation. Each one shall be eager to receive the eulogy from the hand of the priest or the deacon. . . .

29. *We Must Eat with Thanksgiving*

Each one is to eat in the name of the Lord with thanksgiving. What pleases God, after all, is that we prove ourselves better than the pagans by being all united and practicing temperance.

30. *Meals for Widows*

If one invites widows for a meal, they should be women of mature years, and one should send them home before evening. If one cannot (invite them) because of an office one has received, let them be given food and wine and then sent home. They can eat their meal in their own home if they so wish.

31. *Fruits to Be Offered to the Bishop*

The faithful liked to bring for the bishop's blessing the firstfruits they had gathered, as well as flowers — roses and lilies. These offerings remind us to some extent of the offering of firstfruits in the Old Testament. In offering fruits, roses, and lilies, the believer was celebrating the goodness of the God who had given them to him. He read the name of God in the fruits of the earth, and God read the homage of love in the heart of the offerer.

———————————————

As soon as they begin to gather the newly appeared fruit, all shall hasten to present some of it to the bishop. When the latter offers it, he will bless it, name those who have presented it, and say:

> We thank you, O God,
> and offer you the first of the fruits
> you have given us to enjoy.
>
> Through your word you have made them grow;
> you have commanded the earth to bear all its fruits

for the joy and nourishment
of mankind and all the animals.

For all this we praise you, O God,
and for the blessings you give us
when you adorn the whole creation
with all kinds of fruits,
through your Child Jesus Christ, our Lord.

Through him be glory yours
for ever and ever!
     Amen.

32. *The Blessing of Fruits*

The following fruits are blessed: grapes, figs, pomegranates, olives, pears, apples, mulberries, peaches, cherries, almonds, plums; not watermelons, melons, cucumbers, mushrooms, garlic, or any other vegetable. But sometimes flowers too are offered; thus roses and lilies are offered, but no other flowers.

For everything that is harvested the holy God is to be thanked, and it is to be used for his glory.

34. *Deacons Must Be Devoted to the Bishop*

All the deacons, as well as the subdeacons, must be zealous in their service to the bishop.

They are also to tell the bishop of those who are sick, so that if he thinks it good he may visit them. For it is a source of great comfort for a sick person if the high priest is mindful of him.

35. *The Time for Prayer*

As soon as the faithful awake and rise from bed, even before setting about their work, they are to pray to God and only then begin their work. If an instruction is being given on the word of God, the believer will prefer to attend it and hear the word of God so that his soul may be strengthened. Let him be zealous about going to the church, where the Spirit is strongly present.

36. *When We Celebrate the Offering, We Must Receive the Eucharist First, Before Taking Anything Else*

Each believer is to take care to receive the Eucharist before tasting anything else. For if he receives it with faith, and then some deadly poison is given to him afterwards, it will not have power to harm him.

37. *The Eucharist Must Be Kept with Care*

Each person must see to it that an unbeliever, or a mouse or other animal, does not eat the Eucharist,[60] and that no part of it falls to the ground and is lost. For it is the body of the Lord that the faithful eat, and they must not treat it with contempt.

39. *(Deacons and Priests)*

The deacons and priests are to gather daily, at whatever place the bishop orders them.

The deacons must not fail to gather regularly, unless illness prevents them. When all have gathered, they are to instruct any who may be in the church. Then, after prayer, each is to go to his own work.

40. *Cemeteries*

The people are not to be heavily charged for burying their dead in the cemeteries, for these belong to all the poor.

However, the salary of the gravedigger and the price of the bricks are to be regulated. The bishop is to provide those who live and work there with food out of the gifts made to the Church so that these people will not become a burden on the families of the dead.[61]

41. *The Times for Prayer*

IN THE MORNING

As soon as the faithful, men and women, awake from their sleep in the morning, all are to wash their hands[62] and pray to God before undertaking any work whatsoever. Then they will go to their work.

WORD OF GOD AND COMMUNITY PRAYER

If, however, there is an instruction on the word of God, everyone should go to it gladly. He will reflect in his heart that he is listening to God speak through the

---

60. This prudential advice is explained by the fact that Christians kept the Eucharist at home. This custom is attested by Tertullian: *Ad uxorem* 11, 5 (*PL* 1:1295–1297; *CCL* 1:389–90) and *De oratione* 19 (*PL* 1:1183A; *CCL* 1:267–68). It survived until about the eighth century, as we can see from a passage in.Venerable Bede's *Historia ecclesiastica* IV, 24 (*PL* 95:214CD).

61. "To the families of the dead": literally, "to those who come there."

62. A rite of purification (Ps. 26:8) which signifies that the soul, before entering the presence of God, rids itself of its imperfections and faults.

mouth of the one giving the instruction. For if he has prayed in the assembly, he will be able to overcome the evil of the day.

The person who fears God will reflect that it is very wrong not to go to the place where the instruction is given, especially if he knows how to read or if the teacher is coming there.

Let no one among you be slow to join the assembly at the place where the instruction is given. Then it will be given to the speaker to teach what is useful to all, and you, for your part, will hear what you did not previously know, and you will draw profit from what the Spirit gives you through the teacher. In this way your faith will be strengthened by what you hear. They will also tell you there what you should be doing at home. Each person, therefore, should take care to go to the assembly, where the Spirit is strongly present.

On a day when no instruction is given, everyone in his own home is to take a book and read enough from it of what is useful to him.

AT THE THIRD HOUR

If you are at home at the third hour, pray and praise God.[63] But if you are elsewhere at this moment, pray to God in your heart. For at this hour Christ was nailed to the cross. For this reason the Law in the Old (Testament) commanded that at every hour the showbread[64] should be offered, which symbolized the body and blood of Christ, and a lamb devoid of reason should be offered, which symbolized the perfect Lamb. For Christ is the shepherd, and he is also the bread that has come down from heaven.

AT THE SIXTH HOUR

Pray likewise at the sixth hour. For while Christ was nailed to the wood of the cross, day was halted and a great darkness arose. At that hour, therefore, pray with great power, in imitation of him who prayed while all of creation was buried in darkness because of the unbelieving Jews.

AT THE NINTH HOUR

At the ninth hour greatly lengthen your prayer and praise, imitating the souls of the just who bless the true God, who remembered his holy ones and sent his Son, the Word, to enlighten them.

At this hour water and blood came from the pierced side of Christ, and (the Lord) gave light to the day as it declined, and brought it to evening. By thus

---

63. The third, sixth, and ninth hours correspond to 9 a.m., midday, and 3 p.m. The practice of praying three times a day was certainly inherited from Old Testament piety (Ps. 55:18; Dan. 6:11). The custom passed into the Christian community, as *Didache* 8 already shows.

64. The showbread was twelve cakes of the best flour that were set out in the "holy place" and were renewed every Sabbath (see Lev. 24:5-9; 1 Chr. 9:32; 23:29). Num. 4:7 calls them "the bread of perpetual offering" (JB).

beginning a new day[65] at the hour when he began to fall asleep, he gave an image of the resurrection.

IN THE EVENING

Pray also before your body goes to its rest in bed.

NOCTURNAL PRAISE

Toward midnight[66] arise, wash your hands with water, and pray.

If your wife is present, the two of you should pray together. But if she is not a believer, withdraw to another room to pray, then return to bed.

Do not be lazy when it comes to prayer. . . .

When you sign yourself with the moist breath you have gathered in your hand, your body is purified down to your feet.[67] For the gift of the Spirit and the purification by water, both of which rise from the heart as from a spring, sanctify the believer who offers them.

At this hour, then, you should pray. For the ancients who left us this tradition have taught us that at this hour the whole of creation pauses for a moment to praise the Lord. The stars, the trees, and the rivers stop for a moment, and the entire army of angels celebrates and praises God at this hour, together with the souls of the just. That is why believers will be eager to pray at this hour. The Lord himself bears witness to it when he says: "Behold, at midnight a cry resounded, saying: 'The bridegroom is coming! Arise and go to meet him!'" And he concluded: "Watch, therefore, since you do not know at what hour he is coming."[68]

AT COCKCROW

Toward cockcrow, rise again. For it was at this hour, while the cock was crowing, that the sons of Israel denied Christ, whom we have known through faith

---

65. Hippolytus is reckoning the day in the semitic manner; Saturday, the "new day," begins therefore on Friday evening, not at midnight.

66. Nocturnal prayer is an inheritance from Judaism: "At midnight I rise to praise thee, because of thy righteous ordinances" (Ps. 119:62). It is also found in the Qumran texts; cf. *Rule* 10:10, 14: "When day comes and the night, I will enter the Covenant of God; when night and morning depart, I will recite His precepts. . . . When I retire to bed, I will utter cries of joy unto Him" (in A. Dupont-Sommer, *The Essene Writings from Qumran*, tr. by G. Vermes [Oxford, 1961; reprinted, Gloucester, Mass., 1973], pp. 98–99). Cf. also J. Carmignac and P. Guilbert, *Les textes de Qumrân* (Paris, 1961), pp. 70 and 72.

67. The breath of the Christian has been sanctified by the *Breath* of God, that is, by the Holy *Spirit* who dwells in the hearts of the faithful. In signing himself, so to speak, with the Spirit of God, the believer is wholly purified.

68. Mt. 25:6, 13. The way in which the New Testament insists that the return of Jesus will take place in the night is well known: Lk. 12:20; 12:39-20 and Mt. 24:42-43; Lk. 17:34 and Mt. 24:40-41; Mt. 25:1-13; Mk. 13:35-37; 1 Thess. 5:2. These texts seem to echo a hope attested by the Palestinian Targum, which placed the future messianic deliverance in the night of Passover (see Jer. 38:8 LXX), which had become the central night of the whole history of the world and was associated with the night of creation and of the sacrifice of Abraham. See R. Le Déaut, *La nuit pascale* (Rome, 1963).

and in whom we hope for the everlasting light for the resurrection of the dead, with our eyes fixed on that day.

If all of you who are believers act thus, if you keep it in mind, instructing one another and giving example to the catechumens, you cannot be tempted or be lost, for you will always be mindful of Christ.

42. (The Sign of the Cross)

If you are tempted, hasten to sign yourselves on the forehead in a worthy manner. For this sign manifests the Passion which stands against the devil, provided you make it with faith, not for men to see but knowing how to use it like a breastplate. Then the adversary, seeing the power that comes from the heart, will flee. This is what Moses imaged forth through the passover lamb that was sacrificed, when he sprinkled the thresholds and smeared the doorposts with its blood. He was pointing to the faith that we now have in the perfect Lamb.

By signing our forehead and eyes with our hand, we repulse him who seeks to destroy us.

43. (Conclusion)

If you receive these instructions with thanksgiving and right faith, they will edify the Church and bring believers eternal life.

I counsel all prudent men to observe these traditions. For if everyone follows and observes the tradition of the apostles, no heretic, and indeed no human being at all, will be able to lead you astray. The reason why heresies have increased is that leaders have been unwilling to make their own the teachings of the apostles and have acted as they pleased and not as they should have.

Beloved, if we have omitted anything, God will reveal it to those who are worthy of it. For it is he who governs the holy Church so that she may reach the harbor of peace.

10

The Anaphora of Addai and Mari

(third or fifth century)

INTRODUCTION

EASTERN LITURGICAL FAMILIES

Among the Eastern liturgies there are an Alexandrian group, which is connected with the patriarchate of Alexandria, and an Antiochene group, which is connected with the patriarchate of Antioch.

The Alexandrian group comprises the Coptic and Egyptian rites, while the Antiochene group is subdivided into two main types: the West Syrian and the East Syrian.

The West Syrian type includes the Syrian rite of Antioch, the Maronite rite, the Byzantine rite, and the Armenian rite.

The East Syrian type includes the Nestorian rite, the Chaldean rite, and the Malabar rite. It is within this second type that the anaphora of the "holy apostles" Addai and Mari is found; it is used by the Nestorians and by the Christians of the Chaldean and Malabar rites who are united to Rome.[1]

THE ANAPHORA OF THE APOSTLES ADDAI AND MARI

Among the anaphoras written in Syria, that of the "Apostles Addai and Mari" occupies a special place. For, while the anaphoras of Theodore of Mopsuestia and Nestorius betray the fact that they are translations or adaptations of Greek originals, it is very likely that the anaphora of Addai and Mari was first composed in Syriac.[2] On the other hand, its characteristics, both stylistic (redundancy in vo-

---

1. Three anaphoras are used in the Nestorian rite: the anaphoras of Addai and Mari, of Theodore of Mopsuestia, and of Nestorius. The Chaldean rite is followed by the former Nestorians of Cyprus and Chaldea who went over to Rome in the fifteenth and sixteenth centuries and have continued to use a corrected Nestorian liturgy. The Malabar rite is followed by the communities of the Malabar region (India) which were founded by Nestorian missionaries and went over to Rome in the sixteenth century; they have retained the anaphora of Addai and Mari, but not those of Theodore of Mopsuestia and Nestorius. (The Malabar Christians who did not enter into union with Rome form the Malankar Church and follow the West Syrian rite of Antioch.) On the Eastern liturgies, see I. H. Dalmais, *Eastern Liturgies*, tr. D. Attwater (20th Century Encyclopedia of Catholicism 112; New York, 1960); B. Botte, "Rites and Liturgical Groups," in A. Martimort (ed.), *The Church at Prayer 1. Introduction to the Liturgy*, Eng. tr. edited by A. Flannery and V. Ryan (New York, 1968), pp. 3–31.
2. N. Maurice-Denis and R. Boulet write in their *Euchariste* (cf. n. 30, p. 133, above): "We are dealing here with a strictly Syriac document for which we augur no Greek prototype" (p. 301).

cabulary; parallelism in phrasing) and theological, relate it to Jewish prayers for the table. This indicates how old the anaphora must be. B. Botte dates it, at least in its primitive form, as early as the third century, thus making it contemporary with the anaphora of Hippolytus.[3] And L. Bouyer does not hesitate to say: "Everything leads us to believe that this prayer is the most ancient Christian eucharistic composition to which we can have access today."[4]

This anaphora is interesting chiefly for what it lacks, for it contains no account of the institution of the Eucharist. There have been various reactions to this "anomaly," which tests the wits of the historians and liturgists and throws a wrench into all the neat theories.

Some scholars (E. C. Ratcliff, G. Dix, W. E. Pitt) claim that the anaphora never contained the account of institution.[5] In their view, the anaphora in its primitive form contained essentially the prayer of praise, which was perhaps followed by the anamnesis or the *Sanctus*. The fact that the community is authentically celebrating the Lord's Supper is indicated not by the words (those of the institution) that it recites, but by the liturgical action itself that it celebrates. There is no need to make explicit in spoken words that which everyone understands and which is in the process of being done.

On the opposite side, B. Botte, followed by L. Bouyer, has sought to prove that the anaphora must originally have had a fully classical structure (thanksgiving, intercession, account of institution, anamnesis, and epiclesis).[6] Its present state would be the result of textual corruption or later modification.

The authority of Botte is so great and his demonstration so lucid that hardly anyone has dared attack it directly. Scholars have preferred to hold their positions, as in trench warfare, and to retreat each into his own little hole (that is, his personal theory).

There was no reason to think that the data of the problem would ever change. But then W. F. Macomber had the rare good fortune to discover new manuscripts. The oldest of them is from the church of Mar Eša'ya in Mosul and seems to date from the eleventh or twelfth century; it is thus five centuries older than the manuscripts hitherto used in establishing the textus receptus of this anaphora. Evidently this discovery forces a restatement of the problem.

---

3. "L'anaphore chaldéenne des apôtres," *Orientalia Christiana Periodica* 15 (1949), pp. 259–76. See also Botte, "Problèmes de l'anaphore syrienne des Apôtres Addaï et Mari," *Orient Syrien* 10 (1965), pp. 89–106; D. Webb, "La liturgie nestorienne des Apôtres Addaï et Mari dans la tradition manuscrite," in *Eucharisties d'Orient et d'Occident* (Lex orandi 47; Paris, 1970), pp. 25–49.

4. *Op. cit.*, p. 147. Those who do not accept the anaphora of Addai and Mari as being of such great antiquity usually assign it to the fifth century. See A. Raes, "Orientalische Liturgien. B. Einzeltypen," *Lexikon für Theologie und Kirche*[2] 6 (1961), cols. 1089–90.

5. There is a very good discussion of the question in E. J. Cutrone, "The Anaphora of the Apostles: Implications of the Mar Eša'ya Text," *Theological Studies* 34 (1973), pp. 623–42. We wish here to thank Professor Cutrone for the personal help he gave us.

6. See Bouyer, p. 151.

It is true, of course, that all the elements found in the anaphora of the Mar Eša'ya manuscript do not necessarily go back to the primitive text. The least that can be said, however, is that this manuscript provides us with the oldest form now known of the anaphora of Addai and Mari.

Macomber's discovery lets us see the great antiquity of the prayers of intercession, the absence of the account of institution, and the presence of an epiclesis at least in an archaic form. It does not enable us to remove the veil completely as regards the relationship between this Eucharistic prayer and the Jewish blessing, nor as regards the problem of its anamnesis.

TRANSLATION

Our translation follows the critical text that W. F. Macomber has established on the basis of the Mar Eša'ya manuscript.[7]

Whenever the text is incomplete because the copyist assumed that the celebrant would know it and say it by heart, we have completed it from the textus receptus. These additions are printed in italics.

Thanksgiving

Priest: We will give you thanks, Lord,
for the abundant riches of your grace toward us.
For when we were weak sinners,
you made us worthy, in keeping with your great mercy,
of celebrating the holy mysteries
of the body and blood of your Christ.

We implore your help.
Strengthen our souls, that we may celebrate
with perfect charity and sincere love
the gift you have given us.

We praise you, we glorify you,
we give you thanks, we adore you
now *and always*
and forever and ever.[8]

People: Amen.

Priest: Peace be with you.
People: With you and with your spirit.

---

7. W. F. Macomber, "The Oldest Known Text of the Anaphora of the Apostles Addai and Mari," *Orientalia Christiana Periodica* 32 (1966) pp. 335–71.
8. Text completed according to the Latin version in Hänggi-Pahl, p. 375.

Deacon: Give peace to one another
           in the love of Christ.

People: For all the patriarchs.
Deacon: Let us give thanks, and let us pray.

Priest: The grace of our Lord *Jesus Christ,*
           the love of God the Father
           and the fellowship of the Holy Spirit
           be with you all,
           now and always,
           and forever and ever.[9]
People: Amen.

Priest: Raise your minds.
People: They are turned to you,
           God *of Abraham, Isaac, and Israel,*
           King of glory.[10]

Priest: The oblation is offered to God,
           to the Lord of the universe.
People: It is right and fitting.

Deacon: Peace be with you.

Priest: It is right that every mouth should glorify
           and every tongue give thanks
           to the adorable and glorious name[11]
           of the Father, the Son, and the Holy Spirit.
           He created the world in accordance with his graciousness
           and those who dwell in it in accordance with his kindness.
           He saved mankind in accordance with his mercy,
           he has filled mortal men with his great grace.

           Your majesty, O Lord,
           do a thousand thousand heavenly spirits adore,
           and with them the myriad myriads of angels,
           the ranks of (heavenly) spirits,
           the ministers of fire and spirit.
           With the Cherubim and holy Seraphim
           they glorify your name,
           they cry out and give glory.

---

9. Text citing 2 Cor. 13:13, completed according to Hänggi-Pahl, p. 375.
10. Text completed according to Hänggi-Pahl, p. 375.
11. Possible allusion to Phil. 2:9-11, where the praise is addressed to the risen Christ.

Sanctus

People: Holy, holy, holy [12]
the Lord, God almighty.
Heaven and earth are filled with your praises.
Hosanna in the highest (heavens)!
Blessed is he who comes and who will come
in the name of the Lord!
Hosanna to the Son of David!

Priest: With these heavenly armies
we too give you thanks, O Lord,
we your weak, frail, and lowly servants,
for the great grace which you have given us
and for which we can make no return.
For you clothed yourself in our humanity
that you might give us life through your divinity.
You exalted our lowliness,
you raised us up when we had fallen,
you brought our mortal nature back to life,
you forgave our sins.
You justified us when we were sinners,
you enlightened our minds.
Our Lord and our God,
you conquered our enemies,
you gave victory
to our frail, weak human nature
through the abundant mercies of your grace.

For all *your helps and graces to us,*
we offer you praise, honor,
gratitude and adoration,
now and always
and forever and ever. [13]

People: Amen.

Prayers of Intercession

Deacon: In your minds, *pray.*
Peace be with you. [14]

---

12. The *Sanctus* is here completed according to the anaphora of Theodore of Mopsuestia and translated in accordance with Macomber's citation of it (*art. cit.*, p. 363, n. 9).
13. Text completed according to Hänggi-Pahl, p. 377.
14. Text completed according to Hänggi-Pahl, p. 378.

Priest: O Lord, in accordance with your many mercies
which are beyond numbering,
remember with kindness
all the devout and just fathers
who were pleasing to you,
as we now commemorate
the body and blood of your Christ.
We offer him to you upon the pure and holy altar
as you taught us.
Grant us your tranquillity and peace
throughout all the days of this world.

People: Amen.

(Priest):   May all the inhabitants of the world come to know you,
for you alone are God, true Father.
You sent our Lord Jesus Christ.
He is your Son, your Beloved.
It is he, our Lord and our God,
who taught us through his life-giving gospel
all the purity and holiness of the prophets,
the apostles, the martyrs, the confessors,
the bishops, the priests, the deacons,
and all the sons and daughters of your holy catholic Church
who have been marked by the living seal of holy baptism. [15]

And we too, Lord, [16]
your weak, frail, and lowly servants,
who have gathered
and are standing before you at this moment,
we have received from tradition
the rite that has its origin in you.
We rejoice and give glory,
we exalt and commemorate,
we praise and celebrate
this great and awesome mystery
of the passion, the death, and the resurrection
of our Lord Jesus Christ.

---

15. Botte places the account of institution at this point.

16. The liturgical significance of this paragraph is not clear. It might be regarded as an anamnesis if the account of institution had preceded it. As the anaphora now stands, the paragraph may be regarded either as a continuation of the prayer of intercession or as the beginning of the epiclesis.

Epiclesis [17]

Deacon: Be silent *and reverent.*
Pray. May peace be with you.[18]

Priest: May your Holy Spirit come, Lord,
may he rest upon this offering of your servants,
may he bless and sanctify it,
so that it may win for us, Lord,
the forgiveness of offenses and the remission of sins,
the great hope of the resurrection of the dead,
and new life in the kingdom of heaven
with all those who have been pleasing to you.

Doxology

Because of your all-embracing, wonderful plan
which you have carried out in our regard,
we give you thanks and glorify you ceaselessly
in your Church which you have redeemed
through the precious blood of your Christ.
With open mouths and faces unveiled
we present you with *praise and honor,*
gratitude and adoration
to your living, holy, and life-giving name,
now and always
and forever and ever.[19]

People: Amen.

---

17. The archaic character of the epiclesis is emphasized by the fact that the coming of the Spirit is sought, not in order to transform the offerings into the body of Christ (this will be the purpose in later epicleses), but simply in order to bless the offerings and promote the spiritual good of the Church. The importance of the epiclesis is highlighted by the diaconal exhortation that precedes it.
   18. Text completed according to Hänggi-Pahl, p. 380.
   19. Text completed according to Hänggi-Pahl, p. 380.

11

The Didascalia of the Apostles

(beginning of the third century)

INTRODUCTION

THE WORK

The *Didascalia* or *Catholic Teaching of the Twelve Apostles and Holy Disciples of Our Savior* is a Church order dating from the first half or even the first decades of the third century.[1] Its author was a bishop in northern Syria. The work takes the form of a manual or custom-book for the use of a Christian community that had issued from paganism.

In order to give more weight and authority to the teaching and rules that he formulates, the author unhesitatingly presents his work as having been compiled by the apostles and immediate disciples of Christ himself. Such claims no longer surprise or excite the modern scholar, and the writer's stratagem is easily unmasked. Indeed, the author betrays himself by the use he makes of the *Didache*, the apocryphal *Gospel of Peter*, the apocryphal *Acts of Paul*, Ignatius of Antioch, and Irenaeus.

At this period such literary fictions were current practice; they were regarded with indulgence, even complicity, and did not offend the consciences of their readers, still less those of their authors, as long as they served a good cause. The important thing was to edify — in the best sense of the word — the Christian community. It was thought that an authentically Christian work could be produced even with the help of a literary fiction. This was because authenticity was a matter not of authorship but of the spirit of a work.

As a result, we are able today, thanks to a forgery, to understand the essential traits of a Christian community at the beginning of the third century, to marvel at how the spirit of the gospel had permeated the life of clergy and faithful with the splendor of charity, and to stand amazed at the sense of community these Christians had, a sense so strong that, in their view, to fail to attend the assembly was to deprive Christ of one of his members and to rend the body of the Lord (ch. 13). We see the bishop in the act of welcoming a poor man into his church and making him sit on the episcopal throne while he himself sits on the ground (ch. 12). We see deacons and deaconesses prolonging the ministry of the hierarchy in their respective spheres of action (ch. 16). We hear the magnificent penitential "Prayer of Manasseh" (ch. 7) and learn that each local Church must be a community of forgiveness and love (ch. 6). As P. Galtier observes:

---

1. On the date, see P. Galtier, "La date de la Didascalie des Apôtres," *Revue d'histoire ecclésiastique* 42 (1947), pp. 315–51.

The more we study the *Didascalia of the Apostles*, the more evident its interest and importance becomes. Harnack saw in it "a unique and invaluable source of information."[2] No other exists that enables us to enter so intimately into the life of a third-century Church. . . . It enables us to follow the bishop as he carries on his work of teaching, directing, and governing. We see him coming to grips with every detail in the life of his people. Together with his clergy, he is their pastor, leader, and judge. His concern extends and must extend to all and each. Sinners and faithful alike are the object of his care. He is responsible for their souls, but he also provides for their bodily needs.[3]

THE PLAN OF THE WORK

The author has not tied himself down to a logical plan; this, to his way of thinking at least, would have been unsuited to the requirements of the subject he meant to take up. As a matter of fact, he treats topics as they come to his mind; he exercises a great deal of freedom, but at the same time skillfully manages to avoid excessive repetition.

Since there is no plan in the strict sense of the word, we can only list the principal topics. After some instructions for married people (chs. 2–3), the author takes up the qualities and duties of a bishop (ch. 4; he returns to the subject in chs. 7–9 and 11–12). He then turns to repentance and the forgiveness of sinners (ch. 6) and shows clearly that he takes a milder approach than his Western contemporaries, Tertullian, Hippolytus, and Cyprian. We learn next what the qualities and duties of deacons are (chs. 11 and 16) and what good order in the assembly of the faithful requires (ch. 13). Further chapters deal with widows (chs. 14–15), deaconesses (ch. 16), the education of the young and orphans (chs. 17 and 22), the resurrection of the dead (ch. 20), heresies and schisms (ch. 23), apostles and the Church (chs. 24–25), and the abolition of the laws of purity as formulated in the Book of Deuteronomy (ch. 25).

As we work through the text, we find numerous citations from Scripture strewn along the path, some of them quite lengthy. The author of the *Didascalia* clearly knew and loved the word of God and delighted in basing his own words upon it.

TEXTUAL TRADITION

The *Didascalia* was written in Greek, but except for some short fragments this original is lost. It is possible, however, to reconstruct the greater part of it with the help of the *Apostolic Constitutions*, since the first six chapters of this latter document simply take over the text of the *Didascalia*.

An old Latin version, contained in the Verona palimpsest, which dates from the end of the fourth century, reproduces three-eighths of the work.

---

2. Galtier is here quoting Harnack's *The Mission and Expansion of Christianity* 2:157.
3. Galtier, p. 315.

Finally, we possess a complete translation in Syriac. This, like the Latin translation, seems to have followed the text of the original rather closely.[4]

Holy Vineyard of His Catholic Church

Plantation of God,
holy vineyard of his catholic Church,

you the chosen who have put your confidence
in the simplicity of the fear of the Lord,

you who have become, through faith,
heirs of his everlasting kingdom,

you who have received the power and gift of his Spirit,
who have been armed by him,
who have been strengthened in fear,

you who share in the pure and precious blood
poured out by the great God, Jesus Christ,

you who have received the freedom
to call the almighty God "Father,"
who are coheirs and friends of his beloved Son:

listen to the teaching of God,
all you who hope in his promises
and wait (for their fulfillment)!

(ch. 1)

The Pardon of Sinners

Judge then, O bishop, with authority, as almighty God does; receive with love those who repent, as almighty God does. Rebuke, exhort, instruct, for the Lord God has sworn to forgive all those who have sinned, as he says in Ezekiel (33:10-11):

------

4. The situation with regard to the text explains why the *Didascalia* is little known to the general public. H. Achelis and J. Flemming, *Die syrische Didaskalie übersetzt und erklärt* (Texte und Untersuchungen 25/2 [NF 10/2], Leipzig, 1904), complained of this long ago: "It may seem astonishing that a Church Order of the third century, whose great significance for many questions relating to the New Testament and to the history of the Church's constitution and worship is known and acknowledged, should still be inaccessible to the public in Germany" (p. iii).

And you, son of man, say to the house of Israel:
"You have said:
'Our iniquities and our sins weigh upon us
and we rot away beneath them.
How then shall we be able to live?'"
Proclaim to them: "By my life, says the Lord Adonai,
I do not take pleasure in the death of the sinner!
But let the wicked man turn from his way
and live.
Repent therefore,
turn from your evil ways,
and you will not die, house of Israel!"

(God), then, here gives hope to those who have sinned that, when they repent, they will find salvation in their repentance. Let them not despair, let them not abide in their sins, let them not increase them! Let them repent, let them lament and weep for their sins, let them be converted with their whole heart. . . .

(ch. 6)

Teach, therefore, O bishop, rebuke, loose (the bonds of sin) with forgiveness. Know that you take the place of almighty God and that you have received the power to forgive sins. For it is to you, bishops, that it was said:

All that you bind on earth
will be bound in heaven.
And all that you loose
will be loosed (Mt. 18:18). . . .

When the sinner has undergone penance and wept, receive him. And while the people pray for him, lay your hand on him and allow him once again to dwell in the assembly. . . .[5]

As a compassionate shepherd, full of love and pity, filled with concern for his flock, watches and counts it, seek out the lost sheep as the Lord God, Jesus Christ, our good Master and Savior, has demanded: "Leave the ninety-nine in the mountains, go and look for the one sheep that is lost. When you find it, carry it on your shoulders, rejoice because you have found that which was lost. Bring it and reunite it to the flock" (Mt. 18:10-14).

Be obedient then, you too, O bishop: seek out him who has perished, go and find him who is wandering, bring back him who has strayed. For you have power to forgive the sins of him who has fallen, since you have put on the person of Christ.

---

5. Note the community aspect of Christian repentance. Sin is an attack on the holiness of the entire Church; consequently forgiveness requires the reintegration of the sinner into the ecclesial community.

Thus our Lord said to the man who had sinned:

> Your sins are forgiven you,
> your faith has saved you, go in peace! (Mt. 9:2)

Now "peace" refers to the Church, (the refuge) of serenity and rest; those whom you deliver from sin, you bring back full of health and without spot, filled with good hope and eager to undertake hard and painful tasks. Like a wise and compassionate physician, heal everyone, above all those who have strayed in their sins. For "it is not those who are well who need the physician, but those who are ill" (Mt. 9:12).

You too, O bishop, have become a physician in the Church. Therefore do not cease, with her help, to heal those who are diseased with sin. Care for them and heal them in every way, restore them to health in the Church. Thus the word of the Lord: "You rule them with violence and harshness" (Ezek. 34:4), will not apply to you. You are, then, not to guide them with violence; do not be hard or curt or pitiless, do not mock the people who are under your hand, do not hide the words of repentance from them.

(ch. 7)

The Prayer of Repentance Attributed to Manasseh

In the Second Book of Chronicles, the sacred writer relates the history of King Manasseh (687–642), his wickedness, his punishment by deportation to Babylon, his conversion, and his return to Jerusalem (2 Chr. 33:1-20). The author adds that the prayer which the king made to implore pardon and the restoration of his kingship is to be found in the "Chronicles of the Kings of Israel" and in the "Chronicles of the Seer" (2 Chr. 33:18, 20). We do not possess the text of this prayer. So, toward the beginning of the Christian era, in order to fill in what appeared to be a lacuna in the inspired text, a Hellenistic Jew composed an apocryphal prayer which he attributed to Manasseh. This pious artifice succeeded completely; many ecclesiastical writers were taken in by it and accepted the "Prayer of Manasseh" as authentic. It had so great a success that many ancient liturgies adopted it as a prayer of repentance.[6]

It is the text of this prayer that the author of the *Didascalia* has incorporated as a quotation in chapter 7 of his work. Following the traditional structure of Jewish prayers, it is composed of a first part devoted to praise, a second in which forgiveness for sin is implored, and a third which is the final doxology.

---

6. On the history of this text, see J. B. Frey, "Apocryphes de l'Ancien Testament," *Dictionnaire de la Bible: Supplément* 1 (1928), cols. 442–45; P. Grelot, *Introduction à la Bible* 3/1 (1976), pp. 181–82 and bibliography, p. 242. The text used here is the Greek text of the *Apostolic Constitutions* II, 22, 12–15, ed. F. X. Funk, *Didascalia et Constitutiones Apostolorum* (Paderborn, 1905), 1:85–89; see *PG* 1:648–49. See also the edition of the Septuagint by A. Rahlfs, *Septuaginta* 2 (5th ed.; Stuttgart, 1952), pp. 180–81.

Almighty Lord, God of our fathers,
of Abraham, Isaac, and Jacob
and of their just descendants,
you who created the heaven and the earth
with all their splendor,
you who fettered the sea with a word of your will,
you who closed the abyss
and sealed it up with your terrible and glorious name!

The whole universe reveres you
and trembles before your power,
for it cannot sustain the magnificence of your glory,
nor bear the wrath which threatens sinners.
Yet vast and inscrutable
is the mercy that you have promised.
For you are the Lord full of compassion,
patient and rich in mercy (Ex. 34:6),
and you are saddened by the wickedness of men.

For it is you, Lord,
who, in your kindness and goodness,
have promised lenience to repentant sinners.
According to your mercies
you grant pardon to sinners,
and according to the abundance of your compassion
you determine the conversion of sinners
for their salvation.

You, then, Lord, God of the just,
have not established repentance for the just,
for Abraham, Isaac, and Jacob;
they did not sin against you.[7]
But you did establish repentance
for me who am a sinner;
for the number of my sins
is greater than the sand of the sea.

My iniquities are multiplied, Lord,

---

7. The author's reverence for the holiness of the patriarchs is so great that his theology of the universality of sin is somewhat threatened by it. As a matter of fact, however, all men are sinners before God. "The scripture consigned all things to sin, that what was promised to faith in Jesus Christ might be given to those who believe" (Gal. 3:22). The author's position seems to have been influenced by certain rabbinic speculations on the holiness of the patriarchs.

my iniquities are multiplied;
henceforth I am no longer worthy
to lift my eyes
nor to look toward the depths of heaven.
The number of my evil deeds crushes me
like a long chain of iron.
For I have provoked your anger,
"that which is wicked in your eyes, that have I done" (Ps. 51:6).

I have committed abominations,[8]
I have multiplied my offenses.
And now, in my heart,
I bend my knees before you.
I beseech your goodness:
I have sinned, Lord, I have sinned,
and my iniquities, indeed I know them (Ps. 51:5).
I beg and implore you:
Forgive me, Lord, forgive me,
do not destroy me with my iniquities,
do not loose against my faults
an eternal anger.
Do not condemn me to the bowels of the earth.

For you are God,
God of those who turn away from evil.
Show your goodness toward me
despite my unworthiness,
save me according to your great mercy.

I will sing your praises without ceasing
all the days of my life,
for all the powers of heaven
celebrate you with hymns.
To you the glory for all ages!
    Amen.

The Great Church, the Bride Adorned for God

Hear this, you the laity, the Church chosen by God. The (Jewish) people of old was called "Church," but you, you are the catholic Church, holy and perfect,

---

8. Literally: "I have raised abominations." The author is implicitly referring to 2 Chr. 33:2 (this would prove the authenticity of his text) by using the Greek word *bdelygma*, "abomination," which the Septuagint had used in this very passage. The "abominations" were idolatrous worship, with its erection of altars and high places to pagan divinities.

you are a kingly priesthood, a holy community, the people adopted as his inherit-ance,[9] the great Church, the Bride adorned for God the Lord. . . .

THE BISHOP

The bishop is the high priest.[10] He is servant of the word and mediator. After God, he teaches you; he is your father who has begotten you by the water (of baptism). He is your leader and guide, the mighty king who leads you to the place of the Almighty.

THE DEACON

The deacon holds the place of Christ; you are to love him.[11]

THE DEACONESS

The deaconess likewise is to be honored by you as the image of the Holy Spirit.[12]

THE PRIESTS

Priests are to represent the apostles for you.

WIDOWS

Widows and orphans are to be revered like the altar.[13]

(ch. 9)

Good Order in the Assembly

At your assemblies in the holy churches, always hold your meetings in an exemplary manner. Arrange the places for the brethren carefully and with all prudence.

---

9. An allusion to 2 Pet. 2:9. On the kingly priesthood of the faithful, see L. Cerfaux, "Regale sacerdotium," Revue des sciences philosophiques et théologiques 28 (1939), pp. 5–39; reprinted in Recueil Lucien Cerfaux 2 (Gembloux, 1954), pp. 283–315.

10. See J. Colson, "L'évêque dans la Didascalie des apôtres," Vie Spirituelle: Supplé-ment 4 (1951), pp. 271–90.

11. Christian tradition liked to think of Christ as the first "deacon," because he had come precisely to serve, diakonein (Mt. 20:28; Mk. 10:45; Lk. 22:27).

12. The Didascalia often speaks of deaconesses, whose institution seems to go back to the dawn of Christianity (see Rom. 16:1; 1 Tim. 3:11 and 5:9-11). Their ministry was primarily one of prayer and charity. They occupied themselves especially with poor women, with the sick, and with pagan female catechumens; they helped the bishop and substituted for him at the baptism of women for the rites of immersion and anointing. See J. Daniélou, "Le ministère des femmes dans l'Eglise primitive," Maison-Dieu, no. 61 (160), pp. 70–96.

13. Polycarp had already called widows "the altar of god" (Letter to the Philippians 4).

THE PLACE OF THE BISHOP AND THE PRIESTS

For the priests, reserve a place in the eastern part of the house, and set the bishop's throne in the midst of them. The priests are to sit with him.

Laymen are to take their place in the remainder of the eastern part of the house.

It is fitting that the priests be placed in the eastern part of the house with the bishops, then the laymen, and finally the women. In this way, when you stand to pray, the leaders will be able to stand first, then the laymen, and finally the women.

You should pray facing the East. For you know that it is written:

> Give thanks to God
> who rides on the heavens of heavens
> on the eastern side.[14]

THE PLACE OF THE DEACONS

As regards the deacons, let one of them stand continually near the offerings for the Eucharist, and let another stand outside near the door and pay attention to those who enter. Then, when you have made the offerings, let them serve together in the church.

If anyone finds himself in a place not his own, let the deacon who is inside take him, make him get up, and lead him to his proper place. . . .

THE PLACE OF THE YOUNG

Young people are to sit apart, if there is room; if not, they are to remain standing.

Those who are older are to sit apart.

THE PLACE OF CHILDREN

Children are to stay on one side, or else their parents are to take them with them, and they are to remain standing.

THE PLACE OF WOMEN

Again: girls too are to be seated apart; if there is no room, they are to remain standing behind the women.

---

14. Ps. 68:33-34. The psalm is cited according to the Septuagint translation (which in turn is followed by the Vulgate); the Hebrew text reads: "Sing to God . . . sing praises to the Lord, to him who rides in the heavens, the ancient heavens." Christian antiquity, as we know, attached great importance to *orientation*, or facing eastward, in prayer (the rising sun was regarded as a symbol of Christ, following Zech. 6:12 and Mal. 4:2). The orientation of prayer entailed the orientation of churches; this practice became general in the East in the fifth century and traditional in the West in the sixth. On this question the reader may consult especially: F. J. Dölger, *Sol salutis: Gebet und Gesang im christlichen Altertum mit besonderer Rücksicht auf die Ostung in Gebet und Liturgie* (Münster, 1925); E. Peterson,

Married women who are still young and have children are to remain standing apart. Older women and widows are to remain seated apart.

THE ROLE OF THE DEACON

The deacon is to watch and see that each person who enters goes to his own place and does not seat himself anywhere else.

In addition, the deacon is to watch that no one drowses or falls asleep, or laughs or makes signs. For it is fitting that in the church everyone should maintain an attitude full of dignity and keep wakeful in mind, so that his ears may be open to the word of the Lord.

THE PLACE OF BRETHREN WHO ARE PASSING THROUGH

If someone, brother or sister, from another community comes, the deacon is to question them and find out whether he is married, whether she is a faithful widow, whether she is a daughter of the Church or belongs to a heretical group. Then he is to lead them to the place and location that are suitable.

THE PLACE OF PRIESTS AND BISHOPS WHO ARE PASSING THROUGH

But if a priest from another community comes, you, the priests, are to welcome him to your place.

And if he is a bishop, he is to sit with the bishop, who is to judge him as worthy as himself and make him share the honor of his place.

And you, O bishop, are to ask him if he will be kind enough to speak to your people, for the exhortations and advice of strangers are very useful.

THE PLACE OF THE POOR

If a poor man or a poor woman comes, whether they are from your own parish or another, especially if they are advanced in years, and there should be no room for them, then make a place for them, O bishop, with all your heart, even if you yourself have to sit on the ground.[15]

You must not make any distinction between persons, if you wish your ministry to be pleasing to God.

(ch. 12)

Fidelity to the Meetings of the Community

When you are teaching, command and exhort the people to be faithful to the assembly of the church. Let them not fail to attend, but let them gather faithfully

---

"La croce e la preghiera verso Oriente," *Ephemerides Liturgicae* 59 (1945), pp. 52–68; C. Vogel, "Versus ad Orientem," *Maison-Dieu*, no. 70 (1962), pp. 67–99.

15. This rule concerning the place of the poor — even if the bishop himself had to sit on the ground! — is inspired by pure gospel tradition and recalls what is said in Jas. 2:2-4.

together. Let no one deprive the Church by staying away; if they do, they deprive the body of Christ of one of its members!

For you must not think only of others but of yourself as well, when you hear the words that our Lord spoke: "Who does not gather with me, scatters" (Mt. 12:30). Since you are the members of Christ, you must not scatter yourselves outside the Church by failing to assemble there. For we have Christ for our Head, as he himself promised and announced, so that "you have become sharers with us." [16]

Do not, then, make light of your own selves, do not deprive our Savior of his members, do not rend, do not scatter his Body!

(ch. 13)

Deacons and Deaconesses

Bishop, get yourself workers to care for the poor, helpers who, with you, may lead (the people) to life. Choose those who are pleasing to you before all the people and make them deacons, a man to carry out the numerous tasks that are necessary, and also a woman for the service of the women.

DEACONESSES

For there are houses to which, because of the pagans, you cannot send a deacon to look after the women, but you can very well send a deaconess.

In many other cases, too, it is necessary to employ a female deaconess. To begin with, when women descend into the water (to receive baptism), it is required that those who thus descend into the water be anointed by the deaconess with the oil of anointing. Where there is no woman, and especially no deaconess, the minister of baptism must himself be the one who anoints the woman being baptized. [17] But if there is a woman present, and above all a deaconess, it is not

---

16. 2 Pet. 1:4. The argument from Scripture is weak, since the text says in fact: "You have become sharers of the divine nature." Yet the teaching has a real splendor about it. It bears witness that the members of the ecclesial community, when they meet together, make up the body of Christ in a special sense and enjoy the presence of the Lord in a privileged way, according to the promise: "Where two or three are gathered in my name, there am I in the midst of them" (Mt. 18:20).

17. The *Apostolic Constitutions* omits this sentence. It is easy to understand that the rites of immersion and anointing posed delicate problems when they involved young girls and women. John Moschus (540?–619), in *The Spiritual Meadow* 3, relates the case of a monk named Conon, who had been ordained a priest especially for the administration of baptism and who found himself acutely troubled by a beautiful young Persian woman to whom he had to give the rites of anointing. To escape further embarrassing situations, he resolved to leave his monastery and take refuge in solitude, but John the Baptist appeared to him and strengthened him. Upon this, Conon went on baptizing for another twelve years without ever being troubled again. See R. de Journel, *Jean Moschus: Le pré spirituel* (SC 12; Paris, 1946), pp. 48–50.

fitting that the women (being baptized) be seen by men. In this case, give an anointing only on the head, at the time of the laying on of hands. This is the way in which formerly the kings and priests were anointed in Israel. This is the way in which you, similarly, at the laying on of hands, are to anoint the heads of those who receive baptism, whether they are men or women. . . .

When the baptized woman comes up out of the water, the deaconess is to receive her and instruct her in purity and holiness, (showing her) that the seal of baptism is unbreakable.

This is the reason for our saying that the service of a woman, a deaconess, is required and necessary. For our Lord and Savior too was served by women deaconesses; these were Mary of Magdala, Mary the mother of James, the mother of Joses, the mother of the sons of Zebedee, as well as other women.[18]

(ch. 16)

DEACONS

Deacons are to imitate the bishop in their behavior. They are to give themselves up completely to their work, not to seek unjust advantages but to be full of enthusiasm for their service.

Their number is to be proportionate to that of the people of the church, so that they can keep everyone in touch and obtain help for them.

To old people who have lost their strength, to brothers and sisters who are afflicted with illness, they are to render willingly the services of which they stand in need.

The woman (deaconess) must be zealous in the service of the women, and the man, the deacon, in the service of the men. He is to be ready to obey the orders of the bishop. Everywhere that he is sent to be of service and to carry a message, he is to be active and painstaking. For each must know his duty and apply himself to fulfilling it.

Be also of one will, one spirit, one soul, even if you are two in body. Realize what the diaconate is, as our Lord and Savior has defined it in the Gospel:

> He from among you
> who wishes to be your master,
> let him be your servant.
> Thus the Son of man did not come
> to be ministered to but to minister

---

18. The *Didascalia* refers to the group of women who were part of Jesus' entourage and assisted (*diēkonoun*) him with their goods (Lk. 8:2-3). The author joins to this group the women listed among the relatives of Jesus (Mt. 13:55; Mk. 6:3). The assimilation of these women to deaconesses undoubtedly goes beyond the data of the Gospels, but the reference to Scripture makes an excellent scriptural foundation, in the view of the author, for the institution of deaconesses.

and to give his life as a ransom
for the many (Mt. 20:26, 28).

(ch. 16)

Doxology

To him who has power and might
to open the ears of your heart,
so that you may receive
the penetrating[19] words of the Lord
in the Gospel and in the teaching
of Jesus Christ of Nazareth,

To him who, in the days of Pontius Pilate
was crucified and who died
to proclaim to Abraham, Isaac, and Jacob
the end of the world
and the coming resurrection of the dead,

To him who rose from the dead
to proclaim to you
and to give you to know
that he is the pledge of the resurrection,

To him who ascended to the heavens
by the power of God, his Father,
and of the Holy Spirit,

To him who sits at the right hand
on the throne of the Almighty,
above the Cherubim,

To him who is to come
with power and with glory
to judge the dead and the living:

To him be dominion and honor, majesty and kingship
as to the Father and to the Holy Spirit,

---

19. Or "sharp" (Achelis and Flemming, p. 145, translate: "the sharp words"). The text recalls Heb. 4:12: "The word of God is living and active, sharper than any two-edged sword, piercing to the division of soul and spirit."

to (God) "who is, who was, and who is coming,"[20]
now and from age to age
and in all eternity!
Amen.

---

20. A stereotyped formula borrowed from the doxologies of the Apocalypse (1:4, 8; 4:6; 11:17). It is inspired by the divine name, "I am he who is" (Ex. 3:14) and emphasizes the eternity of God.

12

The Euchology of Serapion of Thmuis

of Thmuis

(about 350)

SERAPION, BISHOP OF THMUIS

THE MAN

We possess only fragmentary information about the life of Serapion. We know that he had retired to the desert, where he had become one of the favorite disciples of St. Anthony (who lived *ca.* 250–356). Some time before 339 he became bishop of Thmuis, a small place in Lower Egypt. He seems to have taken part in the Council of Sardica in 343 and to have supported the cause of St. Athanasius of Alexandria (295–373) there. About 356 the latter sent him, with four other bishops and three priests, on an embassy to Emperor Constantius to refute the accusations the Arians had brought against him. Athanasius addressed several letters to Serapion, of which one is on the death of Arius,[1] and some theological writings on the Holy Spirit.[2]

We do not know the year in which Serapion died. But since the correspondence of Athanasius dates from the years 356–362, his death must have taken place after 362.

THE WORK

According to St. Jerome, Serapion united to great holiness of life a brilliant intelligence which won him the surname *Scholasticus*, "the Scholar."[3] All that tradition has preserved of his writings, however, are two letters, a polemical work, *Against the Manicheans* — mentioned by St. Jerome; partially restored by Brinkmann in 1894 and edited in its entirety in 1931 — and a *Euchology*.

It is this last work, discovered in 1894 at Mount Athos, that has especially drawn the attention of theologians and liturgists in our time. It is a kind of Ritual containing thirty liturgical prayers. The first twelve were used in the first part of the Sunday synaxis, the part centered on readings and prayer. There follow the anaphora, which is the most precious document of the whole collection, the prayers for the liturgies of baptism and confirmation, a prayer over the oil of the sick, and another for the dead.[4]

---

1. *PG* 25:685–90.
2. *PG* 26:529–676.
3. *De viris illustribus*, 99; G. Bardy, "Sérapion," *Dictionnaire de théologie catholique*, 14:1908–12.
4. These prayers are given here in the order adopted by F. X. Funk, *Didascalia et Constitutiones Apostolorum* 2:158–94.

Serapion undoubtedly left his own mark on more than one of these texts before transcribing it into his *Euchology*; textual analysis and comparison with other formularies enable us to discover some of these revisions. But the fact that these prayers were meant to represent to some extent the official liturgical prayer at Thmuis in the mid-fourth century, and that some of them certainly date from well before that period, can only enhance their value as witness to the faith of the Church.

The Sunday Synaxis

1. First Prayer for Sunday

We pray you, Father of the only-begotten Son,
Lord of all things,
Creator of the created world,
Author of what exists.

Our pure hands
we hold out toward you;
and our spirits
we raise toward you,

We pray your mercy,
your pity and your goodness;
amend us, increase in us
power, faith, and knowledge.

Cast your eyes on us, Lord,
we lay our weaknesses before you.
Grant pardon and mercy to us all.
Have mercy on your people,
show them your goodness,
make them generous, chaste, and pure.

Send the angelic spirits
that your entire people
may be holy and unspotted.

We pray you,
send your Holy Spirit into our souls.
Grant us to understand
the Scriptures that he inspired,

to interpret them clearly and worthily,
so that all the people here present
may draw profit from them,

Through your only-begotten Son, Jesus Christ,
in the Holy Spirit.
Through him, glory to you and power,
now and for ever and ever!
    Amen.

2. Prayer after the Homily

Savior God, God of the universe,
Sovereign and Creator of all things,
Father of the only-begotten Son,
the living and true Image born of you (Heb. 1:3):
you have sent him for the good of the human race;
through him you have called all men
and you have reconciled them.

We pray you for this people:
Send them the Holy Spirit,
that the Lord Jesus may come to visit them,
that he may speak in the spirit of each,
that he may prepare their hearts for faith,
that he may lead their souls to you,
O God of mercy.
Take possession too
of your people in this town,
take possession of your noble flock,

Through your only-begotten Son, Jesus Christ,
in the Holy Spirit.
Through him, glory to you and power,
now and for ever and ever.
    Amen.

3. Prayer for the Catechumens

Lord of the universe, (our) help,
deliverer of the delivered,
Master of those who are saved,
hope of those who are in your hand!

It is you who have taken away iniquity,
who, through your only-begotten Son, have destroyed Satan,
put an end to his undertakings
and delivered those whom he had enchained.

We give you thanks for the catechumens,
whom you have called through your only-begotten Son,
to whom you have given to know you.

For this reason we beg you
to strengthen them in this knowledge,
so "that they may know you,
you the one true God,
and him whom you have sent, Jesus Christ" (Jn. 17:3).

Keep them in your teachings
and in your pure doctrine;
let them progress in it,
let them become worthy of the "bath of regeneration" (Tit. 3:5)
and of your holy mysteries,

Through your only-begotten Son, Jesus Christ,
in the Holy Spirit,
now and for ever and ever.
       Amen.

4. Blessing of the Catechumens

To you, Master, we lift our hands
and we pray you
to stretch out your own divine and life-giving hand
to bless this people.

Before you, eternal Father,[5] through your only-begotten Son,
see, they have bowed their heads.

Let your blessing descend on this people,
the blessing of knowledge and piety,
the blessing of your holy mysteries,

---

5. Serapion likes the title *agenētos* for the Father (*Euchology* 4, 5, 12, 13, 17, 19, 27), which means literally "that which has not had birth or beginning" and which is translated here by "eternal." The *Apostolic Constitutions* (VII, 41, 4; VIII, 6, 9 and 11; VIII, 14, 3; see below, pp. 218, 223, 238) prefers the title *agennētos*, which means literally "not begotten, not created" and which is translated in this book as "uncreated."

Through your only-begotten Son, Jesus Christ.
Through him, glory to you and power,
in the Holy Spirit,
now and for ever and ever.
    Amen.

5. *Litanic Prayer for the People*

We bless you, O God who love mankind,
we set before you our weakness,
we pray you to be our strength.

Pardon our past sins,
forgive us our former faults,
make of us new men,
make of us servants pure and generous.[6]

We consecrate ourselves to you.
Accept us, O God of truth,
accept this people,
that it may be wholly (your) true (people).

Make them live wholly in innocence and uprightness.
Let them be joined to the heavenly spirits,
let them be counted among the angels,
let them all be chosen and holy.

We pray to you for those who believe and acknowledge the Lord Jesus Christ.
May they be strengthened in faith (Col. 2:7), in knowledge, and in doctrine.

We pray to you for all this people. Pardon them all, show yourself, reveal your
light, that all may acknowledge you, eternal Father, together with your
only-begotten Son, Jesus Christ.

We pray to you for all magistrates. May their government be peaceful, for the
tranquillity of the Church.

We pray to you, God of mercies, for free men and for slaves, for men and women,
for the poor and the rich. Show your goodness to all; extend your kindness to
us; have pity on all; guide their steps toward you; give to all the grace of
conversion.

We pray to you for travelers. Give them the angel of peace to accompany them; let

---

6. "Generous" here and "true" at the end of the next stanza translate the same Greek
word *gnēsios*, which means "of (good) birth," "legitimate" (Titus and Timothy are *true* sons
of the faith: Tit. 1:4; 1 Tim. 1:2); whence the meaning "noble," "generous" (in the old sense
of "nobly descended").

no harm befall them, let them end their voyage and their journeying in great security.

We pray to you for the afflicted, the captives, and the poor. Strengthen them all, save them from their bonds, deliver them from their wretchedness, console them all, you who are consolation and strength.

We pray to you for the sick. Give them health, relieve their illness, grant them perfect health of body and soul.

> You are Savior and Benefactor,
> you are Lord and King of all!

> To you we make our prayer for all
> through your only-begotten Son, Jesus Christ.

> Through him, glory to you and power,
> in the Holy Spirit,
> now and for ever and ever.
>   Amen.

6. Blessing of the People

> May the pure and living hand,
> the hand of the only-begotten Son,
> the hand that removes all evils,
> that strengthens and fortifies all that is holy,
> be stretched out over the bowed heads of this people!

> May this people be blessed
> with the blessing of the Spirit,
> with the blessing of heaven,
> with the blessing of the prophets and the apostles.

> May the bodies of all be blessed
> for purity and chastity;
> may their souls be blessed
> for understanding, knowledge, and the mysteries.

> May all together be blessed
> through your only-begotten Son, Jesus Christ.
> Through him, glory to you and power,
> in the Holy Spirit,
> now and for ever and ever.
>   Amen.

7. *Prayer for the Sick*

We pray you, Guardian and Lord,
Maker of the body and Creator of the soul,
you who fashion man,
who administer and govern,
who save the whole human race,
who reconcile and bring peace
because of your love for mankind!

Be favorable, Lord,
succor and heal all the sick,
control their illnesses,
relieve those who languish.
Glorify your holy name
through your only-begotten Son, Jesus Christ.

Through him, glory to you and power,
in the Holy Spirit,
now and for ever and ever.
 Amen.

8. *Blessing of the Sick*

Lord, God of mercies,
deign to stretch out your hands:
in your kindness, heal all the sick,
in your kindness, make them worthy of health,
deliver them from their present sickness;
in the name of your only-begotten Son, grant them recovery;
let this holy name be their remedy
for health and restoration.
Through him, glory to you and power,
in the Holy Spirit,
now and for ever and ever.
 Amen.

9. *Prayer for the Harvests*

Creator of heaven and earth,
who adorn the heaven with the choir of stars
and illuminate it with sparkling points of light,
who load the earth with fruits

for the use of men:
in your kindness, you grant
to the human race you created
to rejoice in the brilliance and clarity of the stars
and to be nourished on the fruits of the earth.

We pray you, give us
most abundant and fertilizing rains;
grant also that the earth may produce fruits
in great plenty,
because of your love for mankind
and because of your good will.

Be mindful of those who call on you.
Honor your one, holy, catholic Church,
hear our prayers and supplications,
and bless the whole earth
through your only-begotten Son, Jesus Christ.

Through him, glory to you and power,
in the Holy Spirit,
now and for ever and ever.
    Amen.

10. Prayer for the Church

Lord, God of the ages,
God of the heavenly spirits,[7]
God of pure souls
and of all who call on you
in all sincerity and purity,
you who in heaven manifest yourself
and make yourself known to the pure spirits,
you to whom on earth hymns are sung
and who dwell in the catholic Church,
you whom the holy angels and pure souls serve,
you who made of heaven a living choir
to glorify and praise the truth!

Make this Church to be living and pure,
grant her to possess divine powers,
to have at her service the pure angels
so that she may be able to celebrate you purely.
We pray you for all the people of this Church.

---

7. Literally: "(spirits) endowed with reason."

To all, grant your favor,
to all, reconciliation,
to all, pardon of their sins.
Grant them henceforth to sin no more.
Be a rampart for them
and destroy all temptation.

Have pity on men, women, and children.
Manifest yourself to all,
that knowledge of you "may be graven on their hearts."[8]

Through your only-begotten Son, Jesus Christ.
Through him, glory to you and power,
in the Holy Spirit,
now and for ever and ever.
    Amen.

11. Litanic Prayer for Clergy and People

We call on you, Savior and Lord, God of all flesh, and Lord of every spirit, you who are blessed and dispense all blessing.

Make holy our bishop, preserve him from all temptation, give him wisdom and knowledge, grant him to make progress in knowledge of you.

We pray you also for those who are priests with him. Make them holy, give them wisdom, knowledge, and right doctrine; grant them to dispense your holy teaching rightly and without reproach.

Make the deacons holy too. Let them be pure in heart and body, that they may be able to fulfill their ministry with a pure conscience and present the sacred body and blood (of the Lord).

We entreat you also for the subdeacons, the readers, and the interpreters.[9] Be consoler to all the ministers of the Church; to all of them grant pity, mercy, and spiritual growth.

We pray you for hermits and those who live in virginity. Let them finish their race undefiled, their life with perseverance; let them be able to pass all their days in purity and holiness.

Have pity also on all who are married and on all men, women, and children. Give your blessing to all so that they may progress and improve, so that they may be found among the living and elect.

---

8. An allusion to the "new covenant" (Jer. 31:33; Heb. 8:10), in which God is going to engrave his law on the hearts of the faithful.

9. That is, those who translate the readings and homilies for the faithful who would not have heard them in their own native language.

Through your only-begotten Son, Jesus Christ.
Through him, glory to you and power,
in the Holy Spirit,
now and for ever and ever.
    Amen.

12. Prayer at the Genuflection

Father of the only-begotten Son,
full of goodness and mercy,
you who love men and love souls,
Benefactor of all who turn to you,

Hear our entreaty,
grant us knowledge and faith,
piety and holiness.

Curb all passion and all sensuality,
every fault of your people,
grant them all to become pure.
Reconcile them and pardon all their offenses.

For it is before you, eternal Father,
through your only-begotten Son,
that we bend our knees.
Give us a holy spirit, a perfect help,
grant us to seek you and to love you,
to examine and search out your divine words.

Give us your hand, O Master, and lift us up.
Raise us, O God of mercies!
Let our gaze be lifted toward you,
let our eyes be opened!

In your goodness, give us confidence,
do not let us be put to shame,
to be covered with confusion,
or to bring judgment on ourselves.

Cancel "the decree which is against us,"[10]

---

10. An allusion to Col. 2:14. God has canceled "the bond which stood against us . . .
this he set aside, nailing it to the cross," thus manifesting the reality of the pardon he has
granted us through the sacrifice of Christ.

write our names in "the book of life,"[11]
count us among your holy prophets
and among your apostles,

Through your only-begotten Son, Jesus Christ.
Through him, glory to you and power,
in the Holy Spirit,
now and for ever and ever.
    Amen.

The Eucharistic Liturgy

13. Prayer of the Anaphora [12]

PREFACE

It is right and just to praise you,
to celebrate you, to glorify you,
eternal Father of the only-begotten Son, Jesus Christ.

We praise you, eternal God,
inscrutable, indescribable,
incomprehensible to every created nature.

We praise you, who are known to the only-begotten Son,
you whom he reveals and interprets,
whom he makes known to created natures.

We praise you, you who know the Son
and reveal his glory to the saints,
you whom the Son you have begotten knows,
you whom he shows and interprets to the saints.

We praise you, invisible Father
who give immortality.
You are the source of life, the source of light,
the source of every grace and every truth.
You love men, you love the poor,
you reconcile yourself with all,

---

11. See Phil. 4:3; Apoc. 13:8.
12. See B. Capelle, "L'Anaphore de Sérapion: Essai d'exégèse," *Le Muséon* 59 (1946), pp. 425–43; reprinted in his *Travaux liturgiques* 2 (Louvain, 1962), pp. 344–59.

you draw all to you
through the coming of your beloved Son.

We pray you, make living men of us.
Give us the Spirit of light
"that we may know you, the True One,
and him whom you have sent, Jesus Christ" (Jn. 17:3).
Give us the Holy Spirit that we may be able
to proclaim and tell forth your indescribable mysteries!

May the Lord Jesus speak in us
and also the Holy Spirit.
May he celebrate you with hymns through us!

For you are above every Principality,
Power, Force, and Domination,
above every name that is named
in this age as in the age to come.

SANCTUS

You are attended by thousands upon thousands
and myriads upon myriads
of Angels and Archangels,
of Thrones and Dominations,
of Principalities and Powers.

Beside you stand
the two august Seraphim with six wings:
two to cover their face,
two to cover their feet,
two with which to fly.
They sing your holiness.
With theirs, accept also
our acclamations of your holiness:
Holy, holy, holy is the Lord Sabaoth!
Heaven and earth are filled with your glory.
Heaven is filled, earth is filled with your wonderful glory!

THE ACCOUNT OF THE INSTITUTION

Lord[13] of the Powers, fill this sacrifice too

---

13. This paragraph (*Lord of the Powers. . . . holy body*) is undoubtedly an addition to the original text. It is dogmatic in character but composed on an ancient model. The expression "figure of the body" is an archaism that is found again in the anaphora of St.

with your power and your participation.
For it is to you that we have offered[14]
this living sacrifice, this bloodless offering.
It is to you that we have offered this bread,
figure of the body of your only-begotten Son.
This bread is a figure of the holy body.

For the Lord Jesus, the night when he was betrayed,
took bread, broke it,
and gave it to his disciples saying:
"Take and eat, this is my body,
which is broken for you
for the forgiveness of sins."

For this reason,[15] we too,
celebrating the memorial of his death,
have offered this bread, and we pray:
Through this sacrifice, reconcile us all to yourself,
be favorable to us, O God of truth.
For just as this bread,
once scattered upon the hills,
has been brought together and become one,
so too, deign to gather your Church
from every people, from every land,
from every town, village, and house,
and make of her a single Church, living and catholic.

We offer too the cup, figure of the blood.
For the Lord Jesus, after the meal,
took the cup and said to his disciples:
"Take and drink,
this is the New Testament,
that is, my blood poured out for you,
for the forgiveness of sins."

Ambrose: "This offering . . . which is the figure of the body and blood of our Lord Jesus Christ" (*De sacramentis* IV, 5, 21); see B. Botte, *Ambroise de Milan: Des sacrements, Des mystères* (SC 25bis; Paris, 1961), p. 114.

14. The perfect tense in "we have offered" seems to be a deliberate modification. Serapion probably emended the text he was using in order to remind the hearers of the action in which the gifts were offered on the altar.

15. Serapion has boldly introduced into the original text of the account of institution a little anamnesis and a section borrowed from the *Didache* (*For this reason. . . . living and catholic*). This insertion is a prayer for the unity of the Church, from which the Arian heresy had snatched so many of the faithful "from every country, town, village, and house."

For this reason we too have offered
the cup, a figure of the blood.

INVOCATION OF THE WORD [16]

O God of truth,
may your holy Word come down upon this bread,
that it may become the body of the Word,
and upon this cup,
that it may become the blood of the Truth.
Grant that all who communicate
may receive a life-giving remedy,
that will heal every weakness in them
and strengthen them for all progress and all virtue;
let it not be a cause, O God of truth,
of condemnation, confusion, or shame.

MEMENTO OF THE LIVING

For we call on you, O eternal (God),
through your only-begotten Son, in the Holy Spirit:
Take pity on this people,
judge them worthy of progress.
Send your Angels to this people,
to help them triumph over the Evil One
and to strengthen your Church.

MEMENTO OF THE DEAD

We pray you also for all the dead
who have fallen asleep
and whom we now mention.

After recalling the names:

Sanctify these souls, for you know them all.
Sanctify those who have fallen asleep in the Lord.
Number them with your holy Powers,
give them a place and a dwelling in your kingdom.

---

16. It is surprising to read here an invocation of the Word instead of the traditional epiclesis addressed to the Holy Spirit. This anomaly is due "to the innovating genius of the bishop of Thmuis" (Capelle, *art. cit.*, p. 443), who is fond of emphasizing the sanctifying action of the incarnate Word. We glimpse here the friend of St. Athanasius, as well as the anti-Arian struggle. (The Fathers, as we know, liked to use the sanctifying action of the Spirit as the basis for proving his divinity. Serapion uses the same argument to prove the divinity of the Word.) The *Euchology* contains other prayers (19, 22, 25, 29) that ask for the descent of the Word, prayers traditionally applied to the Holy Spirit.

FINAL PRAYER AND DOXOLOGY

Accept the thanksgiving of your people.
Bless those who have presented to you
these offerings and thanksgivings.
Give all this people health,
prosperity, and happiness,
all the blessings of soul and body,

Through your only-begotten Son, Jesus Christ,
in the Holy Spirit,
as he was, as he is and will be,
from all generations
and for ever and ever!
     Amen.

14. *Prayer for the Breaking of the Bread*

Make us worthy also to participate in you,[17]
O God of truth,
and grant that our bodies may progress in purity,
our souls in understanding and knowledge.
Give us wisdom, O God of mercies,
through receiving the body and blood (of Christ).

Glory to you and power,
through the only-begotten Son,
in the Holy Spirit,
now and for ever and ever!
     Amen.

15. *Blessing of the People after the Breaking of the Bread*

I lift my hand over this people
and I pray you to stretch out the hand of truth
and to bless this people here
in the name of your love for men,
O God of mercies,
and in the name of the mysteries that we celebrate.

---

17. "To participate in you": literally, "of your participation." The word for participation, *koinōnia*, is the technical term for participation in God (1 Cor. 1:9 NEB: God "called you to share in the life of his Son"). It is also the word for "communion," which is participation in the body and blood of Christ (1 Cor. 10:16: "participation in the blood of Christ. . . . participation in the body of Christ").

Let the hand of love and power,
the hand of wisdom, purity, and all holiness
bless this people and keep them
so that they may progress and improve,

Through your only-begotten Son, Jesus Christ,
in the Holy Spirit,
now and for ever and ever.
    Amen.

16. Prayer after the Communion of the People

We give you thanks, O Master,
for having called those who were in error,
for having reconciled those who had sinned.
You passed over the threat that weighed upon us:
through your love for men, you withdrew it;
through conversion, you abandoned it;
through your knowledge, you rejected it.

We give you thanks
for having made us "to participate in the body and blood" (1 Cor. 10:10).
Bless us and bless this people!
Grant us to have a share in the body and blood!

Through your only-begotten Son.
Through him, glory to you and power,
in the Holy Spirit,
now and for ever and ever.
    Amen.

17. Blessing of Oil and Water

In the name of your only-begotten Son, Jesus Christ,
we bless these creatures.[18]
We invoke the name of him who suffered,
who was crucified, who rose from the dead
and sits at the right hand of the Eternal,
on this water and this oil.
Give these creatures the power to heal,
let them drive out every fever,

---

18. For the significance of these blessings see above, p. 132.

every demon and every sickness.
Let them become for those who use them [19]
a healing and reviving remedy,
in the name of your only-begotten Son, Jesus Christ.

Through him, glory to you and power,
in the Holy Spirit,
now and for ever and ever.
    Amen.

18. *Laying on of Hands after the Blessing of Oil and Water*

God of truth who love men,
keep your people in the participation
in the body and the blood.

Let their bodies be living bodies,
their souls be pure souls.

Grant your blessing to keep them
in the participation (in the body and the blood),

To procure safety for them
thanks to the Eucharist we have celebrated. [20]

Make them happy, all of them together,
and place them among your elect,

Through your only-begotten Son, Jesus Christ,
in the Holy Spirit,
now and for ever and ever.
    Amen.

Liturgy of Baptism, Confirmation, and Holy Orders

19. *Consecration of the Baptismal Waters*

King and Lord of all things,
Creator of the universe,

---

19. *For those who use them*; literally: "through the act of drinking (this water) and through anointing."

20. The translation here is uncertain; literally: "in the stability (or security) of the accomplished Eucharist."

through the incarnation [21] of your only-begotten Son, Jesus Christ,
you have given to all created nature the grace of salvation;
you redeemed your creation
through the coming of your unutterable Word.
Look down now from the height of heaven
and cast your eyes [22] on these waters,
fill them with the Holy Spirit.

Let your unutterable Word be in them,
let him transform their power.
Let him give them the power to be fruitful,
let him fill them with your grace,
so that the mystery which is to be accomplished
may bear fruit in those who will be regenerated
and may fill with your divine grace
all those who go down (into the baptismal font)
and are baptized.

You who love men, be gracious,
take pity on those you have created,
save your creation, the work of your right hand.
Transfigure all those who are going to be reborn
with your divine and indescribable beauty.
Transfigured and regenerated,
let them thus be saved
and "judged worthy of your kingdom" (2 Thess. 1:5).

Just as the Word, your only-begotten Son,
by descending into the waters of the Jordan
bestowed sanctification upon them,
so let him now descend into these waters
to make them holy and spiritual,
so that the baptized
may no longer be "flesh and blood," [23]
but may become "spiritual."
Let them be able to adore you, the eternal Father,
through Jesus Christ, in the Holy Spirit.

---

21. Literally: "the descent" (*katabasis*).
22. An allusion to Ps. 80:15.
23. See Jn. 3:6: "That which is born of the flesh is flesh, that which is born of the Spirit is spirit." On the basis of this text Didymus observes: "The man who has not received baptism is fleshly, that is, he does not yet participate in the divine light. . . . But he who has been baptized is 'spiritual,' that is, he participates in immortal life" (*De Trinitate* II, 12 [PG 39:673A]).

Through him, glory to you and power,
for ever and ever.
> Amen.

20. *Prayer of Exorcism*

We pray you, O God of truth,
for your servant here.
We ask you to make him worthy
of the divine mystery and your unutterable regeneration.

For it is to you who love men
that we offer him,
it is to you that we consecrate him.

According to your grace, let him share in this regeneration,
let him no longer be under the influence
of any baleful and wicked spirit;
but let him serve you at all times,
let him keep your commandments,
let the Word, your only-begotten Son, guide him.

Through him, glory to you and power,
in the Holy Spirit,
now and for ever and ever!
> Amen.

21. *Prayer after the Renunciation*

Almighty Lord, mark with your seal
the assent your servant here
has now given to you.

Keep firm his moral life and his conduct.
Let him not be henceforth the slave of evil
but serve the God of truth.

Let him submit himself, to the very end,
to you, the Creator of the universe,
and show himself a true (son).[24]

---

24. That is, a legitimate (*gnēsios*) son; see note 6 above.

Through your only-begotten Son, Jesus Christ.
Through him, glory to you and power,
in the Holy Spirit,
now and for ever and ever!
    Amen.

22. *Prayer for the Anointing of the Catechumens*[25]

O Master, who love men
and who love souls,
God of mercy, pity, and truth,
we call on you for those who come to follow you,[26]
and we entrust them to the promises of your only-begotten Son,
who said: "Whose sins you shall forgive,
they shall be forgiven them" (Jn. 20:23).
We mark with this anointing these men and women
who present themselves for this divine regeneration.

We beseech our Lord Jesus Christ
to give them the power that heals and strengthens.

Let him manifest himself through this anointing,
let him remove from body, soul, or spirit
every sign of sin, of iniquity,
or the devil's action.

Let him by his grace
grant them forgiveness.
Freed from sin, let them live for righteousness![27]
Now that they have become a new creation through this anointing
and have been purified by this bath and renewed by the Spirit (Tit. 3:5),
let them have the power henceforth to overcome
all the hostile forces ranged against them
and all the deceits of this life.
Let them be gathered and reunited to the flock
of the Lord and of our Savior Jesus Christ.
Let them share with the saints the promised inheritance!

---

25. See the anointing at the exorcism in the *Apostolic Tradition*, p. 141 above.
26. That is, who become disciples of Christ.
27. Compare with Rom. 6:18: "Having been set free from sin, (you) have become slaves of righteousness." Baptism delivers the neophytes from enslavement to sin but introduces them into a new "service," that of righteousness, a service that bears fruit in holiness and leads to eternal life (Rom. 6:22).

Through him, glory to you and power,
in the Holy Spirit,
now and for ever and ever!
    Amen.

23. *Prayer after the Anointing*

You who love men, Benefactor,
Savior of all who turn to you:

Be gracious to this servant of yours;
let your right hand lead him to regeneration.

Let your only-begotten Son, the Word,
bring him to the (baptismal) font.

Let his new birth be honored,
let your grace not be fruitless.

Let your holy Word be at his side,
let your Holy Spirit be with him,
let him repel and put to flight every temptation.

Through your only-begotten Son, Jesus Christ,
glory to you and power,
now and for ever and ever.
    Amen.

24. *Prayer for the Neophytes after Baptism*

God, O God of truth, Creator of the universe
and Lord of all creation,
fill your servant here with your blessing.
Make him share in the angelic powers,
so that henceforth he who has had a part
in your divine and profitable grace,
may be no longer "flesh" but "spirit" (Jn. 3:6).
Keep him for yourself to the very end,
O Creator of all things,

Through your only-begotten Son, Jesus Christ.
Through him, glory to you and power,
in the Holy Spirit,
now and for ever and ever!
    Amen.

Confirmation

25. *Prayer for the Confirmed*[28]

God of the (heavenly) powers,
Help of every soul who turns to you
and places himself under the powerful hand
of your only-begotten Son, we call on you:
By the divine and invisible power
of the Lord and our Savior Jesus Christ,
carry out through this oil your divine and heavenly work.

Those who have been baptized receive the anointing,
(they are marked) with the impress of the sign
of the saving cross of the only-begotten Son.
By this cross Satan and every hostile power
have been defeated and are led captive[29]
in the triumphal procession.

Regenerated and renewed
by the bath of the new birth,
let these here also share
in the gifts of the Holy Spirit.

Strengthened by the seal,
let them remain "steadfast and immovable" (1 Cor. 15:58),
sheltered from all attack and pillaging,
subjected neither to insult nor to aggression.

Let them live to the very end
in faith and the knowledge of the truth,
in expectation of the hope of heavenly life
and of the eternal promises
of the Lord and our Savior Jesus Christ.

---

28. This prayer has the title: "Prayer over the oil of the postbaptismal anointings." The reference is surely to the postbaptismal anointing that accompanies confirmation (see n. 49, p. 142, above). The neophyte is "under the powerful hand of your only-begotten Son," that is, he has received the laying on of hands and has been marked with the "impress of the sign of the saving cross."

29. The verb *ethriambeuthē* means, in the active voice, "to triumph over" and hence "to lead (captive) in the triumphal procession." There is an allusion here to Col. 2:15: Christ "got rid of the Sovereignties and the Powers, and paraded them in public, behind him in his triumphal procession (*thriambeusas*)" (Jerusalem Bible).

Through him, glory to you and power,
in the Holy Spirit,
now and for ever and ever.
Amen.

Ordination Prayers

26. *Laying on of Hands for the Ordination of Deacons*

Father of the only-begotten Son, who sent your Son, and who arranged the things of the earth with wisdom,

who gave rules and orders to your Church for the profit and the salvation of the flock,

who chose bishops, priests, and deacons to serve your catholic Church,

who through your only-begotten Son chose seven deacons and according to your grace gave them the Holy Spirit:[30]

Appoint also (your servant) here to be a deacon of your catholic Church.

Give him the Spirit of knowledge and discernment so that in the midst of your holy people he may be able to serve[31] in this ministry in a pure and untarnished manner.

Through your only-begotten Son, Jesus Christ,
in the Holy Spirit,
now and for ever and ever!
Amen.

27. *Laying on of Hands for the Ordination of Priests*

We raise our hands over this man, O Master, God of heaven, Father of your only-begotten Son, and we pray you:

Let the Spirit of truth dwell in him.

According to your grace, grant him understanding, knowledge, and a good heart.

Let the divine Spirit be with him so that he may be able to administer your people, be the ambassador of your divine words, and reconcile the people to you, O eternal God.

According to your grace, through the Spirit of Moses you have poured out the Holy Spirit upon the elect: grant to this (man) too, through the Spirit of your

---

30. See the institution of the seven in Acts 6:1-6.
31. The text plays on the double meaning of the verb *diakonein*, which means both "to serve" and "to be a deacon."

only-begotten Son, the Holy Spirit in graces of wisdom, knowledge, and right faith
so that he may be able to serve you with a pure conscience.

> Through your only-begotten Son, Jesus Christ.
> Through him, glory to you and power,
> in the Holy Spirit,
> now and for ever and ever.
>> Amen.

28. *Laying on of Hands for the Consecration of a Bishop*

You who sent the Lord Jesus to buy back the whole world,

you who, through him, chose the apostles and from age to age have ordained
holy bishops, O God of truth:

Make your (servant) here a living bishop, a holy bishop in the succession of
the apostles.

Give him the grace of the divine Spirit that you have granted to all the true
servants, to the prophets and the patriarchs.

Render him worthy to feed your flock; let him abide in the episcopate without
reproach or fault.

> Through your only-begotten Son, Jesus Christ.
> Through him, glory to you and power,
> in the Holy Spirit,
> now and for ever and ever.
>> Amen.

Prayers for the Sick and the Dead

29. *Prayer over the Oil of the Sick, over Bread and Water*

> We call on you,
> who possess all authority and power,
> you who are "the Savior of all men" (1 Tim. 4:10),
> the Father of our Lord and Savior Jesus Christ.

> We pray you to send
> from the height of heaven (where your) only-begotten Son (reigns),
> a power of healing into this oil.
> In those who receive anointing
> or make use of these creatures,
> let it put to flight "every disease and every infirmity";[32]

---

32. Mk. 4:23; 9:35; 10:1.

let it be a counter-poison against every demon,
let it expel every unclean spirit
and drive away every wicked spirit;
let it eradicate every fever
and shivering and every weakness;
let it obtain good grace and forgiveness of sins,
remedy of life and salvation, health and wholeness
of soul, body, and spirit,
and full vitality.

Let every satanic power, Lord,
every demon, every plot of the Adversary,
every plague and every torment,
every suffering and every pain,
every blow, shock, and shadow,
dread your holy name
that we now invoke,
and the name of your only-begotten Son.
Let them depart from your servants
inwardly and outwardly,
so that his name may be sanctified
who was crucified for us,
who was raised up,
who "bore our diseases and our infirmities" (Mt. 8:8),
Jesus Christ, who will come
"to judge the living and the dead" (1 Tim. 1:17).

Through him, glory to you and power,
in the Holy Spirit,
now and for ever and ever.
     Amen.

30. Prayer for a Dead Person

O God, who possess power over life and death,
"God of the spirits and Lord of all flesh" (Num. 16:22),
God who give death and life,
who "lead to the gates of the lower world
and bring back again:"[33]

You create man's spirit in him;
you gather and give rest to the souls of the saints;

---

33. An allusion to Wis. 16:13.

you change, you transform,
you transfigure your creatures
according as it is just and profitable.
You alone are incorruptible, unchanging, and eternal!

We pray you for the sleep
and the repose of this man (or: woman), your servant.
Refresh his soul and his spirit
in the places of pasture, in the dwellings of rest,[34]
with Abraham, Isaac, Jacob, and all the saints.

As for his body, raise it
on the day you have appointed
according to your sure promises.
Grant it, in your holy pastures,
the share of the inheritance that belongs to it.

Do not remember his faults and sins.
Grant that his death be peaceful and blessed.

Heal the sadness of those who live on
through your consoling Spirit.
Grant us all a happy end.

Through your only-begotten Son, Jesus Christ.
Through him, glory to you and power,
in the Holy Spirit,
for ever and ever!
    Amen.

---

34. An allusion to Ps. 23:2.

13

The Strasbourg Papyrus

(4th–5th century)

THE STRASBOURG PAPYRUS

The University Library at Strasbourg contains, under the number Gr 254, several much-mutilated fragments of papyrus which on examination prove to be part of the so-called Alexandrian Anaphora of St. Mark.

The writing dates from the 4th–5th century. In their analysis of this document, M. Andrieu and P. Collomp write: "Until now the Liturgy of St. Mark has been known only through certain late manuscripts. Our manuscript is perhaps seven or eight centuries older. Moreover, it is itself only a copy, already altered, and the text that it contains goes back even earlier. It would not be rash to claim that this version of the Anaphora of St. Mark was already circulating in the time of St. Athanasius."[1]

PREFACE[2]

> *It is truly right and just*
> *to sing of you and celebrate you,*
> to bless you *and adore you* day and night. . . .
> *You created the heavens* and all that they con*tain,*
> *the earth and all that it encloses,*
> the sea and the rivers *and all that people them.*
> You created man *in* your im*age* and likeness.
> You created the universe through your wisdom,
> your true Light,
> your Son Jesus Christ,
> our Lord and Sav*ior.*
> Through him and with him
> and with the Holy Spirit
> we offer you in thanksgiving
> this spiritual oblation,
> this bloodless sacrifice,
> that all peoples offer you,

---

1. "Fragments sur papyrus de l'anaphore de saint Marc," *Revue des sciences religieuses* 8 (1928), p. 514.

2. The passages in italics represent a conjectural emendation based on more recent documents.

from the rising of the sun to its setting, from north to south,
for your name is great among the nations
and in every place they offer incense to your holy name,
a pure offering,[3] a sacrifice and oblation. . . .

PRAYER OF INTERCESSION

We pray and beseech you:

Be mindful of your Church, one, holy, and catholic, of all peoples and of all your fold.

Confirm in our hearts the peace that comes from heaven, but give us also, according to your grace, peace in this life.

Give to the *king* of the earth (to keep in his heart) thoughts of peace toward us and toward your holy name. . . .

We pray you, Lord, to keep the fruits of the earth for the sowing and the harvest, for the sake of the poor among *your peo*ple, for the sake of all of us who call upon *your* name, of all those who hope in you.

(Remember) those who have fallen asleep. Give rest to their souls.

Remember those whom we call to mind today, those who names we *call* out, as well as those whom we do not name. . . .

(Remember) our *holy* fathers and the bishops everywhere who profess the true faith.

Grant us to have part and inheritance . . . in the glorious community of your holy prophets, apostles, and martyrs. . . .[4]

Through our Lord and Savior.
Through him, glory to you,
for ever and ever.
Amen.

---

3. An adaptation of Mal. 1:11.
4. The four following lines are illegible.

14

The Apostolic Constitutions

(about 380)

THE APOSTOLIC CONSTITUTIONS

The *Apostolic Constitutions* is the most extensive liturgical and canonical compilation of antiquity. It purports to give the decrees that Pope Clement of Rome supposedly received from the apostles and sent out "to the bishops and priests."[1] In fact the work is apocryphal. The author has made use of documents already in existence and ascribed his work to Clement in order to give it greater authority.

In Books I–VI he has used the *Didascalia of the Apostles* as his source.[2]

Book VII has two parts. The first is an expansion of the *Didache*;[3] the second is a euchology grouping together some ancient prayers.

Book VIII has for its source the *Apostolic Tradition* of Hippolytus of Rome.[4] It contains formulas for ordinations. It is also the most interesting part of the whole collection, since in describing the ceremonies for the consecration of a bishop, the author has inserted the prayers of the Mass, the so-called Clementine Liturgy.

The work saw the light of day about 380 in Syria or at Constantinople.

The orthodoxy of the author is not entirely above suspicion. Some of his formulas are tinged with Arianism. For this reason the work was condemned at the Council *In Trullo* (691–92) as "falsified by heretics" and has exerted no marked influence in the history of the Church. However, if these "falsifications," which are easily recognized, are omitted, the work remains a valuable witness to the liturgy of the fourth century.

Here I have used principally the prayers of the euchology in Book VII and the liturgy of the "Clementine" Mass in Book VIII.

VARIOUS PRAYERS

THE LORD'S DAY

On the day of the resurrection of the Lord, which we call "the Lord's Day,"

---

1. On Clement, see above, pp. 81–83.
2. See pp. 167–90.
3. See pp. 73–77.
4. See pp. 123–53.

215

you must always gather to give thanks[5] to God and to bless him for all the benefits he has heaped upon us through Christ, by rescuing us from the bonds of ignorance and error.

Let your sacrifice be spotless and pleasing to God, who has said of his ecumenical Church:[6]

> "In every place, they will present to me
> incense and a pure offering.
> For I am a great king,
> says the Lord Almighty,
> and my name is wonderful among the nations" (Mal. 1:11, 14).

(VII, 30, 1-2)

Our Eternal Savior

> Our eternal Savior and King of gods,
> who alone are all-powerful and Lord,
> God of the whole universe,
> God of our holy and spotless fathers
> who have gone before us,
> God of Abraham, of Isaac, of Jacob,
> merciful and compassionate,
> patient and rich in mercies:[7]
>
> Before you every heart is bared
> and every secret thought is uncovered.
> The souls of the just cry out to you,
> in you the saints hope and trust.
>
> Father of those who are without reproach,
> you listen to those who call on you in uprightness,
> you hear even silent appeals.
> Your providence indeed reaches
> even to the heart of man,
> and your knowledge searches the thoughts of each.
> In every region of the earth,
> the incense of prayers and supplications
> rises to you!
>
> You made this world an arena
> (in which we struggle) for righteousness;[8]

---

5. The verb used (eucharistein) signifies the celebration of the Eucharist, which is preeminently the Church's sacrifice of thanksgiving.

6. That is, universal Church.

7. See Ex. 34:6-7; Jl. 2:13.

8. An allusion to 1 Cor. 9:24-25, where Paul compares Christian life to a race in the stadium.

but you have opened the gate of mercy to all.
You have shown every man,
by inborn knowledge and natural judgment,
and by the proclamation of the Law,
that the possession of riches is not eternal,
that the splendor of beauty does not last,
that physical strength vanishes away,
that everything is smoke and emptiness.[9]

All that abides is the consciousness of a pure faith.
With the truth it penetrates
even the very depths of heaven
and takes possession of the joys to be.
Even before it has received,
thanks to the resurrection,
the promise of a new birth,
the soul exults in the joy of hope.

For, from the beginning, when our father Abraham
undertook to walk in the way of truth,
you revealed yourself to him and guided him,
you taught him the true nature of the present age.
His faith preceded his knowledge,
and the covenant accompanied his faith.
For you said to him:
"I will multiply your descendants
like the stars in the heavens
like the sand of the seashore" (Gen. 13:16; 22:27).

So too, in giving him Isaac,
whose life, according to your plan,
was to be like his,
you proclaimed yourself his God, saying:
"I will be your God
and the God of your descendants after you" (Gen. 17:19).

So too again, when our father Jacob
set out for Mesopotamia,
you showed him the Messiah and told him:
"See, I am with you.
I will multiply and increase your posterity" (Gen. 26:3; 17:7).

To Moses also, your faithful servant,

---

9. An allusion to Sir. 1:2.

you said, in the vision of the bush:
"I am who I am.
Such is my name, and all generations
shall remember it" (Ex. 3:14, 15).

Defender of the descendants of Abraham,
blessed be you through the ages!

(VII, 33, 2-7)

We Give You Thanks

We give you thanks, all-powerful Lord,
for all your benefits.
You have not removed from us
your kindnesses and your mercies,
but you save from generation to generation,
you rescue, you come to our help,
and you protect. . . .

For all your benefits, to you (Father),
glory and veneration,
through Jesus Christ,
now and always and for ever!
Amen.

(VII, 38, 1 and 8)

Profession of Faith for Future Neophytes

I believe and I have been baptized,
in the one, the uncreated,[10] the only true God almighty, Father of Christ,
who created and made the universe, and from whom all things come,
and in Jesus Christ the Lord, his only-begotten Son, "first-born of every creature" (Col. 1:15),
who was begotten, not created, before the ages, according to the Father's good pleasure,
through whom all things were made, those in the heavens and those on the earth, the visible and the invisible;
in the last times he came down from heaven, took flesh, was born of Mary, the holy Virgin;
he lived a holy life according to the law of his God and Father,
he was crucified under Pontius Pilate and died for us,
and after his passion he was raised from the dead on the third day;
he ascended into heaven and sits at the right hand of the Father;

---

10. Literally: "not begotten" (*agennētos*); see n. 5, p. 186.

he will come again in glory at the consummation of the age, to judge the living
and the dead, for his kingdom has no end.

I have been baptized also in the Holy Spirit, the Paraclete, who assists all the
saints from the beginning of the world,
  whom the Father sent to the apostles, in accordance with the promise of our
Savior and Lord Jesus Christ.
  and (whom he has sent) since then to all who believe in the holy, catholic, and
apostolic Church,

  and in the resurrection of the flesh,
  in the forgiveness of sins,
  in the kingdom of heaven and in the life of the age to come.

(VII, 41, 4–8)

Confirmation [11]

PRAYER OF ANOINTING

When (the bishop) has administered baptism in the name of the Father, of the
Son, and of the Holy Spirit, he will anoint (the neophyte) with oil. He is to say:

  Lord God, uncreated and without equal,
  Lord of all things,
  who have spread abroad among all nations
  the sweet fragrance of the knowledge of the gospel:
  let this oil be effective for the one baptized;
  through it let the fragrance
  abide in him, strong and stable;
  let it raise and give life
  to him who dies with Christ!

(VII, 44, 1–2)

THE OUR FATHER

After that, (the neophyte) is to stand up and say the prayer that the Lord
taught us.

(VII, 45, 1)

RITUAL FOR PRAYER

He who has been raised up [12] must stand for prayer, since when one is risen

---

11. As in the *Apostolic Tradition* of Hippolytus (see p. 142), the rite of confirmation
follows immediately upon baptism.
12. That is, the newly baptized person.

one stands upright. He who has died and been raised up with Christ will therefore stand upright.

He is to turn to the East when he prays. For it is written in the Second Book of Chronicles that when Solomon had finished building the temple of the Lord, at the Dedication the priests, levites, and singers turned to the East, praising, blessing, and singing:

> "Praise the Lord, for he is good,
> for his mercy is everlasting."[13]
>
> (VII, 45, 1–2)

PRAYER OF THE CONFIRMED PERSON

After the first prayer, he is to say:

> Almighty God,
> Father of your Christ, your only-begotten Son,
> grant me a spotless body, a pure heart,
> a watchful spirit, a knowledge without error.
> Let the Holy Spirit come
> so that I may possess the truth and believe it firmly,
> through your Christ.
>
> Through him, glory to you, in the Holy Spirit,
> for ever!
>   Amen.
>
> (VII, 45, 3)

Glory to God in the Highest Heaven [14]

(MORNING PRAYER)

> Glory to God in the highest heaven
> and on earth peace,
> to men (God's) good will!

---

13. An allusion to 2 Chr. 5:12-13. The author here forces the text, for the latter says only that the levitical singers were standing "at the eastern side of the altar." However, it was traditional in the first centuries to face the East while praying (see above, n. 14, p. 175).

14. The compiler of the *Apostolic Constitutions* has revised the text of the *Gloria* to suit his arianizing theology and has turned it into a hymn addressed to the Father. See below, p. 252, for the text of the *Codex Alexandrinus*, which seems to be earlier. — Note that in the citation from Lk. 2:14, "Glory to God in the highest . . . ," the *Apostolic Constitutions* does not keep the text, "and peace on earth to men of (his) good will," but have instead a two-membered formula that is attested by some manuscripts and early versions.

We sing you, we praise you,
we bless you, we give you glory,
and we adore you through your High Priest,
you the only God, who exist from all eternity, [15]
the only inaccessible one,
for your immense glory.

Lord, King of heaven,
God, the almighty Father!
Lord God, Father of Christ,
the spotless Lamb who takes away the sin of the world,
receive our prayer,
"you who sit above the Cherubim" (Ps. 80:2).

For you alone are holy,
you alone are Lord Jesus,
Messiah [16] of the God of the created universe,
and of our King.

Through him, glory, honor, and adoration to you.

(VII, 47)

Children, Praise the Lord

EVENING PRAYER [17]

Children, praise the Lord,
praise the name of the Lord!

We praise you,
we celebrate you with hymns,
we bless you for your measureless glory,
Lord King, Father of Christ,
the spotless Lamb who takes away the sin of the world.

To you praise,
to you hymns,
to you glory,
God and Father,

---

15. "From all eternity:" literally, "not begotten."
16. "Messiah": literally, "Christ."
17. This evening prayer is made up chiefly from Ps. 113:1, the hymns *Gloria in excelsis* and *Te decet laus*, and the Canticle of Simeon (Lk. 2:29-32).

through the Son, in the Holy Spirit,
for ever and ever!
　　Amen.

Now let your servant depart,
Master, according to your word, in peace.
For my eyes have seen your salvation
which you have prepared in the sight of the peoples,
a Light to enlighten the nations
and a glory of your people Israel.

(VII, 48, 1, 4)

Blessed Be You, Lord

BLESSING FOR MEALS

Blessed be you, Lord,
who have fed me from my youth
and give nourishment to all flesh.

Fill our hearts with joy and gladness
that we may always have what is necessary
and may abound in all good works,
in Christ Jesus, our Lord.[18]

Through him, glory to you,
honor and power, for ever!
　　Amen.

(VII, 49)

THE LITURGY OF THE MASS

Part I: Prayers[19]

Liturgy of the Catechumens

LITANIC PRAYER FOR THE CATECHUMENS

Let the deacon invite the catechumens to pray.

---

18. A scriptural mosaic of phrases from Ps. 119:12, Ps. 136:25, Acts 14:17, and 2 Cor. 9:8.

19. These prayers were said after the readings.

All the faithful then pray for them wholeheartedly, saying: "Kyrie eleison!" Let the deacon pray for them as follows:

Let us all pray fervently for the catechumens!

May he who is good and who loves men listen graciously to their prayers and supplications, may he accept their requests and give them his help, may he grant the desires of their hearts, for their good.

May he reveal the gospel of his Christ to them, may he enlighten them and strengthen them, may he instruct them in his divine knowledge.

May he teach them his laws and his commandments, may he fill them with pure and salutary fear of him.

May he open the ears of their heart, so that they may meditate on his law day and night.

May he strengthen them in devotion, may he unite them and gather them into his holy flock.

May he judge them worthy of the bath of the new birth, of the garment of immortality and true life.

May he rescue them from all wickedness, may the Adversary not be able to attack them, "may he cleanse them from all defilement of flesh and spirit" (2 Cor. 7:1).

"May he dwell and walk in the midst of them" (2 Cor. 6:16) through his Christ, "may he bless their coming in and their going out" (Ps. 121:8), may he bring their plans to completion for their good.

Let us again beg fervently that they may obtain the forgiveness of their sins and become worthy, through initiation in baptism, of the holy mysteries and the community of the saints.

Rise, catechumens. Ask peace of God through his Christ, that your day, as well as your life, may be filled with this peace and be sheltered from sin. (Ask for) a Christian death, for the mercy and kindness of God, for forgiveness of sins. Commend yourselves to the only uncreated God, through his Christ. Bow down and receive the blessing.

To all these intentions which the deacon announces, let the people, especially the children, reply "Kyrie eleison!" as we have already said.

(VIII, 6, 3–9)

BLESSING OF THE CATECHUMENS

While the catechumens bow their heads, the bishop pronounces the following blessing over them:

> Almighty God, uncreated and unapproachable,
> you the only true God,
> God and Father of your Christ, your only-begotten Son,
> God of the Paraclete and Lord of all things,
> who appointed your disciples

teachers of instruction in the truth:
cast your eyes now upon your servants
who are being instructed in the gospel of your Christ.

Give them "a new heart,
renew a right spirit in their breast" (Ps. 51:12),
that they may know you
and may do your will
"with their whole heart and willingly" (2 Macc. 1:3).

Make them worthy of the holy initiation,
join them to your holy Church,
grant them to share in your divine mysteries,
through Jesus Christ, our hope,
who died for them.

Through him, glory to you and adoration,
in the Holy Spirit, for ever!
    Amen.
                (VIII, 6, 10–13)

Dismissal of the Catechumens

After this the deacon is to say: "Catechumens, go in peace!"

                                        (VIII, 6, 14)

Litanic Prayer for the Faithful [20]

The deacon goes on to say: "Let no one come near who has not the right! Let all of us, the faithful, kneel. Let us pray to God through his Christ; let all of us fervently beseech God through His Christ.

Let us pray for the peace and tranquillity of the world and the holy churches. May the God of all things grant us firm and lasting peace; may he make us to persevere and keep us in the fullness of virtue and devotion.

Let us pray for the holy, catholic, and apostolic Church that is spread from one end of the world to the other. May God keep her sheltered from disturbance and the agitation of the waves; may he protect (this Church) that is founded on a rock, even to the end of the world.

---

20. After the intercessory prayer for the catechumens, the community also prays for the "demoniacs" and those considered to be such (VIII, 7), for future neophytes (VIII, 8), for those undergoing public penance (VIII, 9), and finally for the faithful themselves (VIII, 10).

Let us pray for this holy parish. May the God of all things judge us worthy to keep firm possession of his heavenly hope and to render him the constant tribute of prayer.

Let us pray for the episcopate of those who, throughout the world, "rightly dispense the word of truth" (2 Tim. 2:15). Let us pray also for our bishop James and his parishes. Let us pray for our bishop Clement and his parishes. Let us pray for our bishop Evodius and his parishes. Let us pray for our bishop Annanios and his parishes. May the God of mercies, for the sake of their holy churches, keep them in health and honor; may he grant them long life and an honorable old age, in piety and righteousness.

Let us pray too for our priests. May God preserve them from all shame and evil; may he grant them an upright and honorable priesthood.

Let us pray for all deacons and ministers of Christ. May God grant them to serve him without fault.

Let us pray for readers, singers, virgins, widows, orphans, those who live in marriage, and their children. May God take pity on them all.

Let us pray for those who practice a holy continence. Let us pray for those who lead a life of chastity and devotion.

Let us pray for those who in the holy Church present offerings and give alms to the poor.

Let us pray for those who bring oblations and firstfruits to the Lord, our God. May the most good God reward them with his heavenly graces; may he give them a hundredfold in the present world and eternal life in the world to come, eternal goods for temporal ones, heavenly goods for earthly ones.

Let us pray for our brethren who recently received baptism. May God establish and strengthen them.

Let us pray for our brethren who are afflicted by illness. May the Lord deliver them from every weakness and infirmity; may he restore them safe and sound to his holy Church.

Let us pray for those who are traveling by land or sea, for those who are condemned to the mines, to exile, to prison and chains, for the sake of the Lord's name. Let us pray for those who are subjected to an oppressive slavery.

Let us pray for our enemies. Let us pray for those who hate and presecute us for the sake of the Lord's name. May the Lord appease their fury and dissipate their hatred for us.

Let us pray for those who are outside (the Church) and astray. May the Lord convert them.

Let us remember the children in the Church. May the Lord grant them a perfect fear and lead them to maturity.

Let us pray for one another. May the Lord keep us by his grace, protect us to the end, deliver us from evil and from "all the snares of those who do evil" (Ps. 141:9); may he save us and bring us into his heavenly kingdom.

Let us pray for every Christian soul.

In your mercy, save and deliver us, O Lord.

Let us rise. Let us pray fervently for one another and commend ourselves to the living God through his Christ.

(VIII, 10, 1–22)

Prayer of the Bishop for the Faithful

After this the bishop says the following prayer:

> Almighty Lord,
> you the Most High, who dwell in the highest heaven,
> the Holy One who abide in the midst of the saints,[21]
> who are without beginning, who alone are Lord,
> who have given us through Christ the message
> that makes known to us your glory and your name,
> revealed by him to our understanding:[22]
>
> Through him, cast your eyes now
> upon your flock here.
> Deliver them from all ignorance and sin,
> grant them to be filled with fear of you,[23]
> to love you with a great love,
> to worship your glorious face.
>
> Be kind and gracious toward them,
> hear their prayers,
> keep them firm and unshaken,
> so that they may be holy in body and soul,
> "without spot or wrinkle or any such thing" (Eph. 5:27).
> Let them be well disposed,
> let none of them be weak or imperfect.
>
> Mighty defender, who are no accepter of persons,
> come to the help of your people here.
> You have chosen them from countless others,
> you have redeemed them with the precious blood of your Christ.
> You are Master, helper, protector,

---

21. Is. 57:15, cited according to the Septuagint.

22. The text is muddled. It reads literally: "Through Christ you have given us the message of knowledge, for a profound knowledge of your glory and your name, that he [Christ] has manifested to us for understanding."

23. Literally: "to fear you with fear."

guardian, a sure rampart and a strong citadel,
for "no one can snatch anything from your hand" (Jn. 10:29).
There is no other god like you;
"it is on you that our hope rests" (Ps. 62:6).

"Sanctify them in the truth,
for your word is truth" (Jn. 17:17),
you who are above all injustice,
above every error.
Deliver them from every weakness and every infirmity,
from every fault, from all calumny and error,
"from fear of the enemy,
from the arrow that flies by day,
from the pestilence that walks in darkness" (Ps. 91:5-6).
Judge them worthy of eternal life
which is in your Christ, your only-begotten Son,
our God and Savior.

Through him, glory to you and worship,
in the Holy Spirit,
now and for ever and ever!
> Amen.
> > (VIII, 11, 1–6)

Part II: Celebration of the Eucharist

The Kiss of Peace [24]

Next the deacon says: "Let us all be attentive."
The bishop then greets the assembly saying: "The peace of God be with you all."
The people answer: "And with your spirit."
The deacon says to all: "Greet one another with a holy kiss." [25]
The clergy then give the kiss (of peace) to the bishop, laymen give it to laymen, and women to women.
> > (VIII, 11, 7–9)

---

24. As in the catecheses of Cyril of Jerusalem (below, p. 284), the kiss of peace is given before the anaphora. In the West, on the contrary, it came after the Our Father, as St. Augustine attests in *Sermo* 227 (PL 38:1101). The arrangement followed in the East seems to be the more ancient.
25. This formula is borrowed from the letters of Paul: Rom. 16:16; 1 Cor. 16:20; 2 Cor. 13:12.

The Anaphora

ACCLAMATION

Surrounded by the priests and brilliantly adorned, the bishop stands before the altar and begins the prayer. With his hand he signs his forehead with the victorious sign of the cross and says: "The grace of almighty God, the love of our Lord Jesus Christ, and the fellowship of the Holy Spirit be with you all!"[26]

> With one voice all reply: "And with your spirit."
> Then the bishop: "Let us lift up our spirits."
> All: "They are turned to the Lord."
> The bishop: "Let us give thanks to the Lord."
> The entire assembly: "It is right and just."

(VIII, 12, 4–5)

Thanksgiving

This long preface is unique in early liturgical literature by reason of its biblical richness.

It falls into two parts, which are separated by the acclamation of the *Sanctus*. The first part is inspired by the *Seder Abodah* in the Jewish liturgy of Kippur. It is in turn subdivided into three parts: (1) praise of God and his infinite perfections; (2) praise of God in creation; (3) praise of God in the history of Israel. The second part of the preface has for its theme the work of Christ in the new covenant. The whole work of creation and human history in its entirety are brought to their final completion and crowned as it were by the sacrifice of Christ and the Eucharist. L. Ligier rightly remarks that this preface is rather a prayer of anamnesis in which the whole work of God is called to mind.[27] As such, it also plays the role of a confession of faith; a celebration in which so extensive an anaphora is used would evidently not need another creed.

The very length of this preface has made it suspect. Does it represent a purely imaginary liturgy that was composed without any reference to a real assembly, or was it in fact really used, in its full form, in the celebration of the Eucharist? It is hardly possible to give a definitive answer to this question. We may mention, however, that in view of its emphasis on the priesthood, some have thought it might have been meant for a Mass at which a bishop was consecrated.

---

26. This trinitarian blessing is inspired by 2 Cor. 13:13.

27. See L. Ligier, *Péché d'Adam et péché du monde: Bible, Kippur, Eucharistie 2* (*Théologie* 48; Paris, 1961), pp. 289–307. The text of the *Seder Abodah* is given in a Latin translation on pp. 399–403. See also M. Metzger, "La Didascalie et les Constitutions Apostoliques," in R. Johanny (ed.), *L'Eucharistie des premiers chrétiens* (Paris, 1976), pp. 187–210.

PRAISE OF GOD IN HIMSELF

The bishop continues: It is truly right and just to praise you first of all, the only true God who exist before creation, from whom "all fatherhood in heaven and on earth draws its origin" (Eph. 3:15). You alone are eternal,[28] without beginning, King and Sovereign without peer. You have need of nothing, you are the giver of every good thing; existing beyond every cause and every origin, you abide eternally without change. Everything comes from you, from you proceeds everything that comes into existence. You are knowledge that has no beginning, vision that has no end, eternal understanding, inborn wisdom. You are first by nature, you exist alone and beyond all measure. You called all things from nothingness into existence through your only-begotten Son, whom you alone engendered before all the ages by your will, your power, your unequaled goodness. He is the only-begotten Son, God the Word, living Wisdom, "first-born of all creation" (Col. 1:15), messenger of your wonderful plan, your High Priest, King and Lord of every creature endowed with spirit and perception. "He is before all things, and everything subsists through him" (Col. 1:17).

PRAISE OF GOD IN CREATION

Through him, O eternal God, you created everything, and through him you take care of all things in accordance with your prevenient providence. Through him you have bestowed the gift of being, and through him you have bestowed the gift of existing in the good. God and Father of your only-begotten Son, through him you created, in the first place, the Cherubim and Seraphim, the Eons and Armies, the Powers and Authorities, the Principalities and Thrones, the Archangels and Angels.

Through him you then create the visible world and all it contains. You stretch out the heavens like a vault, you unfold it like a tent (Is. 40:22). You set the earth over the void by your will alone, and you put the firmament in place. You create the day and the night. You bring the light forth from your treasury, and when it withdraws, you send the darkness so that the living things that move upon the earth may have their rest. You establish the sun in the firmament to rule over the day, and the moon to rule over the night, with the choir of stars in heaven to sing of your magnificence.

You created the water to slake thirst and cleanse, the life-giving air for breathing and speaking, when the tongue beats the air, and for helping the ear to grasp the word that is being communicated.

You created the fire to comfort us in the darkness, to help us in our needs, to warm us and give us light.

You separated the vast sea from the land. You made the sea navigable and the land firm under our feet. The sea you filled with living things small and large (Ps. 104:25), the land you peopled with animals tame and wild; you adorned it with

---

28. Literally: "unbegotten."

varied trees, you covered it with plants, you crowned it with flowers and enriched it with seeds.

It is you who hollowed out the abyss and surrounded it with mighty deeps. The immense ocean you closed in with double doors (Job 38:8), using the sand on the shores. Sometimes you raise the sea to the tops of the mountains, sometimes you spread it out like a plain; you excite it by unleashing the storm, you make it calm and gentle to give sailors an easy crossing. As with a girdle, your rivers enclose the universe you created through Christ; you furrow it with your torrents, you inebriate it with inexhaustible springs, and the mountains ring the solid land so that it may not tremble.

You have filled your universe and adorned it with plants for scent and for healing, with numerous and varied animals, strong and weak, which can provide food or labor, animals, tamed and wild, serpents that hiss and many kinds of singing birds. You have given the universe the rhythm of the years, the months, the days, and the ordered seasons, and of the racing clouds that spread the rain to ripen the fruits and give aid to living things. You regulate the breath of the winds that at your command stir the many plants and grasses.

PRAISE OF GOD IN THE HISTORY OF MANKIND

Not only did you create the world, but you placed man in it to dwell there. In him you brought into being as it were a world within a world. For in your wisdom you said:

> "Let us make man in our image
> and in our likeness!
> Let him have authority over the fishes of the sea
> and over the birds of heaven" (Gen. 1:26).

You gave him an immortal soul and a destructible body, the one emerging from nothingness, the other from the four elements.[29] You gave him a soul endowed with reason and judgment, capable of distinguishing between godliness and ungodliness, of perceiving justice and injustice. You gave him a body endowed with five senses and with movement.

For it is you, all-powerful God, who, through Christ, planted the garden of Eden in the East. You enriched it with all kinds of edible plants. You set man there as in a splendid dwelling. You implanted the law in him so that in and by himself he might possess the seeds of the knowledge of God.

When you brought him into this paradise of delights, you gave him authority over all things so that he might enjoy them. One thing alone you excluded so that he might learn to hope for even better blessings, and so keep the commandment and receive immortality as his reward. But he scorned your commandment; led astray by the serpent, and at the advice of his wife, he tasted the forbidden fruit. And so you rightly thrust him forth from paradise.

---

29. Air, water, fire, and earth. The biblical cosmology of the author here calls upon the physiology of the Stoics.

But because you are good, you did not wholly reject him in his lost state, for he was your work. You had made creation subject to him; now you allowed him to earn his food by his sweat and toil, while you yourself make the seed germinate, grow, and ripen. Binding yourself by an oath, you called him to return to life after falling asleep for a time, and you promised to release him from the bonds of death so that he might live and rise from the dead.

Not content with this, you made of his descendants a countless multitude. Those who remained faithful to you, you glorified. But those who turned away from you, you punished. You accepted the sacrifice of Abel as that of a just man, but you rejected as wicked the sacrifice of Cain, who killed his brother. After them, you came to the aid of Seth and Enoch. You took Enoch up (to heaven). For you are the creator of mankind and the giver of life; you fill them in their need, you give them your laws, you reward those who observe the laws, and punish those who violate them.

You sent the great deluge upon the world because of its many sins. But Noah, the upright man, together with eight persons, you rescued from the catastrophe by means of the ark. He was the end of the previous race of men and the new beginning of those who would be born later.

You lit the terrible fire against the Pentapolis of Sodom. A fertile land "you changed into a salty waste because of the wickedness of its inhabitants" (Ps. 107:34), but you saved Lot, the upright man, from torment.

It was you who rescued Abraham from the wickedness of his ancestors, you who established him as heir of the world and allowed him to see your Christ beforehand.

You consecrated Melchizedek a high priest for your worship. Amid his great trials, you declared your servant Job victor over the serpent, the source of evil. You made Isaac the child you had promised, and Jacob the father of twelve sons and of the many more that issued from them. You led these last into Egypt, seventy-six in number. Lord, you did not turn away from Joseph, but as a reward for the chastity he preserved on your account, you gave him government over the Egyptians. Lord, you did not abandon the Hebrews when they were oppressed by the Egyptians, for the sake of the promise you had given their fathers, but you rescued them and punished the Egyptians.

Men had corrupted the natural law by imagining creation to be the result of chance or by honoring it beyond its due and comparing it to you, the God and Master of the universe, but you did not leave them to wander astray. You raised up Moses, your holy servant. Through him you gave the written law in aid of the natural law; you showed that creation was your work; you extirpated the error of polytheism.

You honored Aaron and his descendants with the priesthood. You chastised the Hebrews when they sinned, you welcomed them back when they turned again to you.

You struck the Egyptians with the ten plagues. Opening the sea, you let the Israelites pass through. You destroyed the pursuing Egyptians in the waves. With wood you sweetened the bitter water.[30] You cleft the rock and made water spring from it; you made the manna rain down from heaven; you gave them the quail of heaven to eat. You were for them a pillar of fire at night to give them light, a pillar of cloud by day to shelter them from the heat.

You raised up Jesus [Joshua] as leader; through him you annihilated the seven peoples of Canaan. You divided the Jordan, dried up the rivers of Ethan, made the walls (of Jericho) collapse without need of machines or human hand.

For all these benefits, glory to you, all-powerful Master!

(VIII, 12, 5–27a)

HOLY IS THE LORD!

It is you who are adored by the countless companies of Angels and Archangels, Thrones, Dominions, Principalities, Virtues, and Powers, the hosts of eternity, as well as the Cherubim and the Seraphim with six wings, two to cover their feet, two to veil their head, and two to fly. With the thousand thousands of Archangels and the myriad myriads of Angels they sing without respite an uninterrupted song. And let all the people say with them:

> Holy, holy, holy
> is the Lord Sabaoth.
> Heaven and earth are filled with his glory!
> Blessed is he for ever. Amen.

(VIII, 12, 27b)

PRAISE OF GOD FOR THE WORK OF JESUS CHRIST

You are holy indeed, infinitely holy, the Most High exalted for ever.

Holy too is your only-begotten Son, our Lord and God, Jesus Christ! In all things he served you, his God and Father, who are admirable in your creation and worthy of being celebrated for your providence. He did not scorn the human race that was being lost, but after (the gift of) the natural law, after the exhortations of the (divine) law, after the denunciations of the prophets, after the interventions of the angels — now that (men) had violated the natural law and the positive law and had erased from their memory the deluge, the burning of the sinful villages, the plagues of Egypt, and the massacres in Palestine, and when men still on earth were about to perish — he chose, in accordance with your will,

> though Creator, to become a man,
> though Legislator, to submit to the law,
> though High Priest, to become the victim,
> though Shepherd, to be the sheep.

He appeased you, his God and Father, he reconciled you to the world, he rescued mankind from the wrath that threatened it. Born of a Virgin, God the Word became flesh, the beloved Son became the first-born of all creation. In

---

30. The reference is to the waters of Mara (Ex. 15:22-25).

accordance with the prophecies concerning him, which he himself had inspired, he was born of the stock of David and Abraham, of the tribe of Judah.

He was begotten in the womb of a Virgin,
he who makes all things that are begotten.
He took flesh,
he who is not fleshly.
He was born in time,
he who is born from all eternity.

He lived a holy life, taught with uprightness, drove from the midst of men "every disease and every infirmity" (Mt. 4:23), and accomplished signs and wonders among the people. He shared our food, our drink, our sleep, though he feeds all those who need nourishment and "satisfies the desire of all living things" (Ps. 145:16).

He manifested your name to those who did not know it; he dispelled ignorance, stirred piety to new life, did your will, finished the work you had given him to do (Jn. 17:6). Having brought his entire work to completion, he was betrayed by the man who was corroded by wickedness, and delivered into the hands of the impious by the treachery of priests and high priests unworthy of the name, and of a corrupted people. He suffered painfully at their hands, endured every kind of ignominy in accordance with your plan, and was handed over to Pilate, the governor.

He, the Judge, was judged,
he, the Savior, was condemned.
He was nailed to the cross,
he who is impassible.
He underwent death,
he who is by nature immortal.
He was buried, the giver of life.

Thus did he deliver from suffering and rescue from death those for whose sake he had come; thus did he break the bonds of the devil and free men from his deceit.

He rose from the dead on the third day and remained with his disciples for forty days. He ascended to the heavens and is seated at the right hand of you, his God and Father.

Remembering, therefore, the sufferings he endured for our sake, we give you thanks, O almighty God, not certainly as well as we ought, but as well as we can, and we carry out your testament.[31]

(VIII, 12, 28–35)

THE ACCOUNT OF INSTITUTION

For, on the night when he was betrayed,
he took bread in his holy and spotless hands,

---

31. Literally: "disposition" (*diataxis*); whence "testamentary disposition."

and, lifting his eyes to heaven
to you, his God and Father,
he broke it, gave it to his disciples, and said:
"This is the mystery of the New Testament.
Take and eat.
This is my body which is broken for many
for the forgiveness of sins."

He also filled the cup with wine mixed with water,
he said the blessing, gave it to them, and said:
"Drink of this, all of you, this is my blood,
which is poured out for many
for the forgiveness of sins.
Do this in memory of me.
For each time that you eat this bread
and drink of this cup,
you will proclaim my death until I return."

(VIII, 12, 36–37)

Anamnesis

Mindful then of his passion, of his death,
of his resurrection from the dead,
of his return to heaven, of his second coming in the future
when he will come with glory and power
to judge the living and the dead
and render to each according to his works,
we offer you, O King and God,
according to your testament, this bread and this cup.
We give you thanks through him
for having judged us worthy to stand before you
and exercise the priesthood for you.
And we ask you
to look down graciously
on these offerings that we bring you,
O God, who have need of nothing,
and to accept them as pleasing to you,
in honor of your Christ.

(VIII, 12, 38–39)

Epiclesis

Send down upon this sacrifice your Holy Spirit,
"witness of the sufferings of the Lord Jesus" (1 Pet. 5:1),
that he may make of this bread
the body of your Christ

and this cup
the blood of your Christ.

May those who share in it
be strengthened in devotion,
obtain forgiveness of sins,
be delivered from the devil and his errors,
be filled with the Holy Spirit,
become worthy of your Christ,
enter into possession of eternal life,
and be reconciled with you, almighty God.

(VIII, 12, 39)

Litanic Prayer of the Bishop

We pray to you, O Lord, for your holy Church, which stretches from one end of the world to the other, "which you obtained by the precious blood" (Acts 20:28) of your Christ. Keep her sheltered from disturbance and the agitation of the waves, even to the end of the world.

(We pray to you) for the universal episcopate which "rightly dispenses the word of truth" (2 Tim. 2:15).

We pray to you for myself, the humble [celebrant] who presents the offering to you, for the whole college of priests, for the deacons, for all the clergy. Teach them wisdom, fill them with the Holy Spirit.

We pray to you, Lord, for the king, for those who hold authority, for the whole army. May we live in peace, may we pass our whole lives in tranquillity and harmony, glorifying you through Jesus Christ, our hope.

We present the offering to you for all the saints who have been pleasing to you from the beginning, patriarchs, prophets, just men, apostles, martyrs, confessors, bishops, priests, deacons, subdeacons, readers, singers, virgins, widows, lay people, and for all those whose names you know.

We present the offering to you for your people who are here, that they may become "a royal priesthood and a holy nation" (2 Pet. 1:9) to the praise of your Christ, for those who practice virginity and continence, for the widows of the Church, for those who live in a holy marriage and for their children, for the infants of your people. Do not cast out anyone from among us.

We pray to you for this city and its inhabitants, for the sick, for those subjected to harsh slavery, for the exiled, for the proscribed, for travelers by sea and land. To all of them be succor, help, and defense.

We pray to you for those "who hate and persecute us for the sake of your name" (Mt. 10:22), for those who are outside and straying. Lead them back to what is good and appease their fury.

We pray to you for the catechumens of the Church, for those who are tormented by the Adversary, for our brothers who are undergoing penance. As for the first, strengthen them in the faith; as for the second, keep them from the attacks of the Evil One; as for the last, grant to them, as to ourselves, forgiveness of sins.

We present the offering to you for good weather and an abundant harvest. Enable us, who receive your benefits unceasingly, always to praise you "who give food to all flesh" (Ps. 136:25).

We pray to you also for those who are absent with good cause.

Keep us all in our devotion, gather us into the kingdom of your Christ, the God of every visible and rational creature, our King. May we remain unshaken, without fault or reproach.

For to you, Father, Son, and Holy Spirit, is all glory, worship, thanksgiving, honor, and adoration, now and always, and to endless and everlasting ages upon ages!

Let all the people reply: "Amen."

(VIII, 12, 40–51)

Litanic Prayer of the Deacon

The bishop says: "The peace of God be with you all!" All the people reply: "And with your spirit." The deacon proclaims anew: "Let us pray to God once again through his Christ."

Let us pray for the offering we present to the Lord, our God. May God in his goodness accept it, through the mediation of his Christ, upon his heavenly altar as a sweet savor.

Let us pray for this Church and for the people.

Let us pray for the universal episcopate, for the whole college of priests, for all the deacons and ministers of Christ, for the entire assembly of the Church. May God keep and protect them all.

Let us pray "for kings and for those who hold authority." May we dwell in peace, "that we may be able to lead a quiet and peaceful life, in all piety and worthiness" (2 Tim. 2:1-2).

Let us remember the holy martyrs, that we may be judged worthy to have a share in their struggle.

Let us pray for those who have fallen asleep in the faith.

Let us pray for good weather and for the ripening of the fruits.

Let us pray for those who have recently been enlightened by baptism. May they be strengthened in the faith.

Let us pray earnestly for one another.

Raise us up, O God, by your grace. Thus raised up, let us commend ourselves to God through his Christ.

(VIII, 13, 1–9)

Part III: Liturgy of Communion

Preparatory Prayer

The bishop says:

"Great God, whose name is sublime,
who are magnificent in your plans
and mighty in your works,"[32]
God and Father of Jesus,
your holy Son, our Savior;
cast your eyes upon us, upon your people here,
whom you have chosen through Christ
for the glory of your name.

Sanctify us body and soul,
"cleanse us from all defilement
of flesh and spirit" (2 Cor. 7:1).
Grant us the good things here present.
Do not judge any of us unworthy,
but be our help, succor, and defense
through your Christ.

Glory, honor and praise,
glorification and thanksgiving
to you, as to the Son and the Holy Spirit
for ever.

    Amen.

Acclamation of the People

When everyone has answered "Amen," the deacon says: "Attend!"

The bishop then addresses the people with these words: "Holy things to the holy!"

The people answer:

One only Holy One, one only Lord,
Jesus Christ, who is blessed for ever,
to the glory of the Father. Amen.

"Glory to God in the highest heaven,
on earth, peace,
among men, good will (of God)" (Lk. 2:14).

---

32. Jer. 32:18-19, cited according to the Septuagint (Jer. 39:19).

"Hosanna to the Son of David.
Blessed be he who comes in the name of the Lord."
God the Lord has shown himself among us.
"Hosanna in the highest heaven" (Mt. 21:9).

Communion Rites

The bishop then communicates, followed by the priests, the deacons, the subdeacons, the readers, the singers, and the monks; then, among the women, the deaconesses, the virgins, and the widows; then the children; then the rest of the people, in order, with reverence and devotion, without disturbance.

As he gives the oblation, the bishop says: "The body of the Lord." He who receives it is to reply: "Amen."

For his part, the deacon takes the cup and says as he gives it: "The blood of Christ, the cup of life." He who drinks it is to reply: "Amen."

While all are communicating, Psalm thirty-three is recited.[33]

When all the men and women have communicated, the deacons are to take what is left over and carry it to the sacristy.[34]

(VIII, 13, 10–17)

Prayer after Communion

When the psalm-singer has finished, the deacon is to say:

"Having received the precious body and blood of Christ,
let us give thanks to him who has made us worthy
to share in these holy mysteries.
Let us ask him that they be not our condemnation
but our salvation, the well-being of soul and body,
the safeguard of devotion, the forgiveness of sins,
the life of the world to come."
"Let us stand! Through the grace of Christ, let us commend ourselves to the uncreated God and to his Christ."

(VIII, 14, 1–3)

Prayer of Thanksgiving

The bishop is to say the prayer of thanksgiving:

Lord God almighty,

---

33. According to the numbering of the psalms in the Septuagint; Ps. 34 according to the Hebrew Bible.

34. "Sacristy": the word *pastophorion* used here in the Greek text means, in the Septuagint, the chamber of the priest in the Jerusalem Temple. Here it doubtless means "sacristy" rather than "tabernacle."

Father of your Christ, your blessed Son,
you who hear those that call on you in righteousness,
who know even the prayers we say in silence:

We give you thanks for having judged us worthy
to participate in your holy mysteries.
You have given them to us
to strengthen in us the certainty
of the good things we already know,
for the safeguard of devotion,
for the forgiveness of sins,
for the name of Christ has been invoked over us
and we have made our dwelling near to you.

You have separated us from the company of the unjust;
join us to those who are consecrated to you.
Strengthen us in the truth through the coming of the Holy Spirit,
show us that which we do not know,
fill up our deficiencies,
confirm that which we know.

Preserve the priests blameless in your service,
keep kings in peace,
magistrates in justice.
Give us favorable weather,
harvests in abundance.
Keep the world in your almighty providence,
pacify the nations that desire war,
convert those who are in error.

Sanctify your people,
protect the virgins,
keep the married in fidelity,
confirm those who live in chastity,
help the little children to grow,
strengthen the neophytes,
teach the catechumens,
and make them worthy of initiation.
Gather us into the kingdom of heaven
in Christ Jesus, our Lord.

Glory, honor, and worship
to you, to Christ, and to the Holy Spirit,
for ever.
    Amen.
        (VIII, 15, 1–5)

Final Blessing

The deacon says: "Bow your heads before God, through his Christ, and receive the blessing."

The bishop then prays as follows:

> Almighty God, true and without compare . . .
> God of your people who believe in Christ:
> be gracious, hear me for your name's sake,
> and bless those who have bowed their heads.
> "Grant them the requests of their hearts" (Ps. 37:4),
> those which are for their good,
> do not cast any of them out of your kingdom.
> Sanctify them, keep them, protect them, help them,
> deliver them from the Adversary, from every enemy.
> Watch over their dwellings,
> "protect their coming in and their going out" (Ps. 121:8).
>
> Glory to you, praise and splendor,
> worship and adoration,
> and to your Son, Jesus Christ,
> our Lord, God, and King,
> and to the Holy Spirit,
> now and always
> and for ever and ever.
>   Amen.
>   (VIII, 15, 6–9)

Dismissal

The deacon says: "Go in peace."

                    (VIII, 15, 10)

15

The Euchology of Der Balyzeh

THE EUCHOLOGY OF DER BALYZEH

In 1907, at Der Balyzeh, or the monastery of Balyzeh, in the neighborhood of Assiout in Upper Egypt, a number of papyrus fragments written in Greek were found in the ruins of a Greek monastery destroyed more than a thousand years before. The scraps of papyrus were badly damaged, but when they were restored — often conjecturally — it was possible to identify them as Christian prayers. It was generally admitted that they were liturgical texts of the ancient Mass, including the remains of the general intercessions, the creed, and the anaphora.[1]

Everything seemed to have been said on the "anaphora of Der Balyzeh," when the whole subject was opened to question again by the discovery of new fragments that made it possible to complete those already known.[2] The work revealed itself to be not so much a collection of specifically eucharistic prayers, as a more general one, a euchology. The three prayers, "You, our help," "May he give us charity," and "We pray to you, O Master," are "prayers for all times." The creed seems to come from a profession of faith at baptism, like the one found in the ritual of Hippolytus.[3] Lastly, the anaphora does indeed give us the text of the ancient Mass.

The papyrus itself dates from the sixth century, but the text preserves "some very ancient elements."[4] Across the centuries the sparse remains of the Euchology of Der Balyzeh bring us an echo of the ancient prayer that once rose from distant Egypt to the Father of Jesus Christ, "the well-beloved Child."

Note: In this translation the following conventions have been used. Italics represent a conjectural restoration of lacunas in the papyrus. Three continuous dots represent a more important lacuna which it is impossible to restore.

---

1. See, for example, P. de Puniet, "Le nouveau papyrus liturgique d'Oxford," *Revue bénédictine* 26 (1909), pp. 34–51, at p. 40; F. Cabrol, "Canon," *Dictionnaire d'archéologie chrétienne et liturgie* 2 (1910), cols. 1881–95; H. Leclercq, "Messe," *DACL* 11 (1933), cols. 624–26.

2. These new fragments were published, together with the text already known, by C. H. Roberts and B. Capelle in *An Early Euchologium: The Der Balyzeh Papyrus Enlarged and Re-edited* (Bibliothèque du Muséon 23; Louvain, 1949). It is the Greek text of this edition that has been followed here.

3. See p. 142.

4. Roberts and Capelle, p. 52, prudently speak of "a text which has preserved some very ancient elements but which as a whole can be regarded as a witness only for the time when the papyrus itself was written: about the end of the sixth century."

You, Our Help

. . .

You, our help!
Let the pagans not be able to say:
"Where is their God? (Ps. 115:2)
He has not saved them!"
You, our help and our hope,
You, our refuge . . .
You, our protector!
Do not abandon us,
but rescue us from every danger
that threatens us,
and raise us up on the great Day of the just.

Grant us to serve you
through your well-beloved Child, Jesus Christ.[5]
Through him, glory to you, grace, and honor,
now and for *generation* on generation,
and for ever and *ever*.
     Amen.

May He Give Us Charity

. . .

May he give us charity and brotherly love
in the bond of peace.[6]
May he hear the requests of our hearts,
he who alone holds power,
the holy Master,
resplendent with glory and honor,
whose name is Lord.

He dwells in the highest *heaven*
and casts his eyes upon the humble.
He is enthroned in the heavens.
He is blessed throughout the ages.
     Amen.

We Pray to You, O Master

We pray to you, O Master,

---

5. For "Child," see above, n. 3, p. 74.
6. An allusion to Eph. 4:3: "Eager to maintain the unity of the Spirit in the bond of peace."

protector heavenly and divine,
O God of truth
and Father of our Lord Jesus Christ,
who create the universe,
who contain all things
and alone cannot be contained,
who fixed the bounds of heaven and earth,
the sea, the waves, and the rivers,
the ebb and flow of the tides,
who took dust from the ground
and fashioned man in your image!
. . . *We pray to you,*
through Jesus Christ, our Lord,
your only-begotten Son . . .
To you, glory and power,
with your *Holy* Spir*it,*
now and always,
and in the ages *of eternity.*
    Amen.

Profession of Faith at Baptism

The neophyte proclaims the faith:

I believe in God, Father almighty,
in your only-begotten Son, our Lord,
our Lord Jesus Christ,
in the Holy Spirit,
in the resurrection of the flesh,
in the holy catholic Church.

Liturgy of the Mass

PRAYER OF INTERCESSION

May your bless*ing come upon your* people
who do your will.[7]

Raise up the fallen,
bring back those who have strayed,
console the fainthearted.[8]

---

7. This fragment represents the end of the prayer of intercession.
8. These three lines are borrowed from the "Great Prayer" of St. Clement of Rome; see above, pp. 83–84.

For you are above every principality,
power, force, and dominion,
above everything that can be named
in this world and *in the world to come.*

Anaphora

PREFACE

Near to you stand
the thousands of holy *angels*
and the numberless *hosts of archangels.*
Near to you stand
the Cherubim with many eyes.
Around you stand the Seraphim,
each with six wings:
two to hide the face,
two to hide the feet,
and two to fly.
Unceasingly they all proclaim your holiness.
With all their acclamations of your holiness
receive also our acclamation
who sing to you:

SANCTUS

Holy, holy, holy is the Lord,
the God Sabaoth!
Heaven and earth
are filled with your glory (Is. 6:2-3).

EPICLESIS[9]

Fill us too with your glory!
And deign to send your Holy Spirit
on these offerings that you have created,
and make this bread to become
the body of our Lord and Savior
Jesus Christ,
and this chalice to become
the blood of the New *Testament*
of our Lord, God, and Savior,
Jesus Christ.

---

9. It is exceptional to find the epiclesis placed before the consecration, and for a long time this was thought to be the only example. But in 1940 Lefort published an ancient anaphora showing the same peculiarity (*Le Muséon*, 1940, pp. 22–24).

PRAYER FOR THE CHURCH

> *And as* this bread was scattered
> on *the mountains*, the hills, and in the valleys,
> and was gathered to become a single body . . .[10]
> and as this wine,
> sprung from the *holy* vine of *David*,
> and this water, sprung from the spotless Lamb,
> were mixed
> and became a single mystery,
> so too gather the catholic Church
> of Jesus Christ.

ACCOUNT OF THE INSTITUTION

> For our L*ord Jesus Christ*,
> on the night when he *was betrayed*,
> *took bread in* his *holy hands*,
> *gave* thanks and *blessed it*,
> *sanctified and broke it*,
> *gave it* to his dis*ciples and ap*ostles, saying:
> "T*ake and eat* of it, all of you.
> This *is* my body
> which is given for you
> in forgiveness of sins."
>
> Likewise, after the supper,
> he took the chalice and blessed it,
> drank of it and gave it to them, saying:
> "Take, drink of it, all of you.
> This is my blood
> which is poured out for you
> for the forgiveness of sins.
> *Do this in memory of me*."
>
> Each time that you eat this bread
> and that you drink this chalice,
> you announce my death,
> you proclaim my resurrection,
> *you make me*mory of me."

ANAMNESIS

> We announce your death,

---

10. This passage is borrowed from the Eucharistic Prayer of the *Didache*; see above, p. 75.

*we procl*aim your resurrection,
and we pray .   .   .
.   .   .

COMMUNION PRAYER

Give *your servants*
the power of the Holy Spirit,
the confirmation and increase of faith,
the hope of eternal life to come,
through our Lord Jesus Christ.
Through him, glory to you, Father,
with the Holy Spirit,
for ever!
    Amen.

16

Klasmata
or
Various Fragments

> To you the praise,
> to you the hymns,
> to you the glory,
> Father, Son, and Holy Spirit
> forever and ever. Amen.
> (Hymn *Te decet laus*)

KLASMATA . . .

After the miracle of the multiplication of the loaves, Jesus bade his disciples gather up the broken pieces or fragments (*klasmata*), in order that nothing of the miraculous feast might be lost (Jn. 6:12; cf. Mk. 6:43).

Similarly, we have sought to gather in the basket of this penultimate chapter the fragments of spiritual bread that the Spirit multiplied during the first centuries for the feast of tradition. These hymns, epitaphs, and baptismal inscriptions vary in their worth, and their connection with the liturgy is at times rather weak. They are important because of the witness they give to the Church during that springtime in which her faith was flourishing.

HYMNS

Joyous Light

The hymn "Joyous Light" was sung at the evening office of the Lucernary, that is, the service held at the hour when the candles and lamps were lit in honor of the risen Christ who is the Light of the world. The hymn seems to date from the second-third century.[1]

Joyous light of the holy glory
of the heavenly, immortal Father:
holy and blessed Jesus Christ!

Now, at the hour of sunset,
gazing on the evening light,
we sing the Father and the Son
and the Holy Spirit of God.

---

1. The author of the hymn is unknown. Basil of Caesarea writes: "We are unable to say who fathered these words of thanksgiving for use in the lucernary. The people, however, . . . still use the ancient formula: 'We praise the Father and the Son and the Holy Spirit of God'" (*Treatise on the Holy Spirit*, 29; see B. Pruche, *Basile de Césarée: Traité du Saint Esprit* [SC 17bis; Paris, 1968], pp. 508–10). See above, pp. 146–47, the lucernary in the *Apostolic Tradition* of Hippolytus.

O Son of God, the giver of life,
you are worthy at every moment
to be praised by holy voices!
Therefore does the world glorify you.

Glory to God in the Highest Heaven
(Morning Prayer)

Glory to God in the highest heaven,
and on earth, peace,
to men, (God's) good will!

We sing you, we bless you,
we worship you, we glorify you,
we give you thanks for your great glory.

Lord God, King of heaven, God the Father almighty!
Lord, only Son, Jesus Christ,
and Holy Spirit!

Lord God, Lamb of God, Son of the Father,
you who take away the sins of the world,
have pity on us.
You who take away the sins of the world,
receive our prayer.
You who are seated at the right hand of the Father,
have pity on us.

For you alone are holy,
you alone are Lord, Jesus Christ,
to the glory of God the Father. Amen.[2]

---

2. This is the text of the *Gloria* as given in the Codex Alexandrinus. It seems to be earlier than the one in the *Apostolic Constitutions* (see p. 220), although there is no assurance that each of its phrases is equally old. St. Athanasius (295–373) attests that this hymn was part of the morning Office (*Treatise on Virginity*, 20); therefore it goes back at least to the fourth century. It became part of the liturgy of the Mass toward the beginning of the sixth century; see J. A. Jungmann, *The Mass of the Roman Rite: Its Origins and Development (Missarum Solemnia)*, tr F. A. Brunner, 1 (New York, 1951), pp. 346–59; N. M. Denis-Boulet, "Analysis of the Rites and Prayers of the Mass," in A. G. Martimort (ed.), *The Church at Prayer 2. The Eucharist*, Eng. ed. by A. Flannery and V. Ryan (New York, 1973), pp. 87–89.

Benefactor of All Who Turn to You
(Morning Prayer)[3]

Benefactor of all
who turn (to you),
you who make your light shine
in every darkness,
who give growth to every seed,
who make spiritual grace blossom and grow,
have pity on me, Lord.

Build me as a price(less) temple,
look (not) upon (my) sin(fulness),
for if you take account of my iniquities,
I cannot stand before your face.

But, in accord(ance with your great) compassion,
and with the fullness of your mercies,
re(move my) sins through (Jesus Christ),
our Lord, your only-begotten, most holy Son,
the physician of our souls.

Through him, glory to you and power
and all greatness and magnificence
forever and ever,
ceaselessly and always!
    Amen.

                                   (Second century?)

Holy Is the God
(Morning Prayer)

Holy (is the God) who from my youth
has shown me life and light.
Holy is the God and (Father of) the universe. . . .[4]

Holy are you

---

3. With regard to this and the following prayer, F. Cabrol and H. Leclercq, *Monumenta ecclesiae antiqua* 1/2 (Paris, 1913), pp. CLXXXVIII–CXCII, remark: "Note the absence of any reference to the Eucharist; we will perhaps not be rash in seeing here prayers for a morning assembly in a home."

4. The text is damaged; several lines are unintelligible at this point.

and stronger than any power. . . .
Holy are you,
exalted above (all) praise.[5]

Receive (the prayer)
that rises to you
from my heart and soul,
O Ineffable and Inexpressible One
whom men invoke in silence!

I beg you, grant me to know
what concerns my own being.
Bend to me
and make me strong.
This grace I shall then transmit through love
to my brethren who are your children.

To you the glory,
now and always
forever and ever!
        Amen.

You Are Holy, Lord

You are holy, Lord God almighty,
(Father of o)ur Lord Jesus Christ.
O flowering paradise,
roy(al scep)ter, priceless love,
you are the strength that gives us hope! . . .[6]

You are holy, (Lord God almighty),
ladder of heaven,
new covenant. . . .[7]

You are holy, Lord God(almighty),
King of kings (and Lord of lords),
who (al)one are im(mortal),
(who dwell in unapproachable light),

---

5. An allusion to Neh. 9:5: The "glorious name" of God "is exalted above all blessing and praise."
6. Lacuna of eight lines.
7. Lacuna of five lines.

(whom no man has ever seen![8])
(You are throned upon the cheru)bim (Ps. 80:2),
(you walk on the wings) of the wind (Ps. 104:3),
for you create (heaven, earth, and sea)
(and all) that is in them.
Yours is all the earth and the heavens! (. . . .)

You (make spirits your messengers)
(and) flames of fire are your servants (Ps. 104:4).
(You create man in your image) and likeness.

Your span is the measure of the heavens
and your hand the measure of earth.
The universe is radiant with beauty in your sight. . . .

(Third century)

Your Sacred Body
(Eucharistic Hymn)

Your sacred body
that was crucified for us
we eat.

And your blood
that was shed for our salvation
we drink.

Let your body, then, be our salvation,
and your blood, forgiveness of our sins.

Because of the gall
you drank for us,
take from us the devil's gall.

Because of the sour wine
you drank for us,
let our weakness
be changed into strength.

In place of the spittle

---

8. A borrowing from the hymn in 1 Tim. 6:15-16; see p. 36.

you accepted for us,
may we receive the dew of your kindness.

And in place of the reed
with which you were struck for us,
may we receive the perfect dwelling.

In place of the crown of thorns
you accepted for us,
let an immortal crown be given
to those who have loved you.

In place of the shroud
in which you were buried,
may we too be clad
in invincible power.

In place of the new tomb
and your sepulcher,
may we receive the renewal
of soul and body.

For you rose and returned to life.
When we return to life, we will live
and stand before you
at the just judgment!

(Before the third century)

Christ Is Born, Give Him Glory
(Christmas Hymn)

Christ is born:
  Give him glory!
Christ comes from heaven:
  Go and meet him!
Christ is on the earth:
  Rise up (to heaven)!
Sing to the Lord,
  all the earth!

(Third-fourth century)

He Was Born at Bethlehem
(Christmas Hymn)

He was born at Bethlehem,
he was raised at Nazareth,
he lived in Galilee.

We saw a sign in heaven,
a star that showed itself.
The watching shepherds
were filled with wonder.
Falling to their knees, they sang:
  Glory to the Father,
   Alleluia!
  Glory to the Son,
   Alleluia!
  And glory to the Holy Spirit,
   Alleluia, Alleluia, Alleluia!

         (Fourth century)

We Praise You, God Almighty
(Eucharistic Hymn)

We praise you, God almighty,
who sit above the Cherubim
and above the Seraphim,
whom prophets and apostles praise!

We praise you, Lord, with our prayers,
you who came to free us from sin!
We pray you, exalted Redeemer,
whom the Father sent to shepherd the sheep:

You are Christ the Lord, the Savior,
born of the Virgin Mary.
Deliver forever from all sin
us who take this chalice most holy!

         (Fourth century?)

In the Shelter of Your Mercy

"In the shelter of your mercy" (*Sub tuum praesidium*) is one of the earliest prayers addressed to Mary. The newest research shows that it dates from after the beginning of the fourth century.

We give the prayer here in its earliest form, which was found in a Greek papyrus.

In the shelter of your mercy
we take refuge, Mother of God.

Let those who pray to you
not yield to temptation.

But rescue us from danger,
you who alone are pure, alone blessed.[9]

(Fourth century)

O God Almighty

O God almighty,
who made heaven, earth, and sea
and all that is in them!

Come to my aid,
wash me of my sins,
save me in this world and in the world to come!

Through Jesus Christ, our Lord and Savior.
Through him, glory and power to you,
forever and ever!
    Amen.

(Third-fourth century)

Hope, Life, Way

Hope, Life, Way, Salvation, Understanding, Wisdom, Light,
Judge, Door, Most High, King, Precious Stone, Prophet, Priest,

---

9. The text used in the Latin Church reads: "We fly to your protection, O holy Mother of God. Despise not our petitions in our necessities, but deliver us always from all dangers, O glorious and blessed virgin." The words "deliver us always . . . O glorious and blessed virgin" are a slight mistranslation, since the original Greek text has "Deliver us, O always-virgin."

Messiah, Sabaoth, Teacher, Spouse, Mediator,
Scepter, Dove, Hand, Stone, Son, and Emmanuel,
Vineyard, Shepherd, Sheep, Peace, Root, Vine-stock, Olive Tree,
Source, Wall, Lamb, Victim, Lion, Intercessor,
Word, Man, Net, Rock, House:
　　Christ Jesus is everything.

(Pope Damasus, 366–84)

Blood of Jesus Christ

Blood of Jesus Christ,
　　who became flesh for us,
　　who was born of the holy Virgin.

Blood of Jesus Christ,
　　who was born of the holy Mother of God.

Blood of Jesus Christ,
　　who manifested himself in the flesh.

Blood of Jesus Christ,
　　who was baptized in the Jordan
　　by the Precursor.
　　Jesus Christ! Amen.

Blood of Jesus Christ,
　　who offered himself as a victim
　　for our sins.
　　Jesus Christ! Amen.

(Fifth century)

O Night That Is Brighter than Day
(Hymn for the Easter Vigil)

O night that is brighter than day,
O night more dazzling than the sun,
O night more sparkling than the snow,
O night more brilliant than our lamps!

O night that is sweeter than paradise,
O night delivered from darkness,
O night that dispels sleep,
O night that makes us keep vigil with the angels!

O night terrible for the demons,
O night desired by all the year,
O night that leads the bridal Church to her Spouse,
O night that is mother to those enlightened!

O night in which the devil,
sleeping, was despoiled,
O night in which the Heir
brings the coheirs to their heritage!

(Asterius, bishop of Amasea
in Pontus, † 410)

EPITAPHS

Epitaph of Abercius

The epitaph of Abercius is "the queen of all ancient Christian inscriptions."[10] It comes from Asia Minor and probably dates from the end of the second century. Abercius, bishop of Hierapolis in Phrygia Salutaris, had journeyed to Rome and from there to Syria; on the way he visited the Christian churches and shared in their Eucharists. He tells of this journey in a symbolic language that only Christians could understand.

Citizen of a famous city,
I had this tomb built in my lifetime
so that my body might one day rest in it.

My name is Abercius.
I am the disciple of a holy Shepherd[11]
who pastures his flocks of sheep
on the mountains and in the plains,
who has great eyes whose gaze reaches everywhere.
It is he who taught me the truthful Scriptures
that give life.
It is he who sent me to Rome
to contemplate the sovereign majesty

---

10. J. Quasten, *Patrology* 1. *The Beginnings of Patristic Literature* (Westminster, Md., 1950), p. 171.

11. The "holy Shepherd" is Christ; the image "fish from a wellspring" also designates Christ. The letters of the Greek word for "fish," *ichthus*, form an acrostic: *Iēsous Christos, theou huios, sotēr*, "Jesus Christ, God's Son, Savior."

and see a Queen clad in a golden robe
and shod with sandals of gold.

I saw there a people
marked with a gleaming seal.
I saw, too, the plain of Syria,
and all the cities, Nisibis, beyond the Euphrates;
everywhere I found brothers.
Paul was my companion.
Faith was everywhere my guide
and everywhere served me as food:
a fish from a wellspring, very large and pure,
caught by a holy virgin;
she gave it constantly to her friends to eat;
she possesses a delicious wine
that she serves with her bread.

I, Abercius, dictated this text,
and it was engraved in my presence;
I was seventy-two years old.
Let the brother who understands
pray for Abercius.

Let no one place another tomb
above this
under pain of a fine:
two thousand gold coins for the Roman treasury
and a thousand for my famous native place, Hierapolis.

Epitaph of Pectorius

The epitaph of Pectorius was discovered in an ancient Christian cemetery near Autun; it dates from the years 350–400, but the first part of it may well be a citation from an older poem that is close in time to the Abercius inscription. Christ is called "the heavenly Fish"; baptism is "the immortal spring of divine waters," and the Eucharist is the "food, sweet as honey, of the Savior of the saints." When the writer says that people receive the Fish "in the palms of their hands," he is referring to the ancient manner of receiving Communion.

O divine race of the heavenly Fish,
keep your heart pure,
for you, among mortal men, have received

the immortal spring of divine waters.
Friend, refresh your soul
in the eternal streams of enriching wisdom.
Receive the food, sweet as honey,
of the Savior of the saints.
Eat your fill, drink your fill
when you receive the Fish in the palms of your hands.
I pray you, Master and Savior,
give us the Fish for our food.

Let my Mother rest in peace,
I pray you, O Light of the dead.

Aschandius, father beloved of my heart,
with my sweet mother and my brothers,
in the peace of the Fish remember Pectorius.

Epitaph of Amachis

Holy, holy, holy,
greetings to you who see the sweet light
of our heavenly Father.
To us grant rest
in Christ Jesus, our Lord,
and in his Holy Spirit, who gives life.
And may he grant you as well
to leave life after having lived in beauty.
For even I, lowly though I am,
received at the end of my too short life
my share in God's promise.
And do you, Lord, take pity on me!

Epitaph of Leontius

O God, grant him rest
with the devout and the just
in the place of repose and refreshment
in the paradise of delights
whence pain, affliction, and groaning have fled.
Holy, holy, holy are you, Lord Sabaoth!
Heaven and earth are filled with your holy glory.

Epitaph of Magus

Magus, little innocent child,
henceforth you are with the Innocent.
How lasting the life you now possess!
How filled with joy you are,
now that the Church, your Mother, has received you
on returning from this world!
My heart, cease your moaning,
my eyes, cease your weeping.

God of Spirits and of All Flesh

In the name of the Father and of the Son and of the Holy Spirit. Amen.

O God of spirits and of all flesh,
you who conquered death and trod hell under your feet,
you who gave life to the world:
grant rest to the soul of Pasina
in the bosom of Abraham, Isaac, and Jacob,
in the place agleam with light,
the place of refreshment,
where there is no suffering or sorrow or tears.

You are good and merciful:
forgive her all the sins she committed
in word, in action, or in thought,
for no man can live without sinning.
You alone are God, you alone are sinless,
and your holiness is an eternal holiness
and your word is truth.
Grant rest to my soul, the soul of Pasina,
for you are rest and life and resurrection.

We glorify you, Father, Son, and Holy Spirit. Amen.
Monday, the nineteenth of Khoiak,
in her sixtieth year, in the age of martyrs.
Savior, grant rest to him who wrote these lines.

(Fourth century)

ROMAN BAPTISMAL INSCRIPTIONS

Baptistery of Saint Lawrence in Damaso

From this noble spring a saving water gushes,
which cleanses all human defilement.

Do you wish to know the benefits of the sacred water?
These streams give the faith that regenerates.

Wash away the defilement of your past life in the sacred fountain.
Surpassing joy to share in the life the water brings!

Whoever resorts to this spring abandons earthly things
and tramples under foot the works of darkness.

Baptistery of the Lateran

Here a people of godly race are born for heaven;
the Spirit gives them life in the fertile waters.
The Church-Mother, in these waves, bears her children
like virginal fruit she has conceived by the Holy Spirit.

Hope for the kingdom of heaven, you who are reborn in this spring,
for those who are born but once have no share in the life of blessedness.
Here is to be found the source of life, which washes the whole universe,
which gushed from the wound of Christ.

Sinner, plunge into the sacred fountain to wash away your sin.
The water receives the old man, and in his place makes the new man to rise.
You wish to become innocent: cleanse yourself in this bath,
whatever your burden may be, Adam's sin or your own.

There is no difference between those who are reborn; they are one,
in a single baptism, a single Spirit, a single faith.
Let no one be afraid of the number or the weight of his sins:
he who is born of this stream will be made holy.

(Inscription of Sixtus III, 432–440)

Baptistery of Saint Lawrence

You who pass, consider how short life is.
Turn your vessel back toward the shores of Paradise,

return to port to look on the face of the Lord.
Accept grace, you who share in what is holy.

True God, supreme glory, light, wisdom, and power:
from your side, O wonderful might of your love, you pour
both the blood, which on the altar appears like wine,
and the waters of baptism that purify souls.

(Fifth century)

Inscription Placed in the Consignatorium [12]

Here the innocent sheep, cleansed by the heavenly water,
are marked by the hand of the supreme Shepherd.

You who have been begotten in this water, come to the unity
to which the Holy Spirit calls you, to receive his gifts.

You have received the cross; learn to escape the storms of the world:
this is the great lesson of which this place reminds you. [13]

---

12. The *consignatorium* was the place where the anointings of the newly baptized were performed. Here it is undoubtedly the *consignatorium* of the Vatican Basilica that is meant.

13. Possibly an allusion to the martyrdom of St. Peter who, according to tradition, was crucified here.

17

The Catecheses of Cyril of Jerusalem

(about 350)

CYRIL OF JERUSALEM (314–387)

Cyril is surely one of the most attractive Christian personalities of the fourth century. He was born about 313–314, at a time when the so-called "Peace of Constantine" was being established under Emperors Constantine and Licinius in about 313. He became bishop of Jerusalem about 350. His episcopate was not entirely peaceful, since the persecutions that had formerly assailed the Church from without had now been succeeded by theological disputes that were threatening the faith from within. Cyril was involved in these and, as a defender of orthodoxy, suffered the fate history has in store for such men. He was thrice exiled and, in fact, of the thirty-eight years of his episcopate, he spent sixteen in exile. Finally, however, he died peacefully among the faithful of his diocese.

The Church venerates him as a Doctor and celebrates his feast on March 18.

The Catecheses

The work that has given Cyril a permanent place of honor in Christian tradition and especially in the history of the liturgy consists of twenty-four catecheses or instructions that he preached around the year 350 in the Basilica of the Holy Sepulcher. These instructions can be divided into two groups.

The first is a series of nineteen prebaptismal catecheses delivered during Lent. These are addressed to the catechumens who were to receive baptism and the Eucharist during the Easter Vigil. In them, Cyril concentrates chiefly on the various articles of the creed that was used in the Church of Jerusalem. The catechumens of the time used to be called the *photizomenoi*, that is, "those being enlightened," because they were already receiving a light shed upon them by the sacraments of Christian initiation.

The second group of instructions consists of five catecheses given after the celebration of Easter, during the "week of white garments." They are addressed to the newly baptized, who are called the *neophotistoi*, or "recently enlightened." These catecheses are called "mystagogical," that is, catecheses which "initiate (believers) into the mysteries." In them, Cyril is leading the neophytes to a deeper understanding of the mysteries that baptism had accomplished in them.

In these twenty-four catecheses, then, we have the expression of the traditional faith as taught in the Church of Jerusalem to its catechumens and neophytes in the middle of the fourth century. The Greek text that has come down to us was a stenographer's recording of the instructions as they were given during the liturgical celebration. The catecheses are not, therefore, an extraordinary work of a private theologian looking for celebrity by setting forth his personal views. No, they are simply the ordinary teaching of a pastor explaining the Christian faith.

This ordinary teaching is marked, however, by a strange beauty. The catecheses are improvisations, but how splendid they are! They are teachings, but what tender love fills them! What simplicity united to greatness! J. Quasten calls them "one of the most precious treasures of Christian antiquity,"[1] and A. Piédagnel speaks of them, more specifically, as "one of the most priceless treasures of the fourth-century liturgy."[2] The extracts that follow here will enable the reader to confirm these judgments for himself. Perhaps too, as he compares them with the homilies of our twentieth century, he may come to envy the Christians of fourth-century Jerusalem.

We should bear in mind that "catechesis" is essential to the Church's life. She must inevitably teach the catechism (give it the learned name of "mystagogy" if you will) as soon as she has catechumens and neophytes who require instruction. In the period that followed on the Peace of Constantine, candidates for baptism presented themselves in large numbers. Catecheses correspondingly multiplied.

Among those that have survived the ravages of time and have come down to us, we may mention the little treatise *On the Mysteries* of St. Ambrose of Milan, which dates from the end of the fourth century; St. Augustine's *Catechesis of Beginners* (his *De catechizandis rudibus*), which was composed about 405; the eight *Baptismal Catecheses* of St. John Chrysostom, which Father A. Wenger discovered in 1955 in a dusty monastery library at Mount Athos and which date from 390; and the sixteen *Catecheses* of Theodore of Mopsuestia, which were preached at Antioch between 388 and 392. Cyril's work is thus not the only one of its kind. It was the first, however, and it remains unique for its freshness. It is like the fragrance of a liturgical springtime as compared with the heavier scents from the high summer of patristic theology.

A final word on the difficult problem of authenticity which has been posed with regard to the five mystagogical catecheses. In addition to the Greek manuscript tradition that expressly calls Cyril the author of these catecheses, there is one codex that attributes them to John II, Cyril's successor in the see of Jerusalem, while four codices attribute them both to Cyril and to John. On the other hand, the authorship of Cyril seems to be confirmed by the allusions common to the catecheses as a group; all the catecheses seem to proclaim their common authorship.

---

1. *Patrology* 3. *The Golden Age of Greek Patristic Literature* (Westminster, Md., 1960), p. 363.
2. *Cyrille de Jérusalem: Catéchèses mystagogiques* (SC 126; Paris, 1966). This edition gives a critical text, established by J. Piédagnel, and a translation, by P. Paris, of the five mystagogical catecheses. There is a complete French translation of all the catecheses in J. Bouvet, *Saint Cyrille de Jérusalem: Catéchèses baptismales et mystagogiques* (Paris, 1962).

Given the present state of the question, it certainly does not seem prudent simply to deny the Cyrillian authorship of the mystagogical catecheses. It seems even more imprudent, however, simply to ignore the problem. One solution that has been suggested is that the basic text was recorded by a stenographer, then used in subsequent years for the instruction of catechumens and neophytes, and finally revised and reworded by John II of Jerusalem. This would explain why the style, vocabulary, and images are clearly less lyrical in the mystagogical catecheses than in the prebaptismal ones. This literary difference, which is quite evident in the original Greek, is perceptible even in translation.

Whatever the position we may feel obliged to take with regard to the authorship, the question in no way affects the value of the witness given us in these catecheses (even if the definitive redaction of the mystagogical catecheses were to be assigned to a slightly later time). We certainly have here an exposition of the traditional faith of the Church of Jerusalem in the fourth century.

Procatechesis to the Candidates for Baptism

THE FRUITS WILL SURPASS THE PROMISE OF THE FLOWERS

> The perfume of happiness is already being poured out on you,
> O you who are receiving the light![3]
> You are already gathering spiritual flowers
> to plait celestial crowns!
> The Holy Spirit has already breathed his fragrance on you!
> You have already reached the entrance hall of the royal palace!

May you soon be led in to the King! Now that the flowers have appeared on the trees, may the full-grown fruit be not far behind! Your names have now been registered: you have been called up, you carry the torches for the nuptial procession, you yearn for the heavenly city, your purpose is a good one, and hope is its companion. No liar is he who said: "God makes all things work together for the good of those whom he loves" (Rom. 8:28). Yes, God is generous in doing good, but he also expects each person to show sincere good will. That is why the Apostle adds: "Those whom he has called according to his plan" (Rom. 8:28). If you show sincere good will, you take your place among those who are called.

(Procat. 1)

YOUR NAME HAS BEEN REGISTERED

As for us, the ministers of Christ, we have welcomed each of you, and, like men filling the office of porters, we have left the door open. Perhaps you entered with a soul defiled by sins and with a perverse intention. You did enter, however; you have been welcomed, and your name has been registered.

---

3. Literally: "O enlightened ones."

See the venerable appearance of our assembly. Do you observe its order and discipline, the reading of the Scriptures, the presence of religious, the sequence of instructions? Let the place fill you with a holy fear, and allow yourselves to draw instruction from what you see. Go forth today in good time, and return tomorrow with even better dispositions.

If you are wearing the robe of avarice, don another garment and return. Get rid of your lust and uncleanness, and put on the sparkling robe of purity. I give you this warning before Jesus, the Spouse of souls, comes in and sees the garments you are wearing. A lengthy stay is granted you; you have forty days in which to repent; you have plenty of time to put off your garments, wash yourself, put on new robes, and then return.

If you persevere in your evil intention, he who is speaking to you is not responsible for that. But then you must not expect to receive grace. The water may receive you, but the Spirit will not accept you.

If anyone is conscious of wounds, let him seek healing! If anyone has fallen, let him get up! Let there be no Simon among you,[4] no hypocrisy, no prying curiosity!

(*Procat.* 4)

You Have Been Caught in the Church's Net

Perhaps you have come for some other reason? A man may want to please a woman and may come for that reason. The same may be true of a woman. Often too, a slave wants to please his master, or a friend a friend. I take whatever is on the hook, I pull you in, you who came with an evil intention but will be saved by your hope of the good. Doubtless you did not know, did you, where you were going, and did not recognize the net in which you have been caught? You have been caught in the Church's net! Let yourself be taken alive, and do not flee! Jesus has you on his hook, not to cause your death but to give you life after putting you to death. For you must die and rise again. You have heard the Apostle's words: "Dead to sin but alive to righteousness" (Rom. 6:11). Begin today to live!

(*Procat.* 5)

The Pure Gold of Your Souls

Hasten to the catecheses, hasten to receive the exorcisms. The insufflation and the exorcisms over you bring salvation. Think of yourself as gold that is impure and alloyed, a mixture of various things: copper, tin, iron, or lead. What we want is pure gold!

Without fire, gold cannot be purified of alien elements. So too, without exorcisms the soul cannot be purified. . . .

When goldsmiths fan the flame by directing air upon it with a bellows, they

---

4. In Section 2 (omitted here), Cyril had spoken of Simon the Magician (Acts 8:9-24) who "was baptized but not enlightened" (ms A).

melt the gold that is hidden in the crucible, and they obtain what they are seeking. So too, when exorcisms instill fear by the power of God's Breath[5] and make the soul, which is hidden in the body as in a crucible, pass through fire, the hostile demon flees, while salvation and the hope of eternal life remain. The soul is now purified of its sins and possesses salvation.

SONS AND DAUGHTERS OF A SINGLE MOTHER

> Brethren, let this hope strengthen us!
> Let us trust in it, let us hope!
> May the God of the universe, who sees our resolve,
> purify us of our sins
> and grant us a solid hope of those realities!
> May he grant us conversion and salvation!
> God has called; it is you he has called!

(Procat. 9)

You who have enrolled yourselves have become the sons and daughters of a single Mother.

(Procat. 13)

MAY THE DOOR OF PARADISE SWING WIDE!

I shall observe the alacrity of each man; I shall observe the piety of each woman.

> Let your spirits be inflamed with devotion,
> let your souls be forged as on an anvil,
> and the stubbornness of unbelief be hammered away!
> Let the useless iron dross disappear
> and only what is pure remain.
> Let the iron rust disappear
> and only what is true remain!
>
> May God deign then to show you this night
> the darkness that is as bright as day
> and of which it is written:
> "The darkness will not be dark for you,
> and the night shall be as bright as day" (Ps. 139:12).
>
> For each man and woman among you
> may the door of paradise swing wide!
> Enjoy then the perfumed waters:[6]
> they contain Christ.

---

5. That is, the Holy Spirit.
6. The waters of baptism.

Receive the name of Christ
and the power to do deeds that are divine.

From this moment forward, lift up the eyes of your mind, contemplate within you the choirs of angels and the God, the Master of the universe, sitting on his throne with his only-begotten Son, seated at his right hand, and with the Holy Spirit; the thrones and dominations who serve them; and each man and woman among you, also there, saved! From this moment forward, let your ears hear the marvelous song the angels will sing to you when you are saved:

"Happy they whose faults are forgiven
and whose sins are covered over!" (Ps. 32:1).

Then, like stars of the Church, you will enter heaven, your bodies gleaming with light and your souls resplendent.

(Procat. 15)

Great indeed is the baptism you shall receive! It brings ransom for the captive, forgiveness of sins, death to sin, new birth for the soul. It is a garment of light, an indelible seal, a chariot bearing you to heaven. It is the delights of paradise, the gift of the kingdom, the grace of adoptive sonship.

(Procat. 16)

First Prebaptismal Catechesis

Extempore catechesis at Jerusalem, to introduce the candidates for baptism. Reading from Isaiah: "Wash yourselves, purify yourselves, remove from my sight the wickedness of your souls" (Is. 1:16).

CREATE A NEW HEART FOR YOURSELVES

O disciples of the new covenant,
who share in the mysteries of Christ,
now by calling, soon by grace,
create for yourselves a new heart, a new spirit,
so that there may be joy in heaven (Lk. 15:31)!
For if, as the Gospel says, there is joy
at a single sinner who is converted,
how glad will heaven be
at the salvation of so many souls!

You are on the right path, and the most beautiful one as well,
therefore run fearlessly the race of piety.
It is to ransom you that the only-begotten Son of God
stands there ready and says:
"Come, all you who toil and weep under your burden,
and I will comfort you" (Mt. 11:28).

You who wear the deadly garment of your evil deeds,
who are fettered by the chains of your own sins,
listen to the prophet's voice as he proclaims:
"Wash yourselves, purify yourselves,
remove from my sight the wickedness of your souls!"
Then the choir of angels will greet you with the song:
"Happy they whose faults are forgiven
and whose sins are covered over!" (Ps. 32:1).

Now that you have lit the torches of your faith,
keep them ever lit in your hands,
so that he who once on holy Golgotha
opened paradise to the thief in answer to his faith
may let you also sing the marriage song.

(*Cat.* 1, 1)

COME AND BE MARKED WITH THE MYSTICAL SEAL

If there is anyone here who is still a slave of sin, let him prepare himself by faith for the freedom that rebirth through adoptive sonship brings. Let him free himself from the deadly slavery of sin and acquire the blessed slavery of the Lord (Rom. 6:16-18) so that he may be judged worthy of inheriting the kingdom of heaven! Let him, through confession, strip himself of the old self that is being corrupted by evil lusts, and then put on the new man who is being renewed according to knowledge of his Creator! (Eph. 4:22-24).

Acquire the firstfruits of the Holy Spirit through faith so that you may be received into the eternal dwellings. Come and be marked with the mystical seal so that the Master can recognize you. Join the holy and spiritual flock of Christ in order to win a place at his right side and receive the inheritance of life that has been made ready for you.

As for those still imprisoned in the rough wrapping of their sins, they will be on the left side because they have not taken the step toward the grace of God that Christ gives us in the bath of regeneration.

(*Cat.* 1, 1-2)

YOU WILL BE TRANSPLANTED INTO THE SPIRITUAL PARADISE

From then on you will be planted in the spiritual paradise,
you will receive a new name you did not have before.
Hitherto you were "catechumen";
now they will call you "believer."

From then on you will be transplanted into the spiritual olive grove,
and grafted from the wild olive tree on to the true olive tree,
from your sins on to justice,
from your defilements on to purity.

You will participate in the holy vine;
if you remain in the vine, you will grow
as a shoot laden with fruit;
if you do not remain in it, you will be burned in the fire.

Let us therefore bear fruit as we should!
Let our fate be not that of the barren fig tree;
let Jesus not come again today
to curse it for its barrenness!

May we all say: "As for me,
like a green olive tree in the house of God,
I have forever put my hope in the mercy of God!" (Ps. 52:8).
An olive tree that is not material
but spiritual, a bearer of light.

It is for God, then, to plant and water (1 Cor. 3:6)
but for you to bear fruit;
for God to give his grace
but for you to receive and preserve it.

                                                    (*Cat.* 1, 4)

First Mystagogical Catechesis [7]

Baptismal Renunciations and Profession

First mystagogical catechesis to the neophytes. Reading from the First Catholic Letter of Peter, from "Be sober and keep watch," to the end of the Letter (1 Pet. 5:8-14).

THE PURPOSE OF THE MYSTAGOGICAL CATECHESES

Dear and true children of the Church, I have long desired to instruct you in these spiritual and heavenly mysteries of the Church . . . so that you may know the work that has been done in you on this evening of your baptism.

                                                    (*Cat.* 19, 1)

"I RENOUNCE YOU, SATAN!"

First, you entered the vestibule of the baptistery and, standing there, you

---

7. We shall ordinarily follow the critical Greek text established by A. Piédagnel.

listened while facing the West. Then they bade you raise your hand, and you renounced Satan, as if he were actually present.[8]

You must realize that this rite was prefigured in ancient history. When Pharaoh, that very violent and cruel tyrant, was oppressing the free and noble Hebrew people, God sent Moses to rescue them from their terrible enslavement to the Egyptians. They smeared their doorposts with the blood of the Lamb so that the Destroyer might spare the houses that were marked with the blood. The Hebrew people was thus wonderfully rescued. But when the enemy pursued those who had regained their freedom, he saw another marvel: the sea opening before them. Wanting to cross in the same manner, he rushed forward in their tracks, but suddenly he was submerged, and the Red Sea buried him.

Let us pass now from ancient things to new, from figure to reality.

There Moses was sent by God to Egypt; here it is Christ whom the Father sends into the world. There an afflicted people had to be rescued from Egypt; here it is Christ who must liberate men over whom sin was holding tyrannical sway in the world. There the blood of a lamb turned the Destroyer aside; here it is the blood of the spotless Lamb, Jesus Christ, that puts the demons to flight. The tyrant pursued the people of old as far as the sea; as for you, this shameless, impudent demon, the source of all evil, pursues you as far as the fountain of salvation. The tyrant was submerged in the sea; the demon disappears in the waters of salvation.

This is why you were ordered to raise your hand and say to Satan, as if he were actually present: "I renounce you, Satan."

I also want to explain to you, for it is necessary, why you turned to the West.

The West is the land where darkness makes itself visible. Now the devil, who is himself darkness, exercises his power in darkness. It is in order to symbolize this that you looked to the West and renounced the prince of night and darkness.

What did you say then, each of you, as you stood there? "I renounce you, Satan, wicked and cruel tyrant!" And you asserted: "Henceforth, I am no longer in your power. For Christ destroyed that power by sharing with me a nature of flesh and blood. He destroyed death by dying; never again shall I enslaved to you! I renounce you, crafty serpent full of deceit! I renounce you who lurk in ambush, who pretend friendship but have been the cause of every iniquity, who instigated the sin of our first parents! I renounce you, Satan, author and abettor of every evil."

(Cat. 19, 2-4)

"AND ALL YOUR WORKS"

In a second formula, you then learn to say: "And all your works."

The works of Satan are all the sins that must be renounced, just as one who

---

8. The renunciation of Satan was the first act in the baptismal ritual of Holy Saturday evening. In other Churches, it took place on Good Friday, at three o'clock in the afternoon.

flees a usurper must also unconditionally reject the weapons the usurper uses. Sin, in all its forms, is to be numbered among the works of the devil.

In addition, be sure of this: that everything you say, especially at this awe-inspiring moment, is written in the invisible books of God.

It is for this reason that if you do anything contrary to the words you speak here, you will be judged as a perjurer. For you are renouncing all the works of Satan, that is, all the actions and thoughts that are contrary to the word you give.

"AND YOUR WORSHIP"

Then you say: "And your worship." The worship of the devil takes the form of prayer in temples built for idols and of rites in honor of lifeless idols, as, for example, to light lamps or burn incense beside springs or rivers. Some people are deceived by dreams or demons and come to such spots in the belief that they will find there a cure for bodily illnesses. Do not indulge in such practices. Omens, divination, auguries, amulets, inscriptions on leaves of metal, magic, and other evil arts, as well as all practices of a similar kind, are the worship of the devil. Therefore, flee them.

(Cat. 19, 8)

PROFESSION OF FAITH, TOWARD THE EAST

When you renounce Satan, you break off every agreement you have entered into with him, every covenant you have established with hell. Then there opens to you the paradise which God planted in the East (Gen. 2:8) and from which dis-obedience expelled our first parent. It is in order to symbolize this that you turn from the West to the East, the land of light.

Then they asked you to declare yourself: "I believe in the Father, in the Son, in the Holy Spirit, and in a single baptism of repentance."

(Cat. 19, 9)

NEVER AGAIN SHALL YOU WEEP

Draw strength from the words you spoke and be watchful. For, as we have just read, your adversary, the devil, prowls like a roaring lion, seeking whom he may devour. Formerly death was powerful and could devour. But in the bath of new birth God has dried all the tears from every face (Is. 25:8). Never again shall you weep; you shall always be on holiday, for you have put on the garment of salvation, Jesus Christ.

(Cat. 19, 10)

This, then, if what took place outside the baptistery proper. God willing, we shall, in ensuing explanations of the mysteries, enter into the holy of holies and learn the meaning of the rites that are performed there. To God the Father, glory, power, and greatness, with the Son and the Holy Spirit, for ever and ever. Amen!

(Cat. 19, 11)

Second Mystagogical Catechesis: On Baptism

Second mystagogical catechesis, on baptism. Reading from the Letter to the Romans, from the words: "Do you not know that when we were baptized into Christ Jesus, it was into his death that we were baptized?" to the words: "You are no longer under the law, but under grace" (Rom. 6:3-14).

These daily mystagogical catecheses are useful to you, these new instructions that tell you of realities still new to you, for you have been renewed in passing from decrepitude to newness. I must therefore continue yesterday's mystagogical catechesis and show you the meaning of the rites to which you submitted inside the baptistery.

You Stripped Off Your Tunic

As soon as you entered, you stripped off your tunic. This rite signified the stripping off of the old self with all its activities.

Stripped of your garments you were naked and thus resembled Christ on the cross. There, by his nakedness, Christ despoiled the Principalities and Powers and, by means of the wood (of the cross), dragged them after him in his triumphal procession (Col. 2:15). Now, since the hostile powers were hiding in your members, you could no longer be allowed to wear this shabby tunic. I am speaking, of course, not of the garment men see but of the old self that is being corrupted by the lusts that lead astray (Eph. 4:22). May the soul that has stripped off that garment once and for all not put it on again! Let it say, rather, as the Spouse of Christ says in the Song of Songs: "I have stripped off my tunic, how shall I put it on again?" (Song 5:3). What a marvelous thing! You were naked in the sight of all, yet you did not blush. In very truth, you were an image of the first man, Adam, who in the garden was likewise naked and did not blush.

(*Cat.* 20, 2)

The Anointing

Stripped of your garments, you were anointed from the crown of your head to your feet[9] with the oil of exorcism. Here you became a sharer in the true olive tree, Jesus Christ! You have been cut off from the wild olive tree and grafted on to the true olive tree, and therefore you share in the anointing that the true olive tree bestows. For the oil over which an exorcism has been spoken symbolizes our sharing in the anointing of Christ; it removes all the marks left by the hostile

---

9. In order that the symbols might be truly meaningful, the ancient liturgy made them as expressive as possible. Thus the stripping off of garments was complete, the anointing covered the whole body, and the immersion was total. To assure proper order during the celebration, the men were separated from the women, and deaconesses were available to help the women in ministering to the women.

power. Just as the insufflations by the saints[10] and the invocation of the name of God burn like the hottest flame and put the demons to flight, so this oil of exorcism acquires a marvelous power, thanks to the invocation of God's name and the prayer. Not only does it purify all the traces of sin by burning them away, but it also puts to flight the invisible powers of the Evil One.

(*Cat.* 20, 3)

The Triple Baptismal Immersion

Next they led you to the holy font of divine baptism, just as they brought Christ from the cross to the sepulcher that stands over there before you.[11]

They asked each person if he or she believed in the name of the Father, of the Son, and of the Holy Spirit. And you pronounced the salutary profession.

Then you were plunged three times into the water, and three times you came forth. This rite symbolized the burial of Christ for three days. . . . In a single moment you died and you were reborn, and this saving water was both tomb and mother to you.

(*Cat.* 20:4)

The Grace of Salvation

O strange and wonderful event! We were not really put to death, we were not really buried, we were not really crucified, we were not really brought back to life. But, though the imitation was symbolic, the salvation is very real! Christ was truly crucified, truly buried, truly raised up. And all this was given to us by grace in order that we might share his sufferings by imitating them, and thus truly obtain salvation. How vast God's love for men! Christ had his utterly pure hands pierced by the nails, he suffered; and yet it is to me, who share in his sufferings without suffering or experiencing pain, that he gives the grace of salvation.

(*Cat.* 20, 5)

Baptized into the Death of Christ

Let no one think that baptism gives us only the forgiveness of sins and the grace of adoption. It was John's baptism that bestowed only the forgiveness of sins. But (this baptism of ours), which brings purification from sins and also mediates the gift of the Holy Spirit, is also a replica of the passion of Christ. That is why Paul asserted just now:[12]

"Do you not know that when we were baptized into Christ Jesus, it was into

---

10. The rite of "insufflation" ("breathing into") is an exorcism in preparation for baptism. The "saints" mentioned are perhaps the priests who did the insufflation.

11. Remember that the catechesis was being given in the Rotunda of the Resurrection, part of the Basilica of the Holy Sepulcher.

12. Cyril is alluding to the reading from the Letter to the Romans that preceded the catechesis.

his death that were baptized? We have therefore been buried with him through baptism" (Rom. 6:3-4).

He undoubtedly meant his remarks for those who maintained that baptism bestowed only the forgiveness of sins and adoption as God's children and did not involve a sharing, through imitation, in the real sufferings of Christ.

(Cat. 20, 6)

GRAFTED ON TO CHRIST

We must therefore learn that whatever Christ suffered he endured in reality and not in mere appearance, and he did so for us and our salvation. Thus we share in his passion. Paul proclaimed this with perfect accuracy:

> "If we have been grafted on to Christ by a death like his, we shall also be grafted on by a resurrection like his" (Rom. 6:5).

What a splendid word "grafted" is! The true Vine was indeed planted right here.[13] By sharing in his death through baptism, we were grafted on to it.

Pay the greatest attention to the meaning of the Apostle's words. He does not say: "If we are grafted by the death," but "by a likeness of his death." Christ really died, for his soul was really separated from his body. His burial too was real, for his sacred body was wrapped in a clean shroud. In his regard, everything really happened. For us, it is different: we image forth his death and sufferings. But when it comes to salvation, we possess it not in an image but in its very reality.

(Cat. 20, 7)

WALK IN A NEW LIFE

You are now sufficiently instructed on this matter. Hold on to this teaching, I beg of you. Then I too, despite my unworthiness, will be able to say: "I love you because you remember me at all times and maintain the traditions I passed on to you" (1 Cor. 11:2).

Powerful indeed is God, who took you from among the dead and brought you into life, and who enables you to walk in a new life. To him, glory and power, now and for ever. Amen.

(Cat. 20, 8)

Third Mystagogical Catechesis: On the Anointing

Third mystagogical catechesis, on the anointing. Reading from the First Letter of John, from the words: "You have been anointed by God, and you know everything," to the words: "lest we be cast far from him and shamed at his coming" (1 Jn. 2:20-28).

---

13. "Right here": *entautha*. Cyril had only to point to the spot where the cross of Jesus had stood.

Men Call You "Christ" [14]

Having been baptized into Christ and having put on Christ, you have become like the Son of God. Because God predestined us for adoptive sonship, he has made us like the glorious body of Christ. Rightly then do men call you "christs," since you share in Christ. It is of you that God was speaking when he said: "Do not touch my christs" (Ps. 105:15). Yes, you have become christs by receiving the mark of the Holy Spirit. All this was done to you in imaged form, because you are images of Christ.

When Christ bathed himself in the River Jordan, thus communicating to the waters the contact with his divinity, and when he emerged again from the river, the Holy Spirit really rested on him, Like upon Like. In a parallel way, when you came up from the font and its holy waters, you received chrismation and the mark with which Christ was chrismated: the Holy Spirit. Blessed Isaiah, in his prophecy on the person of Christ (Is. 61:1), said of him:

> "The Spirit of the Lord is upon me.
> That is why he has chrismated me,
> he has sent me to bring the Good News to the poor."

(*Cat.* 21, 1)

It was not men who chrismated Christ, using a material oil or balm. No, it was the Father who, after designating him in advance as Savior of the Entire universe, chrismated him with the Holy Spirit, as Peter tells us: "God chrismated Jesus of Nazareth with the Holy Spirit" (Acts 10:38). . . . He was chrismated with a spiritual oil of gladness, that is, with the Holy Spirit, who is called the oil of spiritual gladness. You too have been chrismated with a balm that makes you sharers and associates of Christ.

(*Cat.* 21, 2)

The Consecrated Balm

Yet do not imagine that this was an ordinary balm. For just as the bread of the Eucharist, after the invocation of the Holy Spirit, is no longer ordinary bread but the body of Christ, so this holy balm, after the invocation, is no longer what we might call an ordinary, everyday balm, but it is a gift of Christ, and the presence of the Holy Spirit, of the divinity, makes it efficacious. It serves to chrismate your forehead and other senses. This action is symbolic: while your body is being

---

14. Following J. Bouvet (p. 466), who is followed also by P. Paris (p. 121), in this catechesis we choose to translate the Greek word for "anointing" as "chrism," and the verb "to anoint" as "to chrismate." The awkwardness of the words is compensated for by the fact that we are thus able to retain, as the Greek does, the family unity of the words *Christ, chrism, chrismate,* and *Christian.* The original text constantly plays on this unity, which is lost if we translate these words belonging to the same family by English words of quite different origins: *Christ, anointing, anoint,* and *Christian.*

chrismated by visible balm, your soul is being sanctified by the holy and life-giving Spirit.

(Cat. 21, 3)

THE ANOINTINGS

You were chrismated first on the forehead so that you might be freed from the shame that the first man after his disobedience carried with him everywhere, and so that, with unveiled face, you might reflect as in a mirror the glory of the Lord (2 Cor. 3:18).

Then on the ears so that you might receive ears that are attentive to the divine mysteries. Isaiah foretells, on this point: "The Lord has given me ears with which to hear" (Is. 50:4). And the Lord Jesus says in the Gospels: "Whoever has ears to hear, let him hear" (Mt. 11:15).

Then on the nostrils so that you might breathe in this divine perfume and say, "We are the fragrance of Christ to God, among those who are being saved" (2 Cor. 2:15).

Finally on the breast so that you might put on the breastplate of uprightness and resist the assaults of the devil. For just as the Savior went out to fight the Enemy after his baptism and the descent of the Spirit, so you, after holy baptism and the mystical chrismation, have put on the armor of the Holy Spirit and stand in battle against the hostile Powers; you fight them, saying: "I can do everything in him who strengthens me, Christ" (Phil. 4:13).

(Cat. 21, 4)

THE NAME "CHRISTIAN"

Since you have been judged worthy of this chrismation, you now bear the name "Christians," and your regeneration confirms the legitimacy of this title. For before being judged worthy of the grace of baptism and the Holy Spirit, you did not truly deserve this title. You were only traveling along the road to becoming Christians.

(Cat. 21, 5)

Preserve unspotted and unprofaned the anointing you have received with this holy balm. Preserve it by advancing in goodness and making yourselves pleasing to Jesus Christ, the author of your salvation.

To him, glory for ever and ever. Amen.

(Cat. 21, 7)

Fifth Mystagogical Catechesis: On the Eucharist

Fifth mystagogical catechesis. Reading from the First Letter of Peter: "Put aside therefore all malice, deceitfulness and slander . . ." and what follows (1 Pet. 2:1).

Thanks to God's love for you, you have been sufficiently instructed, at the preceding gatherings, on baptism, on the anointing, and on the reception of the body and blood of Christ. We must now pass on to the next subject and finish today the spiritual edifice of your salvation.[15]

(Cat. 23, 1)

THE WASHING OF THE HANDS

You then saw the deacon present the ablutions to the bishop and the priests who stand around the altar of God.[16] He did not present them because of any bodily uncleanness. No, that was not the point. After all, we did not enter the church with unwashed bodies at the beginning of the service! The meaning of the washing of the hands is that we must purify ourselves of all our sins and failings. The hands symbolize our actions. By washing them, we show that our actions should be pure and beyond reproach. Did you not hear blessed David initiating us into this mystery when he said: "I will wash my hands among the innocent and go about your altar, Lord" (Ps. 26:6)? The washing of hands thus symbolizes purification from sin.

(Cat. 23, 2)

THE KISS OF PEACE

The deacon then says in a loud voice: "Welcome one another and embrace one another!"

Do not think of this kiss as being like the kiss people exchange in the public squares when they meet friends. No, this kiss is not of that kind. It unites souls, it requires that we forget all grudges.

This kiss thus signifies the union of souls with one another, and the forgetfulness of all wrongs done us. This is why Christ said:

> "If you are presenting your gift at the altar, and there you remember that your brother has a grievance against you, leave your offering there before the altar, and go first to be reconciled to your brother; then return and present your offering" (Mt. 5:23-24).

This kiss, then, is an act of reconciliation. That is why it is holy, as blessed Paul proclaims it to be when he says: "Greet one another with a holy kiss" (1 Cor. 16:20); Peter also says: "Greet one another with a kiss of love" (1 Pet. 5:14).

(Cat. 23, 3)

PREFACE

Then the priest says in a loud voice: "Lift up your hearts!" Truly, at this awe-inspiring time we must raise our hearts to God and not let them sink down to

---

15. Literally: "the spiritual edifice of (your) profit."
16. Literally: "to the priest and elders (presbyters)." "Priest" here means the bishop, and "elders" or "presbyters" means the priests. Note that Cyril says nothing of the celebration of the word of God that precedes the Eucharist proper. The reason is that the liturgy of the word was a regular part of the celebrations for the catechumens during Lent; thus the neophytes had a sufficient knowledge of it.

the earth and earthly affairs. The bishop therefore orders us at this moment to abandon all our everyday preoccupations and our domestic cares, and to keep our hearts in heaven, close to God, who loves men.

You then respond: "We turn them to the Lord." You thus give your assen you assert your agreement. Let no one, then, stand there and say with his lips only: "We turn them to the Lord," while his mind remains absorbed by the cares of life. We ought indeed be constantly mindful of God, but if that is not possible because of human weakness, then at this moment above all we must make the effort to have him before us.

The priest says next: "Let us give thanks to the Lord!" We should indeed give thanks to the Lord, for he has called us to so wonderful a grace when we were unworthy of it; he reconciled us when we were still his enemies; he judged us worthy of the Spirit of adoption.

You answer: "That is right and just." When we offer thanks, we do a work that is right and just. As for God, however, he did not merely do what was just, but went far beyond what justice required when he heaped blessings upon us and deemed us worthy of such wonderful gifts.

(Cat. 23, 4)

After this we make mention of heaven, earth, and sea, sun and moon, stars and all creatures, those endowed with reason and those not so endowed, those visible and those invisible: Angels, Archangels, Powers, Dominations, Principalities, Virtues, Thrones, and Cherubim with their many faces. Then with vigor we repeat these words of David:

"Glorify the Lord with me!" (Ps. 34:4)

We also make mention of the Seraphim, whom Isaiah contemplated when he was caught up in an ecstasy by the Holy Spirit. They encircled the throne of God. They had two wings to hide their faces, two wings to cover their feet, and two wings for flying. And they were exclaiming:

"Holy, holy, holy
is the Lord Sabaoth!" (Is. 6:3).

We sing this doxology, which comes to us from the Seraphim, in order that we may participate in the song of the heavenly armies.

(Cat. 23, 6)

EPICLESIS

After having sanctified ourselves by means of these spiritual hymns, we ask God, the lover of mankind, to send the Holy Spirit on the offerings that are set forth there, in order that he may change the bread into the body of Christ and the wine into the blood of Christ. For whatever the Spirit touches is sanctified and transformed.

(Cat. 23, 7)

INTERCESSIONS

After the spiritual sacrifice, the unbloody worship, has been accomplished in this victim that is offered in propitiation, we call on God for peace in all the Churches, for tranquillity in the world, for the emperors, for the armies and the allies, for the ill and the afflicted. In brief, for all those in need of help we all pray and offer this sacrifice.

(Cat. 23, 8)

We then remember also those who have fallen asleep: first, the patriarchs, prophets, apostles, and martyrs, that through their prayers and intercession God would accept our petitions; then, for our fathers who have fallen asleep in holiness, for the bishops, and, in short, for all those who have already fallen asleep. For we are convinced that our prayers, which rise up for them in the presence of the holy and venerable victim, are most profitable to their souls.

(Cat. 23, 9)

THE LORD'S PRAYER

After this you say the family prayer that the Savior taught his disciples. With a pure conscience we address God as our Father and we say: *"Our Father,* who art in the heavens!" O how immense God's love is for men! To those who have gone far from him and fallen into the worst evil he grants so great a pardon for their sins and makes them share so greatly in his grace that they can call him "Father."

"Our Father, *who art in the heavens!"* The heavens may also be those which are in the likeness of the heavenly man (1 Cor. 15:49), in the midst of which God walks and dwells (2 Cor. 6:16)!

(Cat. 23, 11)

"Hallowed be thy name!" Whether or not we call God's name "holy," it is holy by its nature. But since that name is at times profaned among sinners, as it is written: "Because of you my name is constantly blasphemed among the gentiles" (Is. 52:5), we ask that God's name be hallowed among us. Not that it should become holy as though it were not previously holy, but that it may become holy in us when we are sanctified and act in a manner worthy of its holiness.

(Cat. 23, 12)

"Thy kingdom come!" A pure soul can say with assurance: "Thy kingdom come!" For the person who has heeded St. Paul's words: "Let sin, therefore, no longer reign in your mortal body" (Rom. 6:12) and who has achieved purity in action, thought, and words, can say to God: "Thy kingdom come!"

(Cat. 23, 13)

"Thy will be done on earth as it is in heaven." The godlike, blessed angels of God do his will, as David sings in the psalm:

> "Bless the Lord, all his angels,
> who are mighty and strong,
> who fulfill his word!" (Ps. 103:20).

Your fervent prayer, then, has this meaning: "Your will is done in the angels; Master, may it likewise be done in me on earth!"

"Give us this day our substantial bread." [17] The bread over there, which is ordinary bread, is not "substantial." But this bread on the altar, which is now holy, is indeed substantial; in other words, it has been instituted for the "subsistence" of the soul. This bread does not enter the stomach and then pass from it in a private place, but it nourishes you in your entirety, for the good of body and soul. As for the words "this day," they mean "day after day." Paul speaks in a similar manner: "As long as the time called 'today' lasts . . ." (Heb. 3:13).

(Cat. 23, 15)

"And forgive us our debts, as we forgive our debtors." We have many sins, for we stumble in word and thought; we do a large number of condemnable actions, and if we claim "to be without sin, we lie," as John says (1 Jn. 1:8). We enter into a contract with God: we ask him to forgive us our sins, as we forgive our neighbor his debts. Let us consider, then, what we receive and the exchange we are making. Let us not delay, let us not hesitate to forgive one another. The offenses committed against us are small, light, easy to blot out. But those we have committed against God are great, and the only thing we can appeal to is his love. Be on guard, then, lest because of the small and light offenses committed against you, you block God's forgiveness for very serious sins.

(Cat. 23, 16)

"And lead us not into temptation, Lord." Is the Lord teaching us to ask that we never be tempted? But how could we then read elsewhere: "The man who has not been tempted has not been tested" (Sir. 34:10). And again: "Regard it as a supreme joy, my brethren, that you are subject to all kinds of temptations" (Jas. 1:2). But, then, does "entering into temptation" mean "being submerged by temptation"? Temptation is in fact comparable to a torrent that is difficult to cross; those who are not submerged by temptations pass through them; they are excellent swimmers, and the temptations have no power to drag them down. But when those who do not have the same qualities enter the stream, they are swallowed up.

---

17. In Mt. 6:11, the Greek word *epiousios* does not have the stronger meaning of "substantial," but the author gives it this meaning here in order to apply it more easily to the Eucharist.

Judas is an example: he entered into the temptation of avarice; he did not pass through it, but was swallowed up and perished body and soul. Peter entered into the temptation of denial; he entered but was not swallowed up; he swam nobly and was saved from the temptation.

Listen, too, to the choir of the saints who were saved and who offer thanks for having been delivered from temptation:

> "You put us to the test,
> you tried us with fire as they purify silver in a fire,
> you brought us into the net,
> you loaded us down with afflictions;
> you let men tread upon our heads,
> we passed through fire and water.
> Then you led us to the place of refreshment" (Ps. 66:10-12).

You see with what assurance they speak, these men and women who passed through without being swallowed up. "You led us," they sing, "to the place of refreshment." To go to the place of refreshment means to be saved from temptation.

(Cat. 23, 17)

"But deliver us from the Evil One." If the words "Lead us not into temptation" meant never to be tempted, the Lord would not have added: "But deliver us from the Evil One." The Evil One is the devil, the adversary, and we ask to be delivered from him.

At the end of the prayer you add: *"Amen!"* "Amen" means "Let it be so!" With this word you put your seal on the content of the prayer that God has taught us.

(Cat. 23, 18)

"Holy Things to the Holy"

After this the bishop says: "Holy things to the holy!" Holy are the offerings which have been laid here and on which the Holy Spirit has descended. Holy, too, are you who have been judged worthy of the Holy Spirit. The holy things, then, are for those who are holy.

You then say: "One alone is holy, one alone is Lord: Jesus Christ." Yes, truly is he alone holy, and he is so by nature. We too are holy, not by nature, but by participation as well as by the exercise of the virtues and by prayer.

(Cat. 23, 19)

Then you hear the cantor inviting you, in a divine song, to communion in the holy mysteries; he says: "Taste and see how good the Lord is" (Ps. 34:9). Do not judge by bodily taste but by a faith that is free of doubt. Those who taste the Lord do not taste bread and wine but the body and blood of Christ, which the bread and wine signify.

(Cat. 23, 20)

COMMUNION

When you come forward, do not draw near with your hands wide open or with the fingers spread apart; instead, with your left hand make a throne for the right hand, which will receive the King. Receive the body of Christ in the hollow of your hand and give the response: "Amen."

Then, with care, sanctify your eyes by contact with the sacred body. Take it and be on guard lest you lose any of it. For if you lost a particle of it, it would be as if you had lost one of your members! Tell me, if someone gave you some gold-dust, would you not preserve it with the greatest care and be on guard not to let any of it be destroyed and so to suffer the loss of it? Should you not be even more careful of what is far more precious than gold and precious stones, lest you let a particle of it fall?

Then, after sharing in the body of Christ, draw near also to the cup of his blood. Do not stretch out your hands, but bow in adoration and respect, and say: "Amen." Then sanctify yourself further by sharing in the blood of Christ. And while your lips are still wet, touch them with your fingers and sanctify your eyes, your forehead, and your other senses. Then, while waiting for the prayer, give thanks to God who has judged you worthy of such great mysteries.

(*Cat.* 23, 22)

PRESERVE THESE TRADITIONS

Keep these traditions inviolate. Remain spotless. Do not separate yourself from the community. Do not make yourself unclean by sin and so deprive yourself of these holy and spiritual mysteries.

May the God of peace sanctify you wholly, and may your entire being — spirit, soul, and body — be preserved without reproach for the coming of our Savior Jesus Christ (1 Thess. 5:23)!

> To him, glory and power,
> with the Father and the Holy Spirit,
> now and always
> and for ever and ever. Amen.

(*Cat.* 23, 23)

Glossary

Agape, from the Greek *agapē*, "love." A fellowship meal, liturgical in character and accompanied by prayer; an expression of fraternal love. It could be joined to the Eucharist (1 Cor. 11:20-22).

Alleluia, from the Hebrew *Halelu-Yah*, "Praise Yah [=Yahweh]!" A liturgical acclamation at the beginning or end of certain psalms. An acclamation of the elect in the heavenly liturgy of the Apocalypse. A cry of paschal joy and praise.

Alpha and *Omega*, the first and last letters of the Greek alphabet. The beginning and the end of being, Rev. 21:6. A divine title applied to Christ, Rev. 1:8.

Amen, a Hebrew word from a root meaning "firm, permanent." The word means both "Let it be so!" and "Yes, it is so!" A title of Christ, Rev. 3:14.

Anamnesis, from the Greek *anamnēsis*, "remembrance." A prayer recalling the mysteries of salvation that are contained in the Eucharistic celebration. The prayer is based on the Lord's words: "Do this in remembrance of me," and is said after the consecration.

Anaphora, from the Greek *anaphora*, "a raising up," and thus "an offering." The central prayer of the Mass, corresponding to the present-day Eucharistic Prayers of the Roman liturgy.

Apocalypse, from the Greek *apo*, "un-," and *kalyptō*, "hide." A revelation concerning spiritual realities, for example, the person of Jesus, Mt. 11:25-27. — A charism the Spirit bestows on believers, 1 Cor. 14:26. — A name for the book of the New Testament entitled "The Revelation of Jesus Christ," Rev. 1:1.

Apocrypha, from the Greek *apo*, "from," and *kryptō*, "cover"; therefore: "remove from view, keep secret." Writings which claim to be inspired but which do not belong to the official canon of Scripture. They are also called *pseudepigrapha*: writings (*graphai*) whose ascription (*epi*) is false (*pseudēs*). The apocrypha are valuable as witnesses to tradition.

Arianism, a heresy spread by a priest, Arius, at Alexandria, beginning in 315 A.D. Arius wanted to explain the mystery of the Trinity by making the Son subordinate to the Father in such a way as to deny that the two Persons are equally divine.

Azymes, from the Greek *a-zymos*, "without yeast." Unleavened bread used in the celebration of Passover.

Blessing, in Greek *eulogia*, "good *or* kind word." A word or action by which God communicates his gift. Blessing comes from the Father, who gives it in Christ and the Holy Spirit, Eph. 1. Man responds to it with thanksgiving or "eucharist."

Breaking of bread is a Palestinian term for the Jewish meal. It may also designate the Eucharistic meal, 1 Cor. 10:16.

Catechesis, from the Greek *catēchēsis*, "instruction" (see 1 Cor. 14:19).

Catechumen, one who receives instruction (catechesis) with a view to baptism.

Cherubim, from the Hebrew *kerub*. Mysterious heavenly beings who serve God, Gen. 3:24; Heb. 9:5.

Christ, from the Greek *Christos*, "anointed," which is a translation of Hebrew *mashiah*, Jn. 1:41. Jesus is the one whom God has anointed, Lk. 4:18; Acts 4:27; whence the title "Christ" that is given to him, Mt. 1:17. The titles "Jesus" and "Christ" are interchangeable, Acts 8:5; 9:20.

Confess, from the Latin *confiteor*, "acknowledge, proclaim one's faith; acknowledge one's sin."

Copt, derived from the Greek *Aigyptios*, "Egyptian." The Coptic Rite is used chiefly in Egypt.

Didache, a Greek word meaning "instruction, teaching."

Didaskalia, a Greek word meaning "instruction, teaching."

Docetism, from the Greek *dokeō*, "seem, appear." A Christological heresy according to which Jesus was God but had only the appearance of a man. The Letter to the Colossians and the Letters of John, 1 Jn. 1:1-3, are already combatting this heresy.

Doxology, from the Greek *doxologia*, a prayer which expresses (*logos*) the glory (*doxa*) of God, Lk. 2:14; Rev. 7:10.

Epiclesis, from the Greek *epiklēsis*, "invocation." A prayer of the Eucharistic liturgy which calls on (*kaleō*) the Holy Spirit (or the Logos, the Word) to descend upon (*epi*) the offerings.

Eschatology, from the Greek *eschata*, "the last things," and *logos*, "discourse": Discourse about the end of the world, the last Day. The eschatological age has already begun with the coming of Christ, 1 Cor. 10:11, and will end with his glorious coming at the end of time.

Eucharist, from the Greek *eu*, "well," and *charizomai*, "give thanks." The prayer of thanksgiving pronounced over the bread and wine. — The bread over which the prayer of thanksgiving has been spoken.

Euchology, from the Greek *euchē*, "prayer," and *logos*, "discourse; book." A book of prayers.

Eulogy, from the Greek *eu*, "well," and *logos*, "discourse." Words of commendation; therefore: blessing.

Episcopos, from the Greek *episkopos*, "overseer." Originally the name given to those in charge of the Christian communities (Acts 20:28). Later, *the* person in charge, that is, the bishop.

Exodus, from the Greek *exodos*, "going forth; departure." Refers either to the departure of Israel from Egypt or to the departure from this world in the mystery of death, Lk. 9:31.

Gematria, a science which attributes a certain meaning to numbers and interprets it. Thus the number 7 is regarded as a perfect number.

Geniza, an Aramaic word from the root *gnz*, "conceal." In synagogues, the storage room used chiefly for tattered biblical scrolls (which, out of respect for God's word, were not simply destroyed).

Gnosis, from the Greek *gnōsis*, "knowledge." In the broad sense of the term, "gnosis" means a collection of heretical speculation that identified salvation with knowledge of the divine mysteries and, usually, held the material created world in contempt. Gnosticism was on the scene from the first century B.C. to the fourth century A.D.

Haggadah, from the Hebrew word meaning "announce," "narrate." A commentary or homily on a biblical text that deals either with a historical event or with a moral teaching. It often involves amplification with the help of legend or folklore. — The ritual narrative for the Passover meal.

Hosanna, from the Aramaic and Hebrew word meaning "Save!" (see Ps. 118:25). — It had become a popular acclamation equivalent to our "Hurrah!"; Mt. 21:9, 15.

Kerygma, from the Greek *kerygma*, "proclamation." A technical term for the proclamation of the Kingdom, Mt. 4:23, and of the mystery of Jesus, Rom. 16:25. The *kerygma* usually states what God is going to do, while the *didache* teaches what man ought to do.

Logion, plural *logia*, from the Greek *logion*, "word," "sentence." A sentence which does not necessarily belong in the context in which it is found, or which can be detached from this context. An example: Mk. 10:31.

Lord's Day, a stereotyped expression for the Day on which God will definitely triumph over all the forces hostile to him, Mal. 3:19-20. — Sunday, the day for recalling the Lord's resurrection, is called *kyriakē hēmera*, "day belonging to the Lord," Rev. 1:10.

Maranatha, an Aramaic expression meaning "The Lord is coming" (*maran atha*) or "Come, Lord!" (*marana tha*), 1 Cor. 16:22. In Rev. 22:20 it is translated "Come, Lord Jesus!"

Messiah, from the Greek *Messias*, which is a transliteration of the Hebrew *Mashiah* and the Aramaic *Meshiha*, and means "anointed" (*Christos* in Greek). One (a king or priest) who has been consecrated by means of an anointing. A title of Christ, Mt. 16:16.

Mishnah, derived from the Hebrew *shanah*, "repeat." A written collection of laws that had at one time been transmitted orally. It forms the nucleus of the Palestinian and Babylonian Talmuds. It was begun in about the second century B.C. and attained its definitive form in the second century A.D., thanks to the work of Rabbi Judah ha-Nasi (135–217).

Monophysitism, the doctrine of the one (*monos*) nature (*physis*). In the strict sense of the term, monophysitism is the teaching of Eutyches (middle of the fifth century A.D.), who regarded Christ as having but a single nature, the humanity being absorbed into the divinity as a drop of honey is absorbed by the ocean.

Mystery, derived from the Greek verb *myō*, "close [the mouth]." Something hidden or secret. Specifically: God's plan for the establishment of his Kingdom, Mt. 13:11, his wisdom that is revealed in Jesus Christ, Rom. 16:25. — The deeper meaning of certain spiritual realities, as, for example, the destiny of Israel, Rom. 11:25. — A hidden meaning, Rev. 1:20. — In a broader application of the term, the Mass is called "the divine mysteries."

Mystagogic, from the Greek: that which leads or guides (*agō*), i.e., initiates, into the mystery (*mystērion*).

Palimpsest, from the Greek *palimpsestos*, "scraped again." Writing material which is reused after earlier writing has been erased.

Parenesis, from the Greek *parainesis*, "encouragement." An address of exhortation and encouragement. Parenetic: exhortatory.

Parousia, from the Greek verb *par-eimi*, "be present"; the noun means "presence" or "coming." Refers chiefly to the coming of Jesus or of the "Day" of Jesus, 1 Cor. 16:17.

Pauline Corpus: the collection of letters traditionally attributed to Paul the Apostle.

Pericope, from the Greek *perikopē*, "(the action of) cutting," therefore a "section." A passage of Scripture that is to some extent self-contained or that has been chosen to be read during a liturgical celebration.

Presbyter, from the Greek *presbyteros*, "older" or "an elder." The word appears in English as "priest"; originally it designated the "elder," or person in charge of a Christian community, Acts 11:30. Later on it came to mean a priest of a community.

Sabaoth, a transliteration of the Hebrew *Sebaot*, "multitude" or "armies." It may signify the armies of Israel or the multitude of the stars or the multitude of the heavenly powers. The "Lord Sabaoth" is the sovereign God who has all the powers of the universe at his command, Rom. 9:29.

Sacramentary: a liturgical compilation containing the texts for Masses or the rites for the sacraments.

Septuagint: the Greek translation of the Hebrew Bible that was made in the third and second centuries before Christ for the use of Greek-speaking Jewish communities. According to tradition, it was made by seventy scholars in seventy days, whence the name Septuagint (the Latin for "seventy" is *septuaginta*).

Seraphim, derived from the Hebrew verb *saraf*, "burn." The name given in Is. 6:2 to the six-winged beings who stand before God's throne.

Synaxis, from the Greek *synaxis*, "(religious) assembly." The Eucharistic synaxis is the Eucharistic assembly.

Trisagion, from the Greek *tris*, "thrice," and *hagios*, "holy." A hymn in the Eastern Liturgies which invokes the holy God, the mighty God, the immortal God. The name is also given to the hymn which corresponds to the *Sanctus* of the Roman Mass.

List of Sources

THE SOURCES OF JEWISH PRAYER

The Kiddush for the Sabbath and Feastdays
S. Baer, *Seder Avodat Israel* (Tel-Aviv, 1957), pp. 197–98.

Birkat ha-mazon
Primitive text as reconstructed by L. Finkelstein, "The birkat ha-mazon," *Jewish Quarterly Review* 19 (1929), pp. 243–59. Liturgical text according to the Siddur Rav Saadja in I. Davidson, S. Assaf, and B. I. Joel, *Siddur R. Saadja Gaon* (Jerusalem, 1941), pp. 102–3.

Shemone Esre
Palestinian recension in D. W. Staerk, *Altjüdische liturgische Gebete* (Bonn, 1910), pp. 11–14. Babylonian recension in I. Davidson *et al.*, *op. cit.*, pp. 17–19 and 38–39.

Shema Israel, Birkat Yotser
Text in D. W. Staerk, *op. cit.*, pp. 4–6.

The Jewish Kaddish and the Christian Our Father
Jewish Kaddish in Staerk, *op. cit.*, pp. 30–31.

THE ACCOUNT OF THE INSTITUTION OF THE EUCHARIST

Parallel texts in K. Aland, *Synopsis Quattuor Evangeliorum* (Stuttgart, 1964).

DOXOLOGIES, BLESSINGS, AND HYMNS OF THE NEW TESTAMENT

K. Aland, M. Black, B. M. Metzger, and A. Wikgren, *The Greek New Testament* (Stuttgart, 1966).

THE DIDACHE

J.-P. Audet, *La Didaché: Instructions des apôtres* (Paris, 1958), pp. 226–42

(Greek text). — W. Rordorf and A. Tuilier, *La Doctrine des Douze Apôtres* (Sources chrétiennes 248; Paris, 1978).

CLEMENT OF ROME, THE LETTER TO THE CORINTHIANS

F. X. Funk, *Patres Apostolici* 1 (Tübingen, 1905), pp. 98–184 (Greek text with Latin translation).—A. Jaubert, *Clément de Rome, Epître aux Corinthiens* (Sources chrétiennes 167; Paris, 1971).

THE WITNESS OF SAINT JUSTIN

L. Pautigny, *Les Apologies* (Texts et documents 1; Paris, 1904).

THE HOMILY ON THE PASCH OF MELITO OF SARDIS

B. Lohse, *Die Passa-Homilie des Bischofs Meliton von Sardes* (Textus Minores 24; Leiden, 1958). — O. Perler, *Méliton de Sardes, Sur la Pâque et Fragments* (Sources chrétiennes 123; Paris, 1966).

CLEMENT OF ALEXANDRIA

C. Mondésert and A. Plassart, *Clément d'Alexandrie, Le Protreptique* (Sources chrétiennes 2; Paris, 1949). — C. Mondésert, C. Matray, and H. Marrou, *Clément d'Alexandrie, Le Pédagogue, Livre III* (Sources chrétiennes 158; Paris, 1970).

THE APOSTOLIC TRADITION OF HIPPOLYTUS OF ROME

B. Botte, *La Tradition Apostolique de saint Hippolyte: Essai de reconstitution* (Liturgiewissenschaftliche Quellen und Forschungen 39; Münster, 1963).

THE ANAPHORA OF ADDAI AND MARI

W. F. Macomber, "The Oldest Known Text of the Anaphora of the Apostles Addai and Mari," *Orientalia Christiana Periodica* 32 (1966), pp. 358–71 (text).

THE DIDASCALIA OF THE APOSTLES

H. Achelis and J. Flemming, *Die syrische Didaskalie übersetzt und erklärt*

(Texte und Untersuchungen 25/2 [NF 10/2]; Leipzig, 1904 (the translation is closer to the original than that of F. Nau, *La Didascalie, c'est-à-dire l'enseignement catholique des douze apôtres et saints disciples de Notre Seigneur* [2nd ed.; Paris, 1912]). — F. X. Funk, *Didascalia et Constitutiones Apostolorum* 1 (Paderborn, 1905), pp. 2–385 (Greek text along with a Latin translation of the *Apostolic Constitutions*, Books I–VI).

THE EUCHOLOGY OF SERAPION OF THMUIS

F. X. Funk, *Didascalia et Constitutiones Apostolorum* 2 (Paderborn, 1905), pp. 158–95 (Greek text with Latin translation).

THE STRASBOURG PAPYRUS

M. Andrieu and P. Collomp, "Fragments sur papyrus de l'anaphore de saint Marc," *Revue des sciences religieuses* 8 (1928), pp. 489–515.

THE APOSTOLIC CONSTITUTIONS

F. X. Funk, *Didascalia et Constitutiones Apostolorum* 1 (Paderborn, 1905), pp. 2–595.

THE EUCHOLOGY OF DER BALYZEH

C. H. Roberts and B. Capelle, *An Early Euchologium: The Der Balyzeh Papyrus Enlarged and Re-edited* (Bibliothèque du Muséon 23; Louvain, 1949).

KLASMATA, OR VARIOUS FRAGMENTS

Joyous Light
F. J. Dölger, "Lumen Christi," *Antike und Christentum* 5 (Münster, 1936), pp. 11–26.

Glory to God in the Highest Heaven
F. X. Funk, *Didascalia et Constitutiones Apostolorum* 1 (Paderborn, 1905), pp. 455–57 (in a note).

Benefactor of All Who Turn to You
F. A. Cabrol and H. Leclercq, *Monumenta ecclesiae antiqua: Reliquiae liturgicae vetustissimae* 1/2 (Paris, 1913), no. 32, pp. CLXXXVIII–CXCII. [Cited henceforth as: Cabrol-Leclercq, *M.E.L.*]

Holy Is the God
Cabrol-Leclercq, *ibid.*

You Are Holy, Lord
Berlin Papyrus, P. 9794, in *Patrologia Orientalis* 18:431–32.

Your Sacred Body
D. N. Borgia, *Frammenti eucaristici antichissimi: Saggio di poesia sacra populare bizantina* (Grottaferrata, 1932), pp. 37–40.

Christ Is Born, Give Him Glory
J. B. Pitra, *Hymnographie de l'Eglise grecque* (Rome, 1867), p. 75.

He Was Born at Bethlehem
Cabrol-Leclercq, *M.E.L.*, no. 2, p. CXLV.

We Praise You, God Almighty
I. Schuster, *The Sacramentary*, tr. A. Levelis-Marke, 2 (New York, 1925), p. 423.

In the Shelter of Your Mercy
F. Mercenier, "L'antienne mariale grecque la plus ancienne," *Le Muséon* 49 (1939), pp. 229–33. — O. Stegmüller, "Sub tuum praesidium: Bemerkungen zur ältesten Überlieferung," *Zeitschrift für katholische Theologie* 74 (1952), pp. 76–82.

O God Almighty
Cabrol-Leclercq, *M.E.L.*, no. 19, p. CLXXXI. — H. Leclercq, "Papyrus," *Dictionnaire d'archéologie chrétienne et de liturgie* 13:1439–40. [Henceforth: *DACL.*]

Hope, Life, Way
Schuster, *op. cit.*, 3 (New York, 1927), p. 441.

Blood of Jesus Christ
Patrologia Orientalis 18:435.

O Night That Is Brighter Than Day
Asterius, *Homily 19: On Psalm 5* (PG 40:436).

Epitaph of Abercius
H. Leclercq, "Abercius," *DACL* 1:70–75. — F. J. Dölger, *Ichthys* 2 (Münster, 1922), pp. 454–507.

Epitaph of Pectorius
H. Leclercq, "Abercius," *DACL* 1:83. — Dölger, *ibid.*, pp. 507–15.

Epitaph of Amachis
H. Leclercq, "Prière," *DACL* 14:1770.

Epitaph of Leontius
  H. Leclercq, "Prière," *DACL* 14:1769.

Epitaph of Magus
  H. Leclercq, "Eglise," *DACL* 4:2237–38.

God of Spirits and of All Flesh
  H. Leclercq, "Ame," *DACL* 1:1531–32.

Baptistery of Saint Lawrence in Damaso
  Schuster, *op. cit.*, 1:34.

Baptistery of the Lateran
  Schuster, *op. cit.*, 1:23.

Baptistery of Saint Lawrence
  Schuster, *op. cit.*, 4 (New York, 1930), p. xiv.

Inscription Placed in the Consignatorium
  Schuster, *op. cit.*, 1:33.

THE CATECHESES OF CYRIL OF JERUSALEM

PG 33:331–1180. — A. Piédagnel and P. Paris, *Cyrille de Jérusalem, Catéchèses Mystagogiques* (Sources chrétiennes 126; Paris, 1966).

Index

ABERCIUS, Epitaph of, 260.

ACCLAMATION, MESSIANIC, 31. — Acclamation in the dialogue of the Preface, 129–30, 146, 159–60, 228, 285.

ACHELIS, H., 169, 179, 298.

ADDAI, Anaphora of Addai and Mari, 157–63, 298.

AGAPE, 23 (?), 73, 147.

ALAND, K., 297.

ALLO, B., 52.

ALTANER, B., 117.

AMACHIS, Epitaph of, 266.

AMBROSE OF MILAN, viii, 195, 270.

ANAMNESIS, 26, 131, 162, 195, 212, 234, 247.

ANAPHORA. *See:* Eucharist.

ANDRIEU, M., 211, 299.

ANGELS, 16, 40, 41, 55, 60, 160, 173, 179, 184, 194, 229, 232, 246, 274, 285, 287.

ANOINTING in baptism, 141, 142, 279–80. — Catechesis of Cyril of Jerusalem on anointing, 281–83.

ANTHONY, 183.

APOCALYPSE, hymns of the, 62–69.

APOSTOLIC CONSTITUTIONS, 215–40, 299.

APOSTOLIC TRADITION of Hippolytus, 123–53.

ARIUS and ARIANISM, 183, 196, 215.

ASSAF, S., 7, 297.

ASTERIUS, 260.

ATHANASIUS OF ALEXANDRIA, 183, 196, 211, 252.

AUDET, J.-P., 29, 74, 297.

AUGUSTINE, 270.

BABYLON, Lament over, 67.

BAER, S., 297.

BAPTISM, professions of faith in, 46–49, 218–19, 245, 278. — Rites of baptism, 139–42, 199–203. — Mass of baptism, 144–45. — Baptismal catecheses, 271–89.

— Baptismal inscriptions, 264–65. — Immersion at baptism, 141–42. *See also:* Catechumens.

BARDY, G., 114, 183.

BASIL THE GREAT, 93, 251.

BEDE THE VENERABLE, 150.

BÉRAUDY, R., 143.

BEYER, H. W., 29.

BILLERBECK, P., 9, 15.

BIRKAT HA-MAZON, 6–9.

BIRKAT YOTSER, 15–16.

BISHOP, prayer for ordination of, 127–28. — Prayer of the bishop for the faithful, 226–27. — Duties of the bishop according to the Didascalia, 169–71.

BLACK, M., 297.

BLESSING of bread, 6; of wine, 5; of the sabbath, 5–6; for meals, 222; after meals, 6–9. — Eighteen blessings, 9–14. — Yotser blessing, 15–16. — Blessings of the New Testament, 29–37. — Blessing of the people, 188, 197, 240. — Blessing of catechumens, 223–24. — Blessing of the offerings of the faithful, 132–33. — Blessing of oil and water, 198–99.

BOISMARD, M.-E., 41, 42, 43, 55.

BONNER, C., 99.

BONSIRVEN, J., 9, 16, 17.

BORGIA, D. N., 300.

BOTTE, B., viii, 127, 129, 138, 142, 157, 158, 162, 195, 298.

BOULET, R., 133, 157.

BOUVET, J., 270, 282.

BOUYER, L., 7, 10, 15, 158.

BREAD, blessing of, 6. — Prayer over the bread, 206–7. *See also:* Agape.

BREAKING OF BREAD, 6, 77, 197.

BRINKMANN, 183.

CABROL, F., 243, 253, 299, 300.

CALLISTUS, Pope, 123, 124.

303